Bazyli and Anna Jocz

Jewish Christian Victims of the Holocaust

To Peter & Shelagh
With blessings
[signature]

VCF Sun 9 Oct 2022

Bazyli and Anna Jocz

Jewish Christian Victims of the Holocaust

Kelvin Crombie

Heritage Resources Pty Ltd

Published in 2020
Heritage Resources Pty Ltd

Contact details:
Heritage Resources Pty Ltd, PO Box 565, Mundaring 6073, WA, Australia
Email: kelvin@heritageresources.com.au & sales@heritageresources.com.au

Crombie, Kelvin
Bazyli and Anna Jocz: Jewish Christian Victims of the Holocaust

ISBN: 978-0-646-82295-2

Artwork.
Cover by Ophelia Roberts, Minuteman Press, Midvale.

Printed by Minuteman Press, 42-46 Farrall Road, Midvale 6056, Western Australia.

Visual front cover. Bazyli, Anna, Jakob, Pawel and Jan Jocz, 1935. Original belongs to Phil Jocz. (Jocz Collection)

This is a joint publication between Heritage Resources Pty Ltd, Perth Australia and Conrad Schick Library and Archive, Christ Church Jerusalem.

Table of Contents

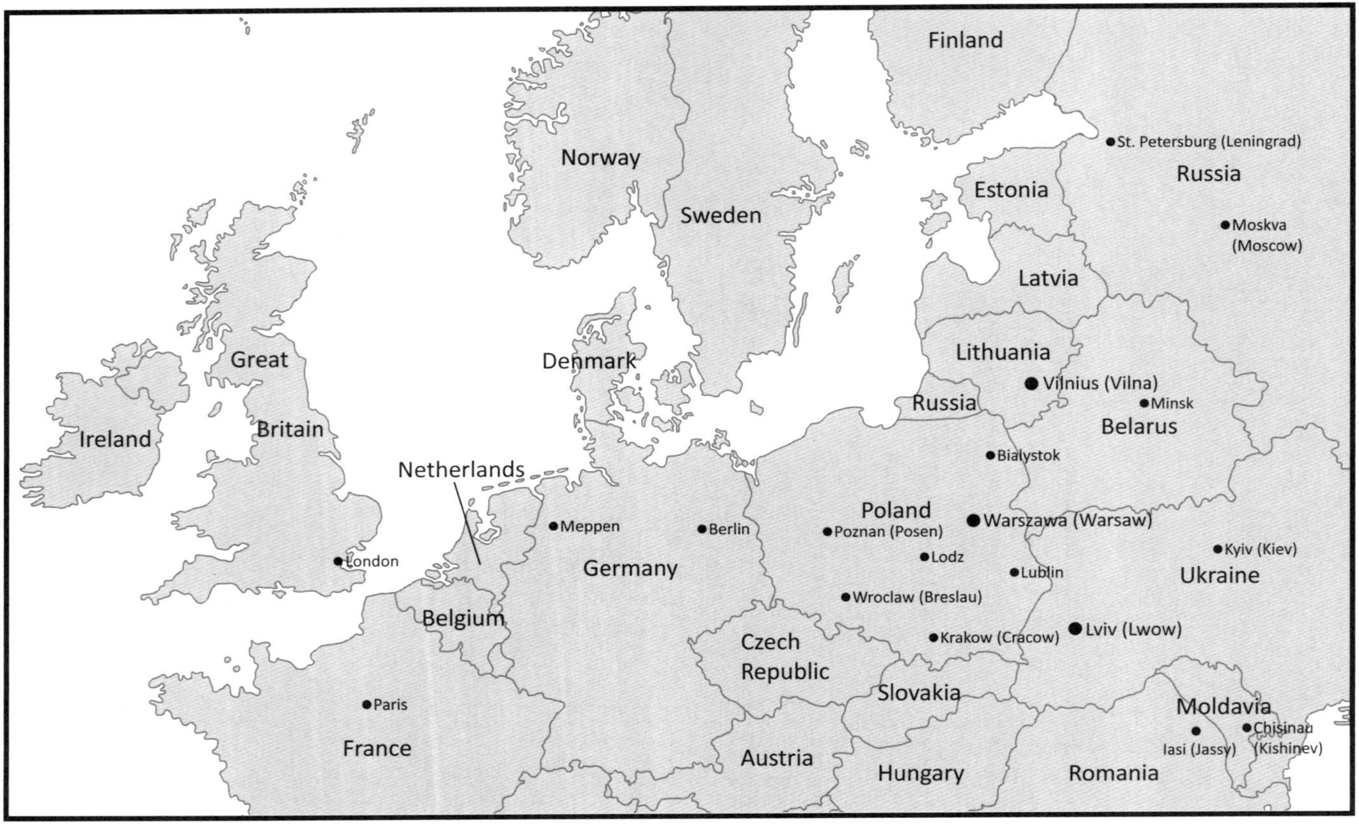
Finland
Norway
Sweden
St. Petersburg (Leningrad)
Russia
Estonia
Moskva
(Moscow)
Latvia
Lithuania
Great
Denmark
Vilnius (Vilna)
Russia
Minsk
Belarus
Ireland
Britain
Bialystok
Netherlands
Poland
Warszawa (Warsaw)
Meppen
Berlin
Poznan (Posen)
Kyiv (Kiev)
London
Lodz
Lublin
Germany
Ukraine
Wroclaw (Breslau)
Belgium
Krakow (Cracow)
Lviv (Lwow)
Czech
Republic
Slovakia
Moldavia
Paris
Chisinau
(Kishinev)
Iasi (Jassy)
France
Austria
Hungary
Romania

Foreword

I was born on 18 May 1942 at the very time when the Nazi's were implementing their plan to totally destroy all Jewish people in Europe – and elsewhere.

At the Wannsee Conference of January 1942 the Nazi architects of the 'Final Solution to the Jewish Problem' presented statistics of where the Jewish people lived in Europe. Included was Great Britain. They had even compiled a list in 1940 of prominent Jewish people who lived in Britain.

Obviously I was not aware of all these happenings. Later, however, this 'Gestapo Arrest List for England' came to the light. My family was on that Blacklist! It is now clear what would have happened to me, even as a baby or small child, had the Germans got their hands on Great Britain – I would most likely have been murdered. Thank God they never did.

Like any person of Jewish heritage the Holocaust is very much a part of me. It is important that we never forget what happened in Europe between 1933-45; that we honour those who suffered; and that we learn from the Holocaust so that we can never repeat that most horrible of historical events.

This book by Kelvin Crombie is primarily about the fate of the Jewish people who were associated with the Church, officially classified as non Aryan Christians. Kelvin has a reputation for rigorous research and leaves no stone unturned. He uncovers another dimension to the Holocaust and one that many have missed. The Nazi fury unleashed against non Aryan Christians.

Some people might dismiss the subject matter, viewing these people as mere apostates from Judaism and converts to Christianity and therefore not Jewish at all. That however was not how they were viewed by the Nazis and their sympathisers, who saw them as 'racially' Jewish. As such it is important that we learn about them and also give them honour as victims of the Holocaust.

This book is relevant for the Jewish people and for the Christian Church. I recommend it to be read by all those who are keen to learn more about the Holocaust as well as this large community of Jewish people who were associated with the Church in Europe prior to and during the Second World War.

Simon Rufus Isaacs - The Most Hon The Marquess of Reading

***

As a child of the post-war boom generation, I have been fortunate to know nothing of privation or war. Growing up as the youngest of four siblings, it did not occur to me to ask my parents about their experiences and nor were they inclined to share painful memories. So for the longest time I remained in ignorance. It was only in later life and after they were gone that I realized I knew very little about my family's history.

In 2018 a confluence of events started me on a journey of discovery. First, Andrew Barron of Jews for Jesus (Toronto) contacted me to ask who owned the copyright to my father's books. It turned out that I and my sisters did and that discovery led to a project involving the digitizing of a number of my father's works. Later that same year, I was contacted by David Williams, Chaplain of the Anglican Mission in Warsaw from 1995-97. He was writing a history of the chaplaincy and was seeking some details from my family. Finally, out of the blue, I received a telephone call from Ruth Brooks. She had just returned from a visit to Israel and had heard about Kelvin Crombie's project there. She was calling to facilitate a visit from Kelvin to specifically discuss the Jocz family history. Clearly, something larger was afoot.

I am indebted to Kelvin. Had I not spent an afternoon with him poring over dusty and long-forgotten papers, I doubt I would have pursued the project to its conclusion. I was surprised by what I found. Documents preserved by my uncle (Paul) were especially revealing. I was finally able to put a name on a picture that had long hung in my father's study that I only knew as "grandfather". The story absorbed me and my wife often joked that I had disappeared "down the rabbit hole". Even now I am discovering facts that have remained hidden for years. Some of them are revealed in the pages that follow.

Living in a stable Western democracy it is easy to forget the capacity for evil that lurks beneath the thin veneer of civility. Reading this book brought with it the sobering reminder that I have more than enough Jewish blood in me to qualify for admission to a Nazi death camp. Let this book serve as a reminder for future generations: when a state starts to persecute some of its own citizens, no one is safe.

Phil Jocz

Introduction

Bazyli and Anna Jocz[1] were two Jewish people living in Lwow Poland[2] when the Germans invaded the country on 1 September 1939. Due to the German-Soviet Non-Aggression Pact of August 1939, Poland was divided and Lwow initially came under Soviet control. However when the Germans attacked the Soviet Union on 22 June 1941 Lwow shortly afterwards came under direct Nazi-German control.

Like all other Jewish people in Poland they were then subject to the anti-Jewish policies of the German Nazi Party. By late 1941 those anti-Jewish policies had determined that all the Jewish people were to be systematically murdered.

Ultimately Bazyli was murdered 'for the crime of being Jewish' in 1944. The arresting Gestapo agents determined that Bazyli was Jewish by conducting a body search. There is no greater sign that a male is Jewish than the sign of circumcision – the sign of the covenant between Almighty God and Abraham, Isaac and Jacob.

Anna almost succumbed to the same fate, but was knocked unconscious by the Gestapo agents, and they left her. When she came to Anna was completely paralysed, but after several months she recovered the use of her upper body. She was paralysed from the waist down for the remainder of her life.

Bazyli and Anna had four sons, three of whom, Jerzy (George), Pawel (Paul), and Jan or Johann (John), were also in Poland during the Second World War, while one son, Jakob (Jacob),[3] happened to be out of Poland the day the War erupted. All of the Jocz family were 100% Jewish according to the Nuremberg Laws, those laws enacted by the Nazi regime which determined if a person was fully, half or quarter Jewish.

But all of the Jocz family were followers of Jesus (Yeshua).[4] Did this make

[1] Jocz is pronounced "Yotch" and rhymes with Scotch.

[2] Lwow was the Polish name of what is now Lviv in Ukraine. In some sources Lvov is also used.

[3] For all four sons sometimes the Polish name will be used and sometimes the Anglicised name, depending on the context.

[4] Jesus' name in Hebrew is Yeshua, which literally means 'Saviour.'

them then less Jewish? They viewed themselves as Jewish or Hebrew Christians, and were part of the Church,[5] but in the Nazi system they were classified as non-Aryan Christians and to the Nazis their affiliation with the Church (in their case, the Protestant Church) meant absolutely nothing. They were 'just Jews.'

There were tens of thousands, perhaps over a hundred thousand, Jewish people who were classified as non-Aryan Christians in Nazi occupied Europe. The majority of Jews within this group suffered the same fate as all other Jewish people.

Israeli scholar Havi Ben-Sasson wrote about this group, relating specifically to the Warsaw Ghetto, in an article in the Yad Vashem Studies:

> It is a basic Jewish principle that even a sinful Jew still remains a Jew. Thus, a Jew remains affiliated with the Jewish community at large (for better or worse) irrespective of his/her actions. During World War II, this tenet of the faith took on practical significance. With the occupation of Warsaw, obviously, the Jews of the city and its surroundings fell into the clutches of the Nazis. However, some 2,000 converts to Christianity who, despite their non-Jewish way of life were perceived by the Nazis as full-fledged Jews based on a racial definition of a Jew, were also at risk.[6]

This book is part of a research study dedicated to this group of Jewish people, and their fate during the period of the Holocaust. This study began in April 2018 following a request by Rev. David Pileggi, Rector of Christ Church Jerusalem (and the director of the Conrad Schick Library located there), and is entitled 'The Jewish non-Aryan Christian Holocaust Research Study.'[7]

---

[5] Today most Jewish followers of Jesus (Yeshua) are referred to as Messianic Jews. In the period under review, however, that term was not used.

[6] Havi Ben-Sasson, 'Christians in the Ghetto: All Saints' Church, Birth of the Holy Virgin Mary Church, and the Jews of the Warsaw Ghetto', in Yad Vashem Studies XXXI, edited by David Silberland, (Yad Vashem Jerusalem, 2003), pp. 153-54.

[7] This is a joint venture between the Conrad Schick Library and Heritage Resources Pty Ltd in Australia, in which I am involved. I am also indebted to Dr Mitch Glaser, Dr Richard Harvey and Dr Gershon Nerel and others who have offered encouragement and assistance.

As part of this research study I have needed to visit libraries, archives, death and concentration camps, Holocaust-related memorials and other related sites, in many countries connected with the subject matter. Thus far much time has been spent in Europe and particularly in Poland. Many of the archives associated with English-speaking missionary societies which operated in Europe during the period 1933-1945 are located in the United Kingdom and the United States. One particular related archive is located at Wycliffe College in Toronto Canada. It is the archive belonging to Jakob Jocz.

Jakob Jocz became a renowned academic and scholar after the Second World War. Shortly after becoming involved with CMJ[8] at Christ Church Jerusalem in 1986 I became aware of the name of Jakob Jocz. However, because Jakob never actually worked in Israel, I never took much of an interest in him – despite the fact that he had written some very significant books on the relationship between Jewish people and Jesus.[9]

It was while writing the CMJ bicentennial history (1809-2009) that I became more interested in Jakob, as this research project covered the work of CMJ world-wide. A very important part of this long and colourful history included Poland and in particular Warsaw.

It was at this time that I became aware of Jakob's parents, Bazyli and Anna. Bazyli had been a long term employee of CMJ, both in Warsaw and in Lwow (formerly Austrian-controlled Lemberg), and according to what I read then he had been murdered by the Gestapo in 1945. At that point I knew nothing of what happened to Anna.

At some point while at Christ Church in Jerusalem I had met Philip Jocz, the son of Jakob, and grandson of Bazyli and Anna, but had not remained in contact with him. Now that I was looking at the lives of the Jocz family (as part of the much larger number of Hebrew Christians who were victims of the Nazi genocide[10]) I made contact with Philip, who lives near Toronto, Can-

[8] CMJ – Church's Ministry among Jewish People, also known as the London Jews Society (LJS) or officially as the London Society for Promoting Christianity amongst the Jews, established in London in 1809.

[9] These include: *Jesus Christ and the Jewish People*, and *The Jewish People and Jesus Christ After Auschwitz*.

[10] The term 'genocide' was first used by lawyer Raphael Lemkin in 1943. He then used it numerous times in his book *Axis Rule in Occupied Europe,* (Washington D.C: Carnegie Endowment for International Peace, 1944), pp. 79-95.

ada.[11] Philip then informed me that he also had some private family archives, which were at his sister Anne's house in Toronto.

In November 2018 I set out on a five week research tour which resulted in visits to seventeen separate archives and collections in Britain, Canada and the US. While in Britain I visited the CMJ archive located at the Bodleian Library in Oxford. Some days later I had the pleasure of visiting the Wycliffe College archive in Toronto, and meeting Philip again. We spent a wonderful half day together going through the family archives at his sister's home.

To use the proverbial saying, 'I was like a kid in a candy (or lollie) store.' Towards the end of our time together Philip produced a thick file and said something like, "I really don't know what to do with this, almost everything is in German." Indeed it was. It contained all the correspondence related to Jakob's attempts to get compensation from the German government after the War for injuries his mother sustained at the hand of Gestapo agents, injuries which resulted in Anna's paralysis from the waist downwards.

My knowledge of German is scant, but I knew enough so that when I leafed through the hundreds of pages of mostly technical material I was able to pick out a number of entries containing important historical and biographical material. Within that material I was able to determine that Bazyli was not in fact murdered in 1945, but on 29 February 1944.

This was a treasure trove and provided me with further insights into the lives of Bazyli and Anna.[12] At the conclusion of my time with Philip I encouraged him to write up something of his family story. This he has subsequently done and it is now available on the website - www.jocz.ca

This present book endeavours to bring the lives of the Jocz family, and especially Bazyli and Anna, out into the open. Bazyli has appeared to me to have been a very faithful, unassuming and dedicated man, and Anna a very faithful and bold woman. They were both ordinary people, committed Jewish follow-

---

[11] This contact was facilitated by Ruth Brooks of Toronto, also Theresa Newell and Andrew Barron, who are both working on Jakob Jocz's literary achievements.

[12] This German material is part of the Jocz Private Collection. The page numbers which show up on the footnotes cited are from the original page numbers of those documents in the original file, which I have named the 'German File.'

ers of Jesus, who were caught up in that tragedy of all tragedies, and who did all they could to survive.

To best understand their lives I have found it necessary to provide considerable information about the environments and times in which they were living, and of the organisation, CMJ, with which they as a family were associated from 1921 until 1956. I am particularly indebted to Elizabeth Myers for information contained in her Masters thesis *The Literary Legacy of Jacob Jocz.* Myers interviewed Joan and Paul Jocz, and others, and has been able to piece together the early Jocz family history. Thanks also to Dr Mitch Glaser who wrote *A Survey of Missions to the Jews in Continental Europe 1950-1900.*

A number of secondary sources have been consulted in order to better understand the historical context of the Holocaust, especially Christopher Browning's *The Origins of the Final Solution*, William Shirer's *The Rise and Fall of the Third Reich*, Timothy Snyder's *Bloodlands,* and Rabbi David Kahane's *Lvov Ghetto Diary.*

Special thanks are also due to: Deborah Pileggi who translated considerable material from German to English; those who have proof read and edited this manuscript; and those who have financially contributed to this on-going research study.

It almost goes without saying that any work is incomplete as some material will most certainly have been missed. However, with the resources at my disposal, I have endeavoured to present to you as best I can the lives of this Jewish Christian couple and their family, and the times in which they lived – and died.

Some basic definitions and outline

Working on a subject related to the Holocaust is very difficult. Working on a subject related to Jewish people who were associated with the Church and who were victims of the Holocaust is difficult, challenging and somewhat controversial. For many Jews a Jewish Christian was a traitor (*meshumad*), while for the Nazis and their collaborators, they were officially classified as a non-Aryan Christian but in real terms they were regarded as 'just Jews.'

In a forthcoming publication, *They Suffered Like Other Jewish People,* I will endeavour to present more detail relating to the plight of the Jewish people who were associated with the Church, not just in Poland but throughout Europe during the period of the Holocaust.

To aid me in this research study I have formulated the following basic definition of who is a Jewish non-Aryan Christian, and a basic outline of the stages or phases leading up to the final and ultimate Nazi solution to 'the Jewish problem'.

Jewish non-Aryan Christians

According to basic Nazi ideology there were Aryans and there were non-Aryans. Germans were Aryans and Jews were non-Aryans.[13] According to basic Nazi ideology the German Church was regarded as a national German institution, in which only Aryans could participate.

What then was the status of Jewish people who were associated with the Church? They were regarded as non-Aryan Christians and as such, according to Nazi ideology, they could not belong to the Church. In Nazi ideology they were Jewish. This was the challenge faced by the Hebrew or Jewish Christians, initially in Germany and then in every area occupied by Nazi Germany. The Jocz family experienced this broader dynamic.

Defining a Jewish non-Aryan Christian is, however, not straight-forward. I have thus far located seven sub-groups which together make up the broad classification of Jewish non-Aryan Christians. These are:

1. One who was genuinely convinced before 1 September 1939 that Jesus was the promised Messiah of Israel.

2. One who 'converted' and was baptised and became a member of the Church mostly for socio-economic reasons, seeing this as being the best avenue for progressing in the host Gentile (or 'Christian') society.

3. One who 'converted' and was baptised into the Church because they were marrying a Gentile or Christian spouse. This person may or may not have had a genuine faith in Jesus as the Messiah.

4. One whose parents or grandparents had 'converted' and were bap-

[13] Roma and Sinta people (Gypsies) were also classified as non-Aryans.

tised, from categories 1, 2 or 3, and who now as a second or third generation person outside of the Jewish community did not perceive themselves as a member of the community of Israel. They were for all intents and purposes fully immersed, or assimilated, into the Gentile world – and this was also how the Jewish community mostly viewed them.

5. One who 'converted' and was baptised after 1 September 1939 due to war time expediency, perceiving this as bettering their chances of survival. There were instances where baptismal certificates were issued which provided their Jewish recipients with the opportunity to survive, and many did. Some from this category might thereafter have continued in the Church, while others in time re-joined the Jewish community.

6. One who as a child after 1 September 1939 was baptised by Christian individuals and institutions that were entrusted with caring for and saving the child. This was a very controversial category, which created considerable angst after the War as some of the children did not want to return to the Jewish community, and some of the Christian people or institutions did not want to return the child to the Jewish community.

7. One who after 1 September 1939 in the midst of the War was genuinely convinced that Jesus was the Messiah of Israel.

There may well be more sub-groupings, but this is my working model, in this publication as well as in the forthcoming more expansive work.

Phases of the Holocaust

My working model for trying to understand the Holocaust is to view it through seven progressive phases. These phases are for the most part not rigid, and there is fluidity between them. However when looking at how and why certain decisions were made, these seven phases assist me in providing a basic context:

Phase One	Until 1933	- Foundations laid
Phase Two	1933-1939	- Intimidation, exploitation and emigration
Phase Three	1939-1940	- The Lublin & Ghettoization Plan

Phase Four	1940-1941	- The Madagascar Plan
Phase Five	1941	- The Eastern Plan
Phase Six	1941-1942	- Initial implementation of Genocide
Phase Seven	1942-1945	- Complete implementation of Genocide

Within this publication mention will often be made to these phases.

Chapter 1

Christianity and the Jewish people

In the land of Israel

Two major events occurred in the 1st century AD which played a huge role in laying a foundation for the lives of Bazyli and Anna Jocz and their family. One was the birth and subsequent life of Jesus of Nazareth and the other was the defeat of the Jewish nation by the Romans, the destruction of Jerusalem and the Temple, and the further exile of the Jewish people from the land of Israel. With the destruction of the Temple the rabbis, led by Rabbi Yochanan ben Zakai, began to develop a faith system which became one of the sources of what today is often called Orthodox Judaism.

While most Jewish people at that time did not accept Jesus as the promised Messiah of Israel, large numbers did. These Jews believed that Jesus fulfilled the Messianic prophecies of the Hebrew Scriptures (the *Tanach*) and that Jesus was the perfect sacrifice to atone for mankind's separation from a relationship with Almighty God (Isaiah 52: 13-15 & 53). This movement was known as 'the Way', the Nazarenes and, later, one branch as the Ebionites.

The separation between the two Jewish faith groups began initially as a result of the different interpretations of *Torah* offered by Jesus in comparison with other Jewish religious leaders. The gap widened following the defeat by Rome in the First Jewish Revolt (66-70 AD). For the most part the Jewish followers of Jesus did not take part in the conflict against Rome, a factor which did not endear them to the nationalist party.[1]

Living in exile in Europe, Africa and elsewhere, or in the land of Israel but bereft of their treasured Temple, the Jewish people needed to 'close ranks' in order to preserve their national distinctiveness. It was at this time, about the year 90 AD, that an addition was made to the daily synagogue declaration, known as the Eighteen Benedictions. This addition, known as the *Birkhat Ha-Minim*, included a pronouncement against the *minim*, or heretics, who at

[1] Wilson, M. *Our Father Abraham*, (Dayton, 1989), p. 76.

this point were seen to include the followers of Jesus (Yeshua) the Nazarene, although they were not specially mentioned by name. Thereafter it was more difficult for the followers of Jesus to openly participate in the synagogue services. It would appear that later the specific word *Notzrim* (Nazarenes) was added to the *Birkat Ha-Minim.*[2]

A foremost authority on Jewish-Christians relations, Dr Jakob Jocz, the son of Bazyli and Anna, wrote in his monumental work, *The Jewish People and Jesus Christ,* about this period: 'The extent of the success of Jewish Christians in the Synagogue is the only possible reason for the introduction of heretics (Christians) in the Hebrew Prayer Book. After political disaster the gospel message offered new hope and vision to a defeated people.'[3]

By 90 AD the separation was becoming evident. Then came the Bar Kokhba Revolt of 132-135 AD, during which a Jewish fighter named Simon Bar Kosiba claimed to be the *Nasi*, or prince. The Messianic title 'Bar Kokhba', Son of the Star, based upon a prophecy from Numbers 24:17, was then conferred upon him by the great Rabbi Akiva. Many Jewish people rallied behind him and fought against the Roman forces. Ultimately they failed and an even worse defeat, destruction and exile from the land of Israel resulted for the Jewish people.

Few Jewish followers of Jesus at the time could follow Bar Kokhba, seeing him as a false messiah – and believing that Jesus of Nazareth was the true Messiah. In the eyes of the majority of the Jewish community those who did not rally behind Bar Kokhba and fight against the Romans were traitors to the national cause, they were *meshumadim.*

The separation in this totally in-house Jewish event was now greatly enhanced. Jakob Jocz stated:

> It must not be forgotten that the decision concerning Jesus of Nazareth was taken at a time when Gentile Christianity was scarcely of any consequence to the Synagogue. The parting of the roads between the Messianic movement and Judaism began upon Jewish soil as a result of a

---

[2] Ibid., pp. 66-69.

[3] Jocz, J. *The Jewish People and Jesus Christ,* (Baker Book House: Grand Rapids, 1979). Author's Note to the Third Edition.

religious controversy between Jews and Jews.[4]

Gentiles become part of 'Messianic Israel'

In time more and more Gentiles became committed followers of Jesus; that is, they repented, were converted from paganism and entered into a new covenant relationship with the God of Israel (Jeremiah 31: 31-34). During the following centuries an ideological and even occasionally a physical battle took place between the two monotheistic faith systems within the Roman Empire - the Jewish religion and this new movement of followers of Jesus.

There was, however, some tension within the 'Jesus movement' between the Jewish and non-Jewish followers, especially as the number of Gentile followers increased. Some of this tension revolved around a central question – 'Was the Jewish nation still in a covenant relationship with Almighty God even though they as a nation had rejected Jesus as Messiah?' This question led to others, such as "Who was now the 'people of God', the 'chosen nation', the 'servant of God'? Was it the nation of Israel or the followers of Jesus, the Church?"

Paul, in particular in his letter to the church in Rome, and the anonymous writer of the Book of Hebrews, both attempted to answer these questions. They provided a clear understanding that the nation of Israel was still beloved of and in a covenant relationship with Almighty God, but, that individual salvation was now attained through repentance and a belief that Jesus was the mediator and sacrifice for the new covenant as prophesied by Jeremiah (Jeremiah 31: 31-34), and no longer through repentance and the offering of an animal sacrifice.

However Gentile Christians,[5] including some of the Church Fathers, failed to fully relate to this duality within God's covenant with Israel – promises to the nation as well as promises to an individual. Some Jewish religious leaders also failed to understand this principle, discouraging their people from reading Isaiah 53 for instance, which speaks of an individual servant of the LORD.

This question of God's elected or chosen people and nation was to plague

---

[4] Ibid., p. 1.

[5] The term 'Christian' was first used to describe Gentile followers of Jesus in Antioch. (Acts 11:26)

the relationship between the followers of Jesus (the Church) and the Jewish nation during the forthcoming centuries, creating considerable angst, especially for the people of Israel. Jewish followers of Jesus were often caught in the middle.

In the Roman Empire

The aforementioned dynamics increased in 313 AD when the Roman Emperor Constantine issued an edict of toleration for the Christian faith in the Roman Empire,[6] and then later in 380 AD when Christianity was proclaimed as the official religion of the Roman Empire. Thereafter many citizens of the Roman Empire became Christians with little requirement for personal repentance and confession of faith in Jesus as the atoning sacrifice. Such people would have little understanding of Almighty God's covenant relationship with the nation of Israel.

The dynamics of Christianity changed at the point that the Roman Empire adopted Christianity. Roman Christianity now became predominant and there was no place for Judaism as an equal. Thereafter the institutionalised Roman Church began adopting a more stringent and negative attitude towards Judaism and the Jewish people. Within this context most of these 'institutional Christians' would have had little understanding of the Jewish-Israel roots of Biblical Christianity. The Church, many of its leaders thereafter maintained, was now the true people of God, even the true Israel. This attitude was retained by both of the main streams of Roman Christianity in Europe, the Roman Catholic Church and the Eastern Orthodox Church.

The terrible result of this growing official antipathy was that the Jewish people were often subjugated and became second-class citizens. They were often portrayed as the 'killers of Christ', and an example of those who are under God's curse. On many occasions there were officially sanctioned massacres of Jewish people – many times on Easter Friday. Also, when a calamity hit a society and a scapegoat was sought, the Jewish people often became that scapegoat.

It was not easy being Jewish during that period, especially when institutional or Roman Christianity was rampant. Interestingly, when Jesus hung on the cross, which was the clearest sign of his rejection by the Jewish religious lead-

---

[6] The Edict of Milan.

ers (and the Roman secular authorities), he said of his persecutors: "Father, forgive them, for they do not know what they do." (Luke 23: 34.)

The separation of these two faith communities resulted because both, being very similar, wanted to establish clear identities from each other. The main issue was (and still is) about the identity of the community.

During the many centuries when institutional Christianity reigned supreme it became virtually impossible for a Jewish person to be a follower of Jesus and at the same time retain his or her Jewish identity. He or she would need to make a choice – one or the other, but not both at the same time. Neither community tolerated 'half-castes.'

The Christians basically viewed the Jews as the 'Christ-killers', while the Jewish people basically viewed the Christians as idol worshippers, and the cross became a constant reminder of all their suffering during those hundreds of years in exile. They called Jesus, *Yeshu,* which is an acronym meaning 'May his name and his memory be blotted out.' There seemed to be little effort made to reveal the true face of Jesus to the Jewish people. What they often saw was the ugly face of institutional Christianity.

What the Jewish people desperately desired and sought for was a land somewhere in Europe where they could live relatively safe lives and where this historic often Church-driven hatred of them would not be so prevalent. Somewhat ironically just such a sanctuary was found in a Roman Catholic dominated country - Poland.

Chapter 2

The Jewish people in Poland

Jewish people first move into Poland

Christianity was introduced into Poland by Catholic monks coming from Western Europe during the Medieval period. Gradually its message made inroads as pagan tribes and even small states were converted, climaxing in 966 AD when Duke Miesko I and his court converted to Christianity. Roman Catholic Christianity then became the official religion of the realm of Poland.

Over the following centuries the region of Poland endured numerous challenges and even territorial losses,[1] but it survived and managed to consolidate. The Roman Catholic Church also consolidated its authority over the people of the land.

During those years some Jewish merchants visited and even on occasion settled within the realm of Poland, especially from the year 1100 AD. However it was after the year 1264, when Prince Boleslaw the Pious signed the Statute of Kalisz which set the 'legal foundations for the presence of Jews in the Wielkopolska region,' that more Jewish people entered into and made their home in Poland.[2]

A high period of Jewish settlement in Poland occurred during the reign of King Casimir (Kazimierz) the Great (1333-1370). Although there was the occasional outbreak of violence against the Jewish people (usually a combination of economic distress, theological prejudice and even parochial nationalism), the Jewish people experienced comparative acceptance and harmony. In many regions their expertise in trade, especially international trade, resulted in them being accepted as great assets by Polish rulers and it was in the best interests of the Jews to retain good relations with the nobles and leaders.

---

1 The regions of East Prussia and Lithuania were captured by the German Teutonic Knights from 1230 AD onwards.

2 Dylewski, A. *Where the Tailor was a Poet – Polish Jews and their Culture*, (Krakow, 2003), p. 12.

The Polish-Lithuanian Commonwealth – 1569

Possibly the most significant event in the development of modern Poland was the Union of Lublin in 1569, whereby the Kingdom of Poland and the Grand Duchy of Lithuania merged together to form the Polish-Lithuanian Commonwealth. This Union saw both entities retaining their autonomy, but being governed by a common king and Sejm.[3]

Both Poland and Lithuania shared a common foreign policy and a single monetary system. The Commonwealth was one of the largest and most diverse states in Europe. It soon became home to the largest Jewish community in Europe.

Many of these Jewish people had come from Germany, mostly to escape the virulent anti-Jewish sentiment prevalent there. One such migrant, the esteemed Rabbi Moses Isserles, stated of Poland in 1572: "Their hatred of us in this country has not overwhelmed us as in the German lands. May it remain so until the coming of our Messiah."[4]

The Protestant Reformation in German lands

This was somewhat of an ironic statement, considering that in the German lands there had recently been a reformation of the Church which witnessed the birth of the Protestant movement. The individual most closely associated with this Reformation in Germany was Martin Luther.

One hallmark of the Reformation was the availability of the Scriptures in the vernacular language. This would mean, ostensibly, that Protestant Christians could then read and understand the covenant relationship between Almighty God and the nation of Israel. One would expect that Protestant Christianity would have a much more tolerant understanding of and attitude towards the Jewish people.

This, however, was not altogether the case. Although Luther at the outset of his ministry was tolerant, his attitude changed when the Jewish people did not readily accept the Protestant Christian message. In 1543 he wrote a vehemently anti-Jewish book entitled *The Jews and their Lies.*

---

[3] Sejm = bicameral parliament.

[4] Moses Isserles, 'She'elot u-tschuvot (*Questions and responses*), before 1572', cited in Polin Museum, Warsaw.

There were, though, other streams within Protestant Christianity which did have a better understanding of God's covenant relationship with the nation of Israel, and which did desire to introduce Jesus as the Messiah to the Jewish people. One of these was the Pietist movement within the Lutheran Church which was initiated by Philip Spener in the 1600s. Others who took an active interest in the Jewish people in Germany were Esdas Edzart in Hamburg, Hermann Francke and John Callenberg in Halle, and Count Nicholas von Zinzendorf and the Moravian movement based in Herrnhut. Additionally there was a positive attitude towards the Jewish people within the Puritan and Evangelical streams within Britain.

Forthcoming hardships for the Jewish people

The Polish-Lithuanian Commonwealth encompassed a huge area, including much of modern day Ukraine. In the far eastern border area lived an autonomous community of warriors named the Cossacks, who were all adherents of the Russian Orthodox faith.

Somc of these Cossacks were employed by the Commonwealth government to defend its extensive borders. But when certain Polish kings and nobles began restricting the freedom of the Cossacks, and reducing the number in their employ, the Cossacks rose in revolt and attacked the Polish nobility, the Roman Catholic clergy and many of the Jewish people. The Cossacks viewed the Jews as being in the pay and service of the Polish nobility.

The largest of these Cossack uprisings occurred in 1648 and was led by Bohdan Chmielnicki (Khmelnytsky). Known in Poland as the Khmelnytsky uprising it decimated the Jewish population in the eastern part of the Polish-Lithuanian Commonwealth.

The consequences of this uprising were disastrous not just for the Jewish population, but also geo-politically for the region, as Russia was drawn into the conflict and ultimately took control over areas of the Ukraine. The Russian bear was now roaring and ready to devour more territory – as too were other neighbours, namely Austria and Prussia.

Interestingly, this uprising climaxed in the same year, 1648, that the disastrous Thirty Years War ended in Germany (the Holy Roman Empire) with the signing of the Peace of Westphalia. This conflict was between those regions and entities which had adopted Protestantism against those which retained allegiance to Roman Catholicism and the Holy Roman emperor.

Both of these events traumatised the Jews of central Europe, and many were confused and disillusioned. In that same year a Jewish man from Smyrna (Izmir in Turkey) named Shabbetai Zvi (1626-1676) began to proclaim that he was the promised messiah who would lead the Jewish people back to the land of Israel. Many, even in central Europe, became his followers. This movement petered out after Shabbetai Zvi converted to Islam while in Turkey in 1666. But the consequences of the movement lingered on in central Europe.

After the disappointment of Shabbetai Zvi's false messiahship significant changes began to occur among the Jewish people. Rabbi Israel ben Eliezer, (Baal Shem Tov) became the figure head of the Hasidic movement that sought to bring joy and intimacy with God through mysticism and prayer. Hasidism was created and nourished in Poland on the eve of its dissolution by the surrounding great powers.

In Western Europe, including Prussia and other parts of 'Germany', many Jews sought to acculturate into Gentile society by embracing secular education and participating fully in society, thus creating a secular Jewish identity. In 'Germany' people such as Moses Mendelssohn were influenced by the Enlightenment and the 'Age of Reason' during the 1700's. A desire now grew among the Jewish population to enter into mainstream German society.

The dissolution of the Poland-Lithuanian Commonwealth

In the eighteenth century the Polish-Lithuanian Commonwealth came to an end. In 1772 the first of three partitions occurred, which would ultimately divide the Commonwealth between the empires of Russia, Austria and Prussia. By 1795 independent Poland had ceased to exist.

The Jewish people of the former Polish-Lithuanian Commonwealth were now divided between three political entities. Thereafter they developed according to the freedoms or restrictions permitted by these great powers.

Development of the Jewish communities

The majority of the Jewish population of the East now lived in the Russian Empire, which encompassed two important cities for the Jewish people - Warsaw and Vilna (also recorded as Wilno, Vilno, Vilnius). Most of this large Jewish population lived in an area known as the 'Pale of Settlement' where they were restricted in movement and exposure to the influences of the West. Warsaw in time became the centre of Jewish life in the Russian Empire.

At the conclusion of the Napoleonic Wars a degree of recognition of Polish autonomy in the Russian controlled area was given at the Congress of Vienna in 1815, but much of this autonomy was dissolved in 1830 by the Russian Czar Nicholas I. His successor, Alexander II, then implemented a stringent Russification policy following a Polish uprising in 1863. Further difficulties for the Jewish population occurred following the assassination of Alexander II in 1881, when the Jews collectively became the scapegoat for his assassination. Terrible pogroms broke out throughout the Russian Empire and thousands of Jewish people were killed, injured and uprooted.

Despite being mostly cut off from the influences of Western Europe, the Jewish communities of the Russian Empire nevertheless experienced some exposure to the Enlightenment (known to the Jewish people as *haskalah*).

This vast region was under the influence of either the Greek Orthodox or Roman Catholic Church, although large areas were also under the sway of the Greek Catholic or Uniate Church.[5] There was little attempt by the traditional churches to introduce Jewish people to the person of Jesus as the Messiah.

The second largest Jewish population at this time lived in the expanded Austrian Empire, living for the most part in the province of Galicia, which included the key cities of Lemberg (Lwow) and Cracow (Krakow). The Jews now living in the Austrian Empire were, for the most part, Orthodox, but were beginning to be exposed to the *haskalah* (Enlightenment). The vast majority of the Jewish population under the control of the Austrian emperor lived far from Vienna.

There was little active endeavour to introduce Jesus to the Jewish people in the predominantly Roman Catholic Austrian Hapsburg Empire (from 1867 known as the Austro-Hungarian Empire). No doubt, though, many Jews did 'convert' mostly for socio-economic reasons.

The smallest of the Jewish populations of former Poland lived within the en-

---

[5] Orthodox in theology and practise, but under the authority of Rome.

larged Prussia,[6] where two key cities were Posen and Breslau.[7] Prussia was the most open to the modernising influences of the Enlightenment, and especially after 1812 when the Prussian government began a process of emancipation for the Jewish people. Jews living in the greater Prussian region therefore had more opportunities to leave the narrow confines of Orthodox Jewish existence, to leave the *shtetl* and become part of the wider community – albeit with certain restrictions. One ultimate result of the Enlightenment was the formation of Reform Judaism in 'Germany.'

The influence of the Protestant Reformation also played a role with the Jewish people, despite Martin Luther's strong anti-Jewish position towards the end of his life. Ever since the 1600s and the formation of the Pietist movement within the Lutheran Church there had been active attempts to introduce Jesus to Jewish people, both in Prussia and in other areas of Protestant 'Germany'. One institution active in this was John Callenberg's *Institutum Judaicum* based in Halle, which had also sent out missionaries into the regions of Poland throughout the 1700s.

Many Jewish people became part of the German Church, for reasons of convenience and conviction. Many saw the only sure way of securing certain key positions was by becoming a Lutheran.[8] Yet throughout these years many individual Jews came to believe that Jesus was indeed the Messiah of Israel, repented, placed their faith in the person of Jesus as the atoning sacrifice and entered into a personal covenant relationship with the God of Israel. (Jeremiah 31: 31-34.)

---

[6] Although Prussia was part of the Holy Roman Empire, it effectively became a Kingdom in 1701 when Frederick the Great was crowned as King of Prussia. The capital moved from Konigsberg to Berlin.
[7] Present day Wroclau in Poland.
[8] For more on this subject see Hertz, D. *How Jews Became Germans*, (Yale University, 2007).

Chapter 3

Early history of CMJ in Poland

Beginnings of CMJ

About the year 1793 a young Jewish man in 'Germany'[1] named Joseph Levi was challenged by a devout German Christian (either a Moravian or Pietist) to consider whether Jesus had been the mediator of the new covenant of Jeremiah 31:31-34.[2]

In time this young man became convinced that Jesus was indeed the Messiah of Israel. After he was baptised he changed his name to Joseph Frey. Several years later Frey was in London en-route to Africa to serve with the London Missionary Society whereupon he noticed the destitute state of his brethren according to the flesh and asked for permission to remain and introduce them to Jesus of Nazareth. Permission was granted and Frey remained in Britain.

This was a period of great messianic and millennial expectancy in Europe, and especially in Britain. Following on from the French Revolution and Napoleon's military incursion into the Middle East and especially the land of Israel, many Christians sensed the imminent end of the age and the return of Jesus. In this period many such Christians (Protestants from various denominations, known collectively as Evangelicals or Pietists) believed that all efforts had to be made to take the message of Jesus out to all the nations.[3]

Many of these very same Evangelical Christians, including William Wilberforce, also believed that it was the time once again to re-introduce Jesus to

---

[1] At that time there was no unified nation called Germany, but the region of Germany was known as the Holy Roman Empire, which was composed of numerous smaller political entities, and two large entities, Austria and Prussia.

[2] In the actual encounter the Christian only quoted from Jeremiah 31:31-33. See Frey, J. *Narrative of the Reverend Joseph C. F. Frey,* (London, 1809), pp. 22-23.

[3] The Evangelical movement is associated with the spiritual revivals in Britain beginning in the mid-1700s in which John Wesley and George Whitfield were instrumental.

the Jewish people. Within this number were many who also believed that all efforts were to be made to encourage the physical restoration of the Jewish people to the land of Israel (Ottoman Turkish Palestine of the time).[4]

In 1809 Frey, together with some supporters, formed a society based upon the aforementioned principles, known as the 'London Society for Promoting Christianity amongst the Jews', which became CMJ.[5]

Following the end of the Napoleonic Wars CMJ also saw the need to take their message to the Jewish people outside of Britain. The first practical move occurred when a CMJ leader, Lewis Way, set out in 1817 on a journey to meet Czar Alexander I of Russia, whom he subsequently met on several occasions. At that point Czar Alexander was open to Evangelical Protestant initiatives, having already permitted the Bible Society to open a branch in Russia.[6]

Accompanying Way was a Polish-born Jewish Christian named Benjamin Nehemiah Solomon, upon whose shoulders the work among the Jews in Russia would hopefully rest. Initially all seemed well, as Solomon was granted a letter and license by Prince Alexander Galitzin the Minister of Religion and National Civilization on 24 February 1818, granting him authority to take up this work.[7]

Czar Alexander then invited Way and Solomon to join him in the region of Crimea in May 1818. While there the Czar commissioned Way to begin to introduce the Jews of the Karaite persuasion to Jesus.[8] Way, though, had other responsibilities, so he entrusted this work to Solomon, who remained in the Crimea.[9]

[4] These Evangelicals were part of the 'restorationist movement' which was birthed during the period of the Puritans in the late 1500 and early 1600s.

[5] CMJ was colloquially known as the London Jews Society (LJS). Wilberforce became a vice-President of this Society.

[6] This openness was due much to the influence which Prince Galitzen (1773-1844) had upon the Czar.

[7] Gidney, W. T. *The History of the London Society for Promoting Christianity amongst the Jews*, (London, 1908), p. 95.

[8] The Karaites only follow the written Torah and not the Talmud and the Oral Law.

[9] Solomon did not fulfill his commission. He later left the services of CMJ, absconding with a sizeable amount of money and was not heard from again.

Foundations of the work in Poland

Throughout his trip Way had been sending reports back to CMJ. His own return to Britain was then delayed when the Czar invited him to attend the Peace Conference at Aix-la-Chapelle (Aachen) in 1818 to address the European leaders and submit a Memorandum on behalf of the Jewish people.[10] Way only returned to Britain towards the end of 1818.

Before his return, however, and as a result of his enthusiastic letters, the CMJ General Committee resolved at a special meeting on 10 July 1818 to open a mission station in Poland.[11] The location would be in Warsaw, the centre of Jewish life in Eastern Europe. A suitable candidate was then selected named Alexander McCaul, a young Dublin scholar and Trinity College graduate.

McCaul, later assisted by a German Christian named William Becker, arrived in 1821 but did not have an altogether easy task initially. However they were ultimately able to establish their presence there. This was quite an achievement considering that CMJ was a Protestant (Anglican) missionary society, while Poland was predominantly Roman Catholic, and Warsaw was then under the political control of the Orthodox Russian Empire.[12] They were able to achieve this due to the personal contact of Lewis Way with Czar Alexander I. Naturally the strong Jewish community resented this incursion into the heartland of Orthodox Judaism.[13]

In her Polish language book *Duszozbawcy*, Professor Agnieszka Jagodzinska wrote about the work of CMJ in Poland: "The 'English missionaries' came also to the Kingdom of Poland, where in the early 1820's they opened their first missionary station in this territory. Poland, with its large Jewish population, was a natural destination for the LSPCJ. The missionaries visited Jewish towns and neighbourhoods, in which they distributed Bibles and missionary writings, and sought to engage Jews in religious disputes."[14]

---

[10] This Conference was organised in order to review the situation in Europe following the Congress of Vienna (which had been convened at the end of the Napoleonic Wars).

[11] Gidney, pp. 58-59.

[12] Russia adopted Eastern, Orthodox or Byzantine Christianity in 988 AD.

[13] Gidney, pp. 96-100.

[14] Jagodzinska, A. *Duszozbawcy,* (Wydawnictwo Austeria: Krakow. Budapeszt, 2017), p. 487. LSPCJ – London Society for Promoting Christianity among the Jews.

Their task was interrupted with the outbreak of the Crimean War in 1854, when Britain was engaged in war against Russia. The CMJ staff had to retreat, and although the conflict was finally resolved in 1856, they were not permitted to return until 1875. With the arrival of Rev O. Ellis in 1877 the work became more firmly established.[15]

During the same period work did continue or begin in other areas of what is now Poland. CMJ operated branches in several cities in Prussian controlled Poland, especially Posen and Breslau (today Wroclaw), and also in Austrian Poland (Galicia), primarily in Cracow (Krakow) and Lemberg (Lwow).

CMJ's involvement in Lemberg began in 1867 with the arrival of Rev. J. H. Bruhl. There were many restrictions placed upon him but Bruhl carried on as best he could until he left in 1871. A number of Jewish people in Lemberg were quite economically well-off so they could more easily hinder missionary work. With Bruhl's departure the work was carried on by successive workers during subsequent years.

Once CMJ was re-established in Warsaw after 1875 they expanded their work there. In 1910 Rev. Herman Charles Zimmerman (a Hebrew Christian who later changed his name to Carpenter) arrived. Zimmerman had previously worked at the CMJ station in Bucharest. By mid-1914, 1077 Jewish people had been baptised by the Society's workers since 1821.[16] They were full of expectation for the future.[17]

Birth of Germany and growth of nationalism – and rationalism

The nineteenth century witnessed a surge in nationalism. In Poland it spilled out into violence against the Russians in 1863. Then in 1871 German nationalism resulted in Prussia becoming the major component of the new nation of Germany - which quickly became an economic powerhouse. The new Germany was also known as the Second German Reich and was led first by

[15] Gidney, pp. 162-163, 165, 221-224, 284-286, 441-443, 541, 600-601.

[16] Gidney, p. 601; Adeney, J. H, *Digest of the Annual Reports from 1908 till 1952,* (No publication details, original copy in Conrad Schick Library), p. 18.

[17] The British-based Mildmay Mission to the Jews (MMJ) also established a presence in Russian Poland in 1905, eventually with stations at Warsaw, Minsk, Odessa and Lublin. See Mitchell Glaser, A Survey of Missions to the Jews in Continental Europe 1900-1950, (Dissertation for Fuller Theological Seminary, October 1988), p. 30.

Kaiser Wilhelm I and then by Kaiser Wilhelm II.

But other forces were also growing in Germany which in time would have a dramatically negative influence upon Jewish people throughout Europe. These were the academic forces of rationalism, which when combined with the fashionable teachings of Charles Darwin, led in turn to a dangerous form of nihilism - the basic belief that rejects all forms of religious and moral principles and that perceives life as essentially meaningless.

During this same period some of the perspectives of the rationalists influenced some Protestant (mostly Lutheran) Christians, leading to the development of an influential stream best known as liberal Christianity. This stream basically taught that the Bible and the teaching of the Church had to be viewed in a pragmatic, rationalistic way. There was little room for faith, or belief in the supernatural. The Bible as well as the people of the Bible, both the true followers of Jesus and the Jewish people, now began to be devalued.

An apt description of this trend is given by a Hebrew Christian leader, Rev. Arnold Frank of the Jerusalem Church in Hamburg, who wrote some years later of the inner collapse of Germany:

> ... the bulk of the people has long ceased to believe in Biblical Christianity, in the Word of God, in the Divinity of Christ, in a future life. Rationalism has undermined the Christian faith in the land of Luther, writers, teachers and preachers having made philosophy intelligible and popular. Most of the theological professors in Germany were also influenced by this rationalism. The Bible was treated irreverently, they explained away Christ's Sacrifice, and denied His Resurrection. The majority of the theological students came from homes where vital Christianity was unknown. Their reason for entering the ministry was that the pastorate was an honoured and a well-paid profession.[18]

Ironically while Christianity was losing much of its spiritual fervour in the land of Luther, another form of spirituality, namely occultism, was spreading its influence. Then towards the end of the nineteenth and beginning of the twentieth century there was a fervent increase in a form of German nationalism, both in Germany and in Austria. Some streams of this German nation-

---

[18] *The Hebrew Christian*, Volume XIII, 1939-1940, p. 49.

alism merged with the occult movement, and within this emerging movement there was also an emphasis on reconnecting with the pre-Christian Germanic deities.

These ultra nationalists desired to return to the Germany of pre-800 AD, the year in which Charlemagne (Charles the Great) was crowned as the Roman emperor. In that year Roman Catholicism was officially accepted as the religion of Germany.

The growing German nationalist movement in its many forms saw little place for anyone who was not a pure German. This perspective was quite strong in Vienna in the 1890s and early 1900s. The mighty Austro-Hungarian Empire ruled over a vast number of 'non-German' ethnic groups causing many Germans in the Empire to desire union with the German nation. In such an environment a distinction was being made between 'pure Germans' (Aryans) and all the others, especially the Slavs – and the Jews. The Jewish people in particular were viewed as a non-European and therefore an alien ethnic group.

During that period there was a large and culturally diverse Jewish population in Vienna. Such a Jewish influence disturbed many of these staunch German nationalists. One of these was a young man who was beginning to formulate his philosophical and political views of life. His name was Adolf Hitler.

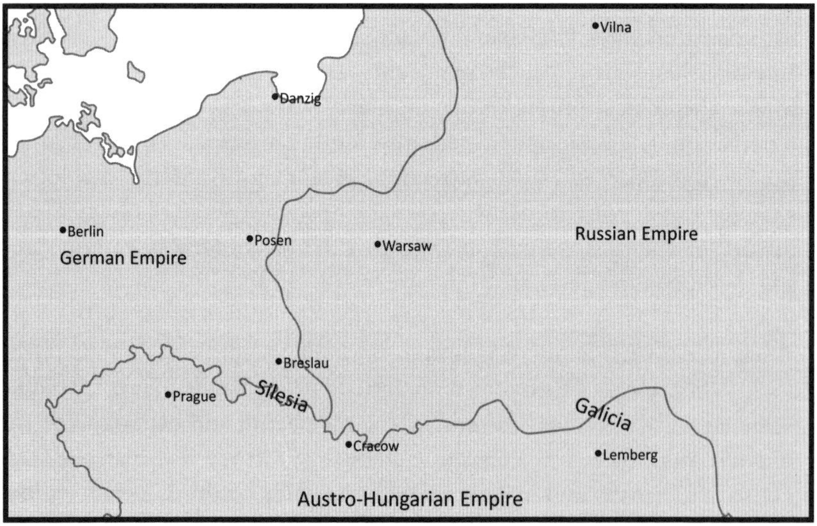

Poland pre-1914

Chapter 4

Early lives of Basilius Jocz and Chana Don

Vilna, Wilno, Vilnius

Another city with a vibrant Jewish community was Vilna, located in the border region of Poland and Lithuania. The Jewish community there was associated with a famous rabbi named Elijah ben Solomon Zalman (1720-1797). In early times in the Middle East the term *gaon* was given to rabbis and Talmudic scholars of great importance. Elijah ben Solomon Zalman was so renowned that he was dubbed the Ga'on of Vilna, or the Vilna Ga'on.

The Jewish population in Vilna in the early 1880s numbered some 40,000[1] and by the turn of the twentieth century had grown to around 76,000 people. The city had numerous educational facilities,[2] many of which were Talmudic schools, known as *yeshivot*, often associated with the teachings of the Vilna of Ga'on.

But Vilna had more to offer than just the Ga'on and Talmudic studies. It was also a centre of the *haskalah*, the Jewish Enlightenment. Additionally in 1897 the *Bund*, the General Jewish Workers Union in Lithuania, Russia, and Poland, was founded there,[3] something which later caused a measure of grief to the Jocz family.

Another significant Jewish movement was also birthed in 1897 – the Zionist movement, which began in Basel, Switzerland, through the vision of Theodor Herzl. Herzl's vision was to establish a Jewish national entity in Palestine, a vision which other groups, known as the *Chovevei Zion* and *Biluim,* had been attempting to bring about in the land of Israel since 1882.

---

[1] *Yivo Encyclopaedia,* Jews in Eastern Europe, www.yivoencyclopedia.org/Vilnius
[2] Yad Vashem, The Jewish Community of Lithuania, www.yadvashem.org.
[3] *Yivo Encyclopaedia,* Jews in Eastern Europe, www.yivoencyclopedia.org/Vilnius

The birth of Basilius (Bazyli) Jocz and Chana (Anna) Don

It was in this vibrant city that Basilius Jocz (henceforth Bazyli)[4] was born on 23 October 1880 to Yankel and Ita Jocz.[5] Little is known of Bazyli's early life, apart from him having had little education.[6] However as a young boy Bazyli must have shown some academic potential, for he became a rabbinical student in the Vilna Ga'on Yeshiva.[7]

In the same year that Bazyli was born a baby girl was born in the *shtetl*[8] of Zossle (Zelse, Zosli, Soschli) near to Vilna. Chana Don (henceforth Anna) was born on 18 November 1880, to Jochanan and Sara Don.[9] Jochanan was, according to Elizabeth Myers, a milkman.[10] Seemingly Anna never had much education, and it is recorded that she attended elementary school in 1890.[11]

Anna Don's accident

One day in the *shtetl* Anna was sent by her mother to summon the midwife to attend to a woman in labour in the house next door to the Dons' house. The year was either 1894 or 1900.[12] The midwife asked young Anna to stay

---

[4] For much of his life he was known as Bazyli Jocz.

[5] Form from International Red Cross (Koln) for an International Tracing Service, Number ZK 705 848, German File relating to compensation for Anna Jocz, in Jocz Private Collection, p. 113. Henceforth German File.

[6] The Attorney Erich Rocholl to the Ministry of Financial Compensation, 3 June 1958, German File, p. 19.

[7] I cannot find a reference to a particular *yeshiva* matching this name, but there were *yeshivot* associated with the teachings of the Vilna Ga'on.

[8] A *shtetl* was a very small Jewish community.

[9] In a sworn statement made in 1959 Anna stated: 'I, Anna, previously known as Chana Jocz, nee Don…' Her father's given name was Jochanan, and her mother's maiden name was Sadewicz. Her husband's name was Basilius or Wasilej. See German File solemn declaration from Anna Jocz, 8 January 1959, witnessed by Steven Pozel, A Commissioner and Notary Public, p. 55. This information differs a bit from 'Translated letter from Russian and Ukrainian to German', German File, p. 13. The reason, as Jakob Jocz explained in his letter of 20 December 1958 to Attorney Rocholl, German File, p. 39, was so that Anna could hide her Jewish identity from the Nazi and/or Soviet authorities.

[10] Elizabeth Myers, *The Literary Legacy of Jacob Jocz*, (M.A. Thesis, Fuller Theological Seminary, 1989), p. 1.

[11] Form filled out by Erich Rocholl, no date, German File, p. 18. 12 According to the account given by Myers, Anna was fourteen years of age and the year given was 1900. However according to the records, Anna was born in 1880, which would have made her twenty years of age.

in her house in her absence.

By the time Anna was able to return home it was late, and as it had been snowing, she decided to go through the Gentile cemetery. Unfortunately the village fool was lurking in the cemetery and he leapt at Anna from behind a tombstone and startled her, causing her to fall and twist her back. Anna passed out, and after she came to she noticed a throbbing pain in her back, but she managed to return home.[13]

The parents were obviously concerned about the welfare of their daughter as she wasn't recovering quickly, and were informed that there was a certain Dr Frohwein in Vilna who might be able to help. But some people warned Jochanan to be careful as Dr Frohwein was "... kind of a Jew and yet not a Jew."[14] Dr Paul Frohwein was a Jewish follower of Jesus[15] associated with the Lutheran Mission. Primarily as a result of the Pietist influence, the Lutheran Church had an Evangelical stream, and the Lutheran Medical Mission in Vilna was part of this stream.

Jochanan and Anna visit Dr Frohwein

At some point after the accident Jochanan plucked up courage, took his horse and buggy and drove Anna into Vilna in search of the Lutheran Mission. He successfully located it and took his daughter inside. Naturally he was apprehensive. Dr Frohwein was obviously aware of this and as he took Anna into the examination room, he offered Jochanan a warm drink as he waited outside.

While in the waiting room Jochanan noticed a small black book on the table, and curiously picked it up. On it was written in Hebrew *Brith Ha Hadashah* (The New Covenant or The New Testament). Dr Arthur Glasser tells us that: 'Upon opening it, he encountered almost immediately something that he had not heard before, that Jesus was "the son of David, the son of Abraham."'[16] 'The astonished milkman,' wrote Elizabeth Myers 'found that the

[13] Myers, p. 1.

[14] Myers, p. 1.

[15] Within the Jewish community Jewish followers of Jesus were often known by the derogatory Polish name of *meches*, which is similar to *meshumad*.

[16] Arthur F. Glasser, 'The Legacy of Jakob Jocz', *International Bulletin of Missionary Research*, April 1993, p. 66.

little book spoke of Jesus, the son of Abraham. Bazyli then asked himself: 'What had Abraham to do with Jesus?"'[17] When Dr. Frohwein reappeared and noticed Bazyli's interest, the doctor encouraged him to take the book home with him.[18]

Jochanan comes to faith in Jesus and the family moves to Vilna

During the following days Jochanan would get up after everyone else had gone to bed, and would 'light a candle and read the Hebrew text.'[19] As a result of his reading Jochanan came to believe that Jesus (Yeshua) was indeed the Messiah of Israel.

Shortly afterwards the Don family moved from Zelse to Vilna to escape the pogroms that were spreading through the rural areas.[20] Pogroms were destructive riots which periodically broke out in the Russian Empire, and were mostly aimed at the Jewish people. There was tension in the late 1890s during what were termed the 'Storms in the Negev' pogroms in the south of Russia, while in 1900 a Gentile woman spread the false rumour in Vilna that Jewish people had tried to kill her to use her blood for the Passover.[21] Outbreaks of violence against Jewish people invariably occurred whenever this absurd accusation was broadcast.

Jochanan managed to find a suitable Christian congregation close to their new home, and was baptised there. His wife Sarah apparently was not pleased with this move. However, not long afterwards Jochanan died, and in order to earn an income Sarah took in a lodger. He was Bazyli Jocz, then still a student at the Vilna Ga'on Yeshiva. Myers states of Bazyli at this time:

> Bazyli was a keen, thoughtful student with an eager, enquiring mind. And one day, reading through Yeshayahu haNavi [Isaiah the prophet], he came across a passage which he could not understand. Going to the teacher, he asked, "Tell me, of whom does the prophet speak?" But the rabbi struck him on the head, saying, "Du shaygets [you Gentile, you detestable one]! You have seen the missionaries already. Don't ask foolish questions.

[17] Myers, p. 2.

[18] Glasser, p. 66.

[19] Myers, p. 2.

[20] Myers, p. 2.

[21] Yad Vashem, The Jews of Lithuania, www.yadvashem.org/yv/en/exhibitions/vilna.

Study!"[22]

The response of the rabbi deeply affected Bazyli and it caused him to want to look further into the matter. Somehow Bazyli knew about Dr Frohwein, as his clinic offered free services to the Jewish community. As a result he visited the doctor, who informed Bazyli of whom the prophet was speaking. It was about Jesus, and as a result of his conversations with Dr Frohwein, Bazyli Jocz also came to believe that Jesus was the Messiah of Israel.

Bazyli continued living as a guest in the Don household while still studying at the *yeshiva.* During this time he also learnt the trade of carpentry, specialising as a cabinet-maker. All the time he seems to have kept quiet about his faith in Jesus.[23]

It was during this very same period that there were ominous signs for the Jewish people within the Russian Empire. About the year 1902 an anti-Jewish booklet entitled *The Protocols of the Elders of Zion* was produced in Russia. A major thrust of this book was that the rich Jews were planning to take political control of the world. This fraudulent booklet helped spread anti-Jewish sentiment throughout Russia, and later elsewhere. Several decades later a German nationalist from Austria would utilise this forged booklet to substantiate his anti-Jewish policies.

Then in 1903 there was a horrendous pogrom in Kishinev in Bessarabia which resulted in the deaths of many Jews. This event, as well as a failed revolution against the Czarist regime in 1905, resulted in the exodus of a very large number of Jews from the Russian Empire. It was an unsettling time for the Jewish population of Russia.

Interestingly one of the most significant movements of Jews becoming followers of Jesus was birthed in Kishinev in the early 1880s by Joseph Rabinowitz. This short lived movement was named the 'Israelites of the New Covenant.'

Bazyli confesses his faith in Jesus

Although no doubt aware of the larger political issues of his time, Bazyli

[22] Myers, p. 2.

[23] Myers, p. 3.

Jocz had other matters on his mind, or shall we say, in his heart, at this time. Bazyli had become quite fond of Anna Don, but he knew he would have to confess to her about his belief in Jesus. Elizabeth Myers, who refers to Anna as Hannah, describes what then happened:

> One day, in the Vilno park where Bazyli and Hannah would sit together on an afternoon, he said to her, "Hannah, I have a secret."
> "What is your secret?"
> "My secret is that I am a Jew who believes that Yeshua haNotzri is the Moshiach of Israel"
> Hannah looked at him and said, "I too have a secret."
> "What is your secret?"
> "My father also was a believer in the Messiah. Before he died, he told me never to forget about Yeshua."[24]

Marriage and beginnings of a family

It is unclear exactly when this happened but we are then informed that Bazyli and Anna were married in Vilna on 11 November 1905[25] - just a week before Anna's twenty-fifth birthday. According to Anna, they then lived in Vilna until after the First World War.[26]

Their first child was Jakob, who was born in Vilna on 14 October 1906, followed by Jerzy (George) on 30 December 1908 and then Pawel (Paul) who was born on 17 August 1911, also in Vilna.[27] Throughout this time it seems that Bazyli was employed as a carpenter, and worked for quite some time with the Lutheran Mission. It is unclear when this employment began, but it is clear that Bazyli was close to Dr Frohwein. The doctor's son, Dr Gottfried Frohwein, testified in 1959:

> I lived in Wilno from 1902 until 1918 and knew the claimant Mrs. Anna Jocz as well as her husband Basilius Jocz, who often came to the office

[24] Myers, p. 3.

[25] 'Translated letter from Russian and Ukrainian to German', German File, p. 13.

[26] Solemn declaration from Anna Jocz, German File, p. 55.

[27] Letter from Steven Pozel to Erich Rocholl, 9 February 1962, German File, p. 171. *A Brief History of the Jocz Family*, (henceforth *A Brief History*), www.jocz.ca. states the year of Jerzy's birth is 1909. However it also states that he was forty when he died on 31 October 1949, therefore the birth year must be 1908.

> of my father, a doctor in Wilno. I knew that both had Jewish parents and they had converted to Christianity.[28]

It is unclear when Bazyli was baptised, but Anna later testified: 'My husband and I are both of Jewish origin and all of our parents were Jews. We got married in the year 1905. My husband became a Christian after we got married and I got baptized in the year 1918.'[29]

It seems more likely that Anna was baptized in 1908 so it's possible that 1918 was a typing error. Additionally, as it appears that Bazyli was already a committed follower of Jesus, Anna might have been referring to his baptism, when he became 'officially' a member of the Church. In his *Curriculum Vitae* to CMJ in 1924 Jakob wrote: 'I was born in 1906 in Vilna (Polish Lithuania) and was baptized in the Lutheran Church there.'[30]

It seems highly likely that the Jocz family were closely associated with the local Lutheran Church during these years. Jakob wrote of his early education: 'In Vilna I finished the five classes of the Evangelical Church School, where I received a good and Christian education… After completing my studies in the Church School I entered the Gymnasium (High School) but could not finish the third class because of the difficult conditions caused by the World War.'[31]

---

[28] Statutory declaration of Gottfried Emil Hermann Frohwein, 30 January 1959, German File, p. 59.

[29] Statutory declaration by Anna Jocz, 9 January 1959, German File, p. 55.

[30] Jacob Jocz to Mr Gill, 22 September 1924, *Curriculum Vitae,* Bodleian Library, Dept CMJ, File on Warsaw, d. 51.4. (Jocz usually signed his letters to CMJ with his Anglicised name of Jacob.)

[31] Jacob Jocz to Mr Gill, 22 September 1924, *Curriculum Vitae.*

Chapter 5

The First World War

The war in the East

The beginning of the First World War on 4 August 1914 had little immediate effect upon the Jocz family in Vilna. The nearest they were to fighting at that point was when the Russians attacked East Prussia to the west on 17 August, crushing the Germans within four days.

The Germans then introduced a new commander, General von Hindenburg, who quickly counter-attacked and defeated the Russians in what became known as the Battle of Tannenberg between 26-31 August 1914. The Germans later won a further decisive battle at the Masurian Lakes, and had now effectively driven all Russian soldiers from East Prussia.

Further to the south the Russians also invaded the Austro-Hungarian province of Galicia, and gained considerable territory. These Russian victories forced the Germans to form the Ninth Army in order to halt the westward movement of the Russian Army. Russia already controlled the greater part of present day Poland. This new German Army went on to the offensive in late 1914.

The Second Battle of the Masurian Lakes in East Prussia was fought during the winter of 1914-1915 and caused considerable losses to the Russian Army, as well as stopping any further Russian movement westwards. These battles were fought not far from Vilna.

It was during this period that Elzick Don, Anna's only brother, was executed. He was, wrote Myers, 'tortured and shot by the Russian police when his connections with Der Bund, the anti-Tsarist revolutionary movement, were uncovered.'[1]

In April 1915 a major German and Austro-Hungarian offensive against the

[1] Myers, p. 5. Der Bund - General Jewish Workers Union.

Russians began, with one arm of the German offensive heading into Lithuania and the other arm pushing towards Warsaw. Warsaw was captured by the Germans on 4-5 August 1915. On the Lithuanian front there was terrible fighting in Vilna itself, until it too was captured by the Germans on 19 September 1915.

During this period hundreds of thousands of people were forced to flee and became destitute refugees. Life for those who remained was also difficult, as Jakob Jocz later recalled:

> Half of the population of the City fled, the other half stayed a prey to hunger and cold and need. In the chaos of destruction neither Schools nor teachers were left. Their place was taken by "Time" which inculcated that which no school can teach: to hold on patiently, to pray, trust and hope.
>
> Many of our friend[s] succumbed through hunger and epidemics, but thanks be to God, who did not forsake His own, in spite of the terrible trials we were kept safe.[2]

It would appear that throughout the war years Bazyli remained in the employment of the Lutheran Mission in Vilna.[3] This would seem probable considering that from 1915 until 1918 Vilna was under German control. More than likely he was employed as a general tradesman, as his trade was a carpenter and cabinet maker.

Anna's sister, Reisel, married a German officer during the time of the German occupation.[4] Yet despite these German connections the Jocz family still encountered prejudice. Dr Arthur Glasser states how, 'On one occasion a nun denied young Jakob relief food, simply because he was Jewish – and she told him so in no uncertain terms.'[5]

Conditions in Warsaw

Warsaw was not exempt from the deprivations of war. As much of the fight-

---

[2] Jacob Jocz to Mr Gill, 22 September 1924, *Curriculum Vitae.*
[3] Ibid.
[4] Myers, p. 5.
[5] Arthur F. Glasser, 'The Legacy of Jakob Jocz', p. 66.

ing was occurring in regions where hundreds of thousands of Jews lived, tens of thousands of Jewish refugees made their way to Warsaw. When the War broke out Herman Carpenter (formerly Zimmerman) was not in Warsaw but was in Moscow, temporarily filling in for the Anglican chaplain there. He returned to Warsaw in May 1915 but it was a short stay as the Germans then drove towards the city and, being associated with a British organisation, Carpenter and other British subjects were forced to leave.

After the German Army captured Warsaw two local Hebrew Christians, Abraham Eisenman (Ajzeman) and Markus Bregman, continued on with the work in Carpenter's absence. While Carpenter saw out the war years in Britain, another Warsaw worker, Miss Emily Parkhurst, spent much of the war period in Moscow. Both waited for the opportunity to return.[6]

Conditions for the Jewish people on the Eastern Front were very difficult as they were often in areas being fought over by the Russians and the Central Powers (Germany and the Austro-Hungarian Empire). During these challenging times numerous aid agencies and Christian organisations raised funds to aid destitute Jewish refugees.[7]

A period of upheaval and confusion begins

The period from 1918 to 1921 was one of tremendous turmoil in the region. The two revolutions in Russia in March and October 1917 resulted in the formation of a Bolshevik-led government in Russia.

During this same period the nationalities which had been under Russian control, such as Lithuanians and Poles, saw an opportunity for re-establishing their independence. The occupying Germans wanted to ensure that not only would Russia withdraw from the War, but that regions occupied by Germany which had previously been part of the Russian Empire, would remain under Germany's influence in one form or another. Germany sponsored a State Council of Poland, which would rule in the region of Poland that had formerly been occupied by Russia.

---

[6] Adeney, J. H. *Digest of the Annual Reports 1908-1952*, (unpublished, Conrad Schick Library), p. 51; Crombie. K. *CMJ - 200 Years Serving the Jewish People*, (Heritage Resources: Perth, 2016), p. 132.

[7] See Mitchell Glaser, *A Survey of Missions to the Jews in Continental Europe 1900-1950*, p. 33. CMJ also gave aid to these refugees.

The Lithuanians did not want to come under direct Polish control, so they established a National Council in Vilna (Vilnius to the Lithuanians) on 18 September 1917. They also issued a declaration to the German Government that they desired independence, and on 16 February 1918 proclaimed an independent Government of Lithuania with Vilnius as the capital.

Only several weeks later on 3 March 1918 the new Bolshevik government in Russia led by Vladimir Lenin concluded a separate peace agreement with Germany at Brest-Litovsk. As part of that agreement Russia relinquished control over all territories west of the region of Ukraine, which included the regions of Poland and Lithuania.

The end of the First World War in the East did not mean the coming of peace, however, as forces loyal to the former Czarist regime (White Russians) now battled the forces loyal to the Bolshevik or communist government (Red Russians).

When it became clear that the War was soon to end in the West and that Germany would be defeated, German forces began retreating from Lithuania. A whole new dynamic now developed in Germany. On 9 November 1918 Kaiser Wilhelm II abdicated and left no instructions for succession. A republic now became the *de facto* form of government in Germany.

In Warsaw the State Council of Poland asserted its independence and a new independent Polish government was declared on 11 November 1918 with General Jozef Pilsudski playing a leading role.

On that same day, 11 November 1918, an Armistice with the leadership of the new Germany was signed, thereby ending hostilities on the Western Front. There was to be no such cessation of conflict on the Eastern Front however, as the Brest-Litovsk Agreement between Bolshevik Russia and the previous German government was annulled by the Allies. A whole new geo-political dynamic was about to engulf the region of Lithuania and Poland, in which the Jocz family found themselves deeply immersed.

Chapter 6

Bolsheviks, Lithuanians and Poles

With the annulment of the Brest-Litovsk Agreement new challenges arose for the regions of the East. As the German Army withdrew, the newly formed Lithuanian government took control over Vilnius. But this situation was short lived, for the new Bolshevik government in Russia then invaded the regions of Lithuania and Poland and began attacking Vilnius. The Lithuanian Army was forced to withdraw from Vilnius on 5 January 1919 and the Bolsheviks took control.[1]

Jakob Jocz wrote of this difficult period:

> With the coming of the Bolsheviks our greatest suffering also came, not only physical but mental torture was our lot. Though still a young boy I was compelled to leave my father's home and town and seek shelter amongst strangers where by means of hard work I learnt to earn my daily bread and to help my father. I had to suffer a great deal from the Jews who knew that I was baptized. Not seldom would they point to me and say "May such be the lot of all baptized Jews and traiters [sic]" or addressing me would say: "See, your God has deserted you, whereas our God is with us." These experiences called forth in my young heart both pain and compassion, because I was convinced that the Lord had not forsaken me and that they themselves were ignorant of the present [sic – presence] of God. In spite of my material need, their need was greater because of their spiritual condition. This thought evoked audible expression of joy in me, for was I not also a Jew and only through love of the Saviour was I not in the same condition as they?[2]

Vilna (Vilnius) incorporated into Poland

The Bolshevik control over Vilnius was itself short-lived. By this time the newly-formed Polish Army was on the offensive and began attacking the city

[1] *Encyclopaedia Britannica*, 1975, Vol. X, p. 442.

[2] Jacob Jocz to Mr Gill, 22 September 1924, *Curriculum Vitae.*

with the object of capturing it, and of 'forcing Lithuania to enter into a federal union with Poland…'[3]

The Polish Army defeated the Red Army on 20 April 1919 and subsequently occupied the city, which now again became Vilna. Peace did not prevail, however, as the Lithuanians rejected the plans of the Polish commander, Jozef Pilsudski, to create a federal union. The object of this federal union was to create a sizeable buffer between the powerful bastions of Russia on one side and Germany on the other.

Full-scale fighting between Poland and Lithuania was averted when the Allies created a demarcation line, known as the Foch Line, which separated the two sides but which left Vilna on the Polish side.

Peace still evaded Vilna, however, for in the summer of 1920 the Soviet Red Army once again attacked, and captured the city. The Soviets in turn ceded the city to the Lithuanians on 12 July 1920 and Lithuanian troops subsequently occupied it – which displeased the Poles. The League of Nations brokered a partial armistice in October 1920, which the Polish government did not accept, and they subsequently drove the Lithuanians out again.

Negotiations concerning the future status of this strategic city continued and despite Lithuanian objections, Vilnius was ultimately incorporated into Poland in 1923 and again became Vilna.

Bazyli goes to Warsaw with the Polish Army

At some time within this period when Poland controlled Vilna, Bazyli Jocz was drafted to serve in the Polish Army and was taken to Warsaw. The Jocz family history on their website states of this period:

> These were difficult years in Eastern Europe. Even after the First World War ended, fighting continued between Poland, Russia and Lithuania. Uprisings, brutal repression and famine were common features of life until war finally ended with the Treaty of Riga in 1921. During that period the family was briefly separated. Bazyli had been drafted to serve in Polish army barracks in Warsaw and Jakob went with him leaving Anna, George

---

[3] *Encyclopaedia Britannica,* 1975, Vol. X, p. 442.

and Paul in Vilnius.[4]

It is unclear how long Bazyli served or what exactly his role was, but he may well have worked in his trade as a carpenter.

A new Germany

Aside from the battles being fought over Lithuania, during the period of 1919-1920 there were other military battles being fought on both sides of Poland. Following the abdication of Kaiser Wilhelm II, Germany operated as a *de facto* republic – but in practice a political vacuum had been created.

Many German soldiers had felt betrayed by the surrender to the Allies on 11 November, and could not believe that it was due to their defeat on the battlefield. They were looking for scapegoats to blame for why it happened. It was in this environment that the 'Germany was stabbed in the back' slogan was birthed. This myth basically maintained that civilians on the home front had undermined the war effort, especially through profiteering. Prominent among these so-called profiteers were the Social Democrats (who were held responsible for ending the Second German Reich and instituting the new form of government), the Communists – and the Jews.

Bolshevik agitators were at the same time attempting to gain control and fill the vacuum left by the collapse of the Second Reich. Skirmishes were being fought throughout the country, and especially in Berlin. On many occasions the Bolshevik agitators were opposed by para-military groups known as *Freikorps*, composed of former German soldiers. One disillusioned former soldier was Adolf Hitler, who now began his rise to prominence.[5]

In view of the political turmoil the German government left Berlin and convened in the city of Weimar. There, from 6 February till 11 August 1919, they worked on a new constitution for the new Germany. In time this new republic became synonymous with the city where the new constitution was drawn up, and Germany also became known as the Weimar Republic.

Poland defeats the Soviets

From the East the Soviets continued their drive westwards in order to join

[4] *A Brief History*, p. 2.

[5] Hitler had joined the German Army while living in Bavaria in 1914.

and bolster the Communist or Bolshevik 'revolution' in Western Europe. After subduing the region of Ukraine they moved into Poland. The Polish government wanted to stop the Soviets breaking through to Germany, but by early 1920 the Red Army was closing in on Warsaw.

The Western powers became anxious. But the Poles, led by General Pilsudski, won a decisive victory over the Soviets in what became known as the Battle of Warsaw in March 1920. Both Poland and Western Europe were saved from Bolshevism. Pilsudski and his forces then went on the offensive and pushed the Soviets well back into Ukraine. One leading Soviet commander who felt deeply humiliated by this defeat was Joseph Stalin, who would later replace Lenin as leader of the Soviet Union (USSR).

During this campaign as many as 30,000 Jewish people were killed by the Polish armies, partly as a result of some cooperating with the Bolsheviks.[6]

Eventually the Soviets sought a cease-fire with Poland in October 1920, resulting in the Treaty of Riga which was signed on 18 March 1921. The demarcation lines between Poland and the Soviet Union were now basically established. In time Lemberg (Lwow), Vilna and Warsaw all became part of Poland.

The Jocz family could be excused for not remembering what name to call their home city anymore due to the number of times it had changed hands. But its present name and status would no longer greatly affect them as they were on the move - to Warsaw.

[6] Sachar, H. *The Course of Modern Jewish History,* (Delta Publishing: New York, 1977), p. 356. (Henceforth *The Course.*)

Chapter 7

The Jocz family moves to Warsaw

The work of CMJ re-established in Warsaw

Immediately at the conclusion of the War CMJ made known its intention to send Rev. Carpenter back to Poland and, they wrote, 'trust that in God's good time it may be possible to carry out their long-desired plans for a great extension of evangelistic work throughout Poland.'[1]

The internal political and economic situation delayed Carpenter's return to Warsaw until 14 September 1919. His initial task when he arrived was to fulfil the position of chaplain for the English Church.[2] However on 15 December he reported 'difficulties in the matter of recognition by the Polish Government of the status of the English Church – and indirectly the future of work amongst the Jews.'[3]

The new political reality meant that he now had to deal with the Polish government, instead of the former Czarist Russian government. The British Consul, Mr Savery, was thereafter actively involved in pursuing this matter through the Department of Foreign Affairs and the Department of Cults.[4]

In the end an affirmative answer was forwarded from the Minister of the Department of Cults to the Polish Minister of Foreign Affairs on 3 February 1920:

---

[1] CMJ Report 1918-1919, p. 32.

[2] Carpenter sent CMJ a copy of a Memorandum sent to the Polish Government - 'Memorandum - The Status of the Church of England Chaplaincy in Warsaw', Miscellaneous Papers 370B, stamped 27 October 1919, Bodleian Library, Dept CMJ, Warsaw d. 51.4.

[3] Carpenter to Gill, 15 December 1919, CMJ General Committee 23 January 1920, Minute 2575, Bodleian Library, Dept CMJ, Minute Book, Dept CMJ, c. 37.

[4] This term can be misleading to Westerners of today, but in Poland at that time it related to all religious bodies other than the Roman Catholic Church.

> It being stated that the Anglican Mission amongst the Jews reckons nearly 100 years of history in Poland, where its activities were exercised from 1821 to 1854, and from 1875 to 1914, on the basis of the Authorisation by the competent authorities of this epoch, the Minister of Cults and public instruction, taking into consideration that this authorisation has not formally been withdrawn, does not wish, on his part, to cause any inconvenience to the work of the Mission, until the time when religious questions will be definitely regulated by legislation.[5]

Upon receipt of this notification Carpenter was naturally thrilled, although he had to comply with certain restrictions, including being able to operate only within a certain region of Poland. This was primarily due to the ongoing conflict with the Russians in the East. He was also required to supply full details of those who would be involved. These would be: Marcus Bregman, Abraham Ajzeman, Abraham Chinenburg (Ginsburg), and Dora Parkhurst.

Carpenter asked Savery to seek clarification concerning when they could re-establish their presence elsewhere, considering that in the past CMJ had stations at Posen and in Lwow.[6] Despite this minor set-back, Carpenter was pleased that 'for the time being we are in the same position as we were under the Russians, this is a point gained.'[7]

Another minor problem was that their activities 'must be limited to persons of the Israelite Religion.' This matter he sought to re-dress, for if a person who was not Jewish partook of Anglican or CMJ related meetings, then there could be subsequent problems for CMJ. Savery pursued these questions, and in a communication to Carpenter on 8 March 1920, informed him that there

---

[5] The Minister of Cults and Instruction to the Minister of Foreign Affairs, 3 February 1920, Bodleian Library, Dept CMJ, Warsaw d. 51.4. This communication was forwarded to Consul Savery and then to Carpenter. According to the CMJ Report 1920-21 they received a special "Ukas" (decision, ruling, judgement, verdict) to continue their work.

[6] Carpenter to Savery, 20 February 1920, Bodleian Library, Dept CMJ, Warsaw d. 51.4.

[7] Carpenter to Gill, 23 February 1920, Miscellaneous Papers 370B. Bodleian Library, Dept CMJ, Warsaw d.51.4. He also mentioned that he gained his independence from being under the Lutheran Consistory, which, he said 'will facilitate our work a great deal and spare us any more annoyance which has been our lot for the last forty-five years.'

would be no problems if non-Jewish people attended their meetings.[8]

By April 1920 all of the workers had received official permission to re-commence the work of CMJ in Poland. They began in earnest, with Bregman already reporting in June that he and Chinenberg 'had visited twelve centres of big Jewish populations.'[9] They were not always well received, for at that time of turmoil in the region there was considerable anti-Semitism, and many Jewish people in turn responded harshly to the message about Jesus. Many Jews viewed anti-Semitism and the Church as synonymous.

These missionary journeys would continue throughout the following years and many of the large and even smaller scattered Jewish communities were visited. Additionally, in time the other mission agencies operating in Poland also had similar endeavours, and between them large numbers of Jewish people were introduced one way or another to the person of Jesus of Nazareth.

One of the most effective means of engaging with Jewish people was through classes to teach the English language. Miss Dora Parkhurst oversaw these classes for Hebrew Christians as well as for other Jews. Invariably one of the main textbooks used for teaching English was the Bible. In addition a Bible Depot (Shop) was also opened.[10]

The character of the Jewish community

The character of the Jewish community in Warsaw after 1920 was slightly different to the pre-1914 period. Most of the thousands of refugees who had descended upon the capital city during the War had remained. These for the most part were more Orthodox and poor. They joined the already large Orthodox Jewish community resident in Warsaw who had lost none of their historic antipathy to the person of Jesus of Nazareth. To them *Yeshu* was still an arch enemy of the Jewish people, and any Jew who would follow him would be cut off from his people and classified as a *meshumad*, or traitor.[11]

Throughout the 1920s, though, the secular Jewish community continued to grow and expand. There were some who wanted to assimilate into Polish

[8] Savery to Carpenter, 8 March 1920, Miscellaneous Papers 370, Bodleian Library, Dept CMJ, Warsaw d.51.4.

[9] CMJ Report 1920-21, p. 51.

[10] CMJ Report 1920-21, p. 52.

[11] A local Polish term also used was *meches*.

society while others sought to escape their marginalization through Marxism or Zionism. All these secular groups largely agreed that traditional Judaism was in part to blame for the woes of the Jewish people. They were mirroring what had already been occurring in pre-War Germany.

In Germany many Jews, in order to become 'better Germans', had converted to Christianity and most had joined the Lutheran Church. These could be termed 'socio-economic' Jewish Christians. Others converted to Christianity in order to marry a Christian or Gentile spouse. In most such instances in Poland these Jewish people became Roman Catholics, and for the most part they sought assimilation into the host culture. A representative of this group was the renowned medical scientist, Dr Ludwik Hirszfeld.

There were also in Warsaw those adhering to various political persuasions, including the General Jewish Workers' Union, the *Bund*. But now to a greater extent than before, there were the Zionists, whose vision was closer to fulfilment. On 31 October 1917 the British War Cabinet had issued what became known as the Balfour Declaration, promising the establishment of a national home for the Jewish people in Palestine. This promise was embodied into a Mandate for Palestine which was offered to Britain at the San Remo Conference in 1920, and accepted by the British Government in 1922 and then endorsed by the League of Nations in the same year.

As a result the Zionists were now a more vocal force within the Jewish community. They too were of different streams, mostly secular but also religious. For the Zionists, Jewish nationalism was paramount and the message of Jesus of Nazareth was seen as having a conflicting message to Jewish nationalism.

Whereas pre-1914 any missionary to the Jewish people in Poland had to have a good understanding of Orthodox Judaism while an awareness of the other influences and movements was less important, now the missionary needed to be aware of all of these ideological streams within the Jewish community.

Bazyli Jocz finds employment with CMJ

It was during this period and in this environment that Bazyli Jocz was attached to the Polish Army in Warsaw.[12] Being a Jewish follower of Jesus, and CMJ being an Evangelical work in Warsaw reaching out to Jewish people, it is

[12] *A Brief History*, p. 2.

likely that Bazyli attended one of the services at the Anglican Church.

In the CMJ Report for 1921-22 there is reference to a certain 'A. Jodsch' being on staff.[13] Bazyli himself states: 'In 1921, my first year of work in Warsaw'.[14] But the first reference to Bazyli in the CMJ Minutes was in the meeting of the General Committee on 22 May 1922 in response to letters from Carpenter dated March and April 1922. These letters referred to the impending departure of Abraham Ginsburg from employment as a colporteur[15] with CMJ, and asked if they could employ Mr B. Jotsch to replace him. The Minutes stated that 'the Committee are willing that the amount of his salary should be transferred to Mr B. Jotsch.[16]

It could be that Bazyli was somehow involved with CMJ while still serving in the Polish Army before becoming a full-time salaried staff member, which appears to be in 1922. Interestingly in the same CMJ Report of 1921-22 mention is given to the 'storm of opposition raised by Orthodox Jewry because a learned member and his family in their community were receiving Baptismal instruction.'[17] The man in question was Rabbi David Paul Weiss.

Family life in Warsaw

At some point during this time Bazyli had returned to Vilna to prepare the family for the move to Warsaw. Bazyli, Anna and Pawel moved first while Jakob and Jerzy remained in Vilna 'to make arrangements for the rest of the family.' Myers stated that: 'Hannah's sister, Reisel, had married a German officer and it was Jakob's responsibility to obtain papers for her and grandmother Sarah to travel to Konigsberg.'[18] Bazyli, Anna and Pawel were able to find accommodation at Wolomin, a *shtetl* about sixteen kilometres from Warsaw.[19] Jakob and Jerzy joined them several months later.

---

[13] CMJ Report 1921-22, p. 52.

[14] CMJ Report 1925-26, p. 73.

[15] A colporteur distributes religious materials, especially Bibles.

[16] CMJ General Committee Minute Book 1921-1930, 12 May 1922, Minute 351, Bodleian Library, Dept CMJ, c. 37. Elizabeth Myers states that Bazyli began his service with CMJ in 1920, while Adeney, 81, states 1921.

[17] CMJ Report 1921-22, p. 53.

[18] Myers, 5. Konigsberg was the capital of East Prussia, and is now Kaliningrad in Russia.

[19] Myers, p. 5. About ten miles.

While Bazyli began his life as a colporteur and evangelist with CMJ, the family was also active. Jakob stated that he was Confirmed in the 'English Church' in 1923.[20] In the same year another son, Jan (Johann, John), was born on 9 July while they were in Wolomin.[21]

Increasing economic pressures against the Jewish people

In the period when the Jocz family was settling into life in Warsaw, Polish society itself was in the midst of a socio-economic crisis. The new Poland had inherited a huge landmass, which included some eleven million non-Catholic Poles, among whom were about six million Ukrainians (mostly Orthodox and Uniate), one million White Russians (Belarus of today) and some three million Jews. The nineteen million 'ethnic' Poles therefore had to contend with a very high proportion of non-ethnic Poles.[22]

One can well imagine that the economic pressures upon a newly constituted nation which had just fought a very intense war against the Bolshevik Soviets would have been significant. They needed to make some cost cuts somewhere, and the large Jewish minority was hit. Howard Sachar states:

> ... the Polish government cynically began to reduce its subsidies to the Jewish school and welfare system. Shortly thereafter, in 1923, the government devised the "cold pogrom," the policy of systematically eliminating Jews from the economic life of the country. In justification, government officials explained that the Jews were "superfluous," their economic position in the country was an "intrusion," and their elimination in favour of "purely Polish" elements was desirable and necessary.[23]

This policy was orchestrated by the finance minister Wladyslaw Grabski, 'who', as Sachar writes 'nationalized those branches of industry and commerce in which Jews were most heavily represented, then dismissed Jewish employees in favour of Poles. As a result fully a third of the nation's Jewish

[20] Jacob Jocz, *Curriculum Vitae*. Confirmation basically confirms the promises of commitment to follow Jesus made at baptism. If the person being Confirmed was a child at baptism, then those promises were made either by the parents or godparents on the baby's behalf.

[21] Letter from Steven Pozel to Rocholl, 9 February 1962, German File, p. 171.

[22] Sachar, *The Course*, pp. 355-56.

[23] Ibid., p. 357.

merchants were driven to bankruptcy.'[24] The only positive result of this policy is that thousands of such Jewish merchants migrated to the land of Israel, in what became known as the 'fourth *aliyah*.'[25]

One further observation from Sachar is worth noting: 'In addition, Jews were completely frozen out of all civil service positions, and from all government contracts.'[26] This was indeed a season of a different kind of anti-Semitism in Poland. If a Jewish person thereafter desired to remain in Poland, and also desired to contribute to the development of the new Polish nation he or she would have little choice but to at least outwardly fully assimilate.

As had already been the case in Germany for over a hundred years, the most effective way for such a Jewish person to assimilate would be to convert to the host Christian religion, and in Poland's case it was Roman Catholicism. As one could imagine, such an action would not be well received by the conservative Jewish population.

Ironically there was a slight decrease in this wave of anti-Jewish sentiment from 1926. In that year Pilsudski led a *coup d'etat* and took control over the government, essentially becoming a dictator. Sachar wrote: 'One of Pilsudski's first acts was to end the government's policy of anti-Semitism; for much as he loathed Jews personally ... he recognized that the officially condoned policy of Jew-hatred had proved a blind for corruption. Yet Pilsudski's ban on "official" anti-Semitism came too late to help the Jews. Less than three years later the world Depression struck Poland.'[27]

An ominous awakening in Germany

During the same period that Bazyli and Anna were embarking upon a new season in their lives - a season synonymous with the emergence of a different kind of anti-Semitism in Poland - a new season was beginning in neighbouring Germany. After the end of the First World War one of the outcomes of the battles between the various entities vying for control in Germany (mostly different groups against the Communists) was the emergence of Adolf Hitler. Hitler headed up a small entity known as the National Socialist German

[24] Sachar, H. *A History of Israel,* (Alfred A. Knoft, New York, 1996), p. 154.
[25] Sachar, ibid, p. 154. *Aliyah* is the term used for a wave of Jewish immigration into the land of Israel. It actually means 'going up.'
[26] Sachar, The Course, p. 358.
[27] Ibid., p. 358.

Chapter 8

Consolidating the Evangelical presence

Significant events for the Hebrew Christian movement in Poland

Several significant events occurred in 1922 which impacted the growth and development of the local Hebrew Christian movement in Poland. Carpenter wrote:

> May the 6th stands out as the "Red Letter" day in the history of our Mission in Poland. On this day the Bishop of North and Central Europe (Dr. Bury), confirmed some twenty-seven Hebrew Christians who all took communion the following Sunday evening; both of these occasions were most inspiring.
>
> Thus after many years of labour and removal of restrictions the foundation was laid for the first time of a Hebrew Christian congregation. Patience and prayer has thus received its consummation.[1]

Bazyli and Anna became active members of this congregation and Bazyli continued his work as a colporteur working alongside Ajzeman and Bregman. Bregman wrote at this time: 'The good tidings of Christ have been carried not only to the Jews of Poland, but also to Russian Jews, the refugees who were fleeing to seek new homes in the United States of America and elsewhere.'[2]

Another significant event occurred in December 1922. It was the calling together of the many Hebrew Christians scattered throughout Poland for a six day conference in Warsaw, the purpose of which, Carpenter wrote, was:

> The unifying of the scattered members and the constituting of a union of

---

[1] CMJ Report 1922-23, p. 55. CMJ General Committee 21 July 1922, Minute 458.

[2] CMJ Report 1922-23, p. 58. Many of these refugees made their way to Rotterdam in the Netherlands where they awaited passage to North America. There CMJ had a centre there known as 'Elim' which provided help and support to them.

> Hebrew Christians irrespective of the community they locally belonged to. Representatives came from several parts of the country at short notice. Many could not stay with us all the six days of the conference… It was a time of great and definite blessing, and culminated in a large meeting of public testimony, where over five hundred Jews were gathered and witnessed some twenty Hebrew Christians testifying to their faith in Jesus the Messiah and acknowledging their oneness with the Jewish nation.
>
> There was a disturbing element, emissaries of orthodox Jewry, who succeeded in causing a commotion at the commencement, but when these were removed, the audience listened most attentively. They were struck, both by the message and the numbers of Hebrew Christians delivering it and identifying themselves with it.
>
> The intention was to hold a similar meeting the following day, but this had to be abandoned on account of the assassination of the President.[3]

This conference laid the foundations for the future formation of the Polish branch of the Hebrew Christian Alliance. It also highlighted the opportunity for more Evangelical involvement among the Jewish people.

Vision for a Training Home for Jewish Workers

Herman Carpenter recognised that in view of the large Jewish population of Poland what was now required were more Polish-born Jewish followers of Jesus to be raised up and trained for the task of presenting Jesus as Messiah to this large population.

With this objective in mind Carpenter sent a letter to the CMJ General Committee on 7 December 1922 with a proposal for establishing a training institute. The Committee took the matter seriously.[4] In January 1923 Carpenter had already supplied the names of Victor Buksbazen and Victor Weisman as prospective candidates for just such an institute.[5] By 16 March 1923 permission had been granted to provide finances for the training of these two men, as well as Joseph Yurman, and later Leon Smoljar and J. Prentki.[6] Towards

[3] CMJ Report 1922-23, 55. President Gabriel Narutowicz, the first president of Poland, was assassinated on 16 December 1922, just five days after taking office.

[4] CMJ General Committee, 15 December 1922, Minute 682.

[5] CMJ General Committee, 19 January 1923, Minute 716.

[6] CMJ General Committee 16 March 1923, Minute 785; 18 May 1923, Minute 886; Minute 1400, 20 June 1924.

the end of the year it was agreed that an actual 'Training Home for Jewish Workers' would be opened, and the General Committee thereupon informed the other Mission societies operating in Poland of this plan.[7]

Poland strategic planning meeting

At a CMJ Committee meeting on 19 January 1923 mention was made that Rev. Samuel Schor, the recently appointed Director of the Barbican Mission to the Jews (BMJ), was soon to depart for Poland in order to establish a work there among the Jewish people. Schor had previously been associated with CMJ for many years and obviously saw the need for co-operation or co-ordination with CMJ and indeed the other Evangelical societies operating or desiring to operate in Central Europe.

Upon Schor's suggestion a meeting took place on 26 October 1923 at Darley Ash near Bovingdon in Hertfordshire. Present were representatives of the British Jews Society (BJS), Barbican Mission (BMJ), CMJ, United Free Church of Scotland Jewish Mission (UFC) and Mildmay Mission (MMJ). Schor emphasised that the purpose of the meeting was 'to avoid overlapping in Eastern Europe and to consider possibilities of co-ordination of the work of the various societies.'[8]

Schor stated that the BMJ 'had staked out as its parish the Eastern Section of Poland from Grodno in the North to Rovno in the South,' which included such towns as Bialystok, Brest Litovsk, Kovel, Slonim and Pinsk. Rev. Gill of CMJ stated that that they would remain in Warsaw, with the desire also of re-occupying 'Lemberg as soon as permission was given by the Government.' Rev. Dr J. Macdonald Webster of the UFC stated that the Scots Mission was 'likely to develop its work in Czecho-Slovakia.' Rev. Exley stated that the BJS had thought of Vilna or south-west Poland.[9]

One other item raised was the need for establishing a Training Home 'for enquirers.' It was felt 'that the needs of Poland could not be adequately met outside Poland, and the name of Rev. I. Landsman was suggested as that of

[7] CMJ General Committee, 16 November 1923, Minute 1105.

[8] Minutes 'Conference of Work Amongst Jews in Central Europe' Bodleian Library, Dept CMJ d.51/4.

[9] Minutes 'Conference of Work Amongst Jews in Central Europe' Bodleian Library, Dept CMJ d.51/4.

a possible Director if a new College could be started in Warsaw.'[10] It was thereupon determined that all the agencies would support the development of the CMJ Training Home.

Development of other Evangelical societies

Following his visit to Poland in 1923 Rev. Schor established a Barbican Mission presence at Rovno and another Jewish Christian pastor, Rev. Piotr Gorodishz (also known as Peter Gorodisch), who had previously worked for BMJ in Odessa, became the head of the work. He later moved the centre of the operations to Bialystok. Gorodishz would be murdered in the Holocaust.

In 1924 the British Jews Society (BJS) opened their work in Krakow. They also established a presence in Vilna, working together with the Society of the Friends of Israel Mission of Basel (SFOI).[11] The Mildmay Mission also returned to Poland, and its work was headed up in time by S. Joffe (Yoffe) and later by Nathan Sendyk. Slowly throughout the 1920s many of the Evangelical societies who desired to introduce Jesus to the Jewish people began to establish their presence throughout the vast region of Poland.[12]

The early activities of Jakob Jocz

It would appear that soon after he was confirmed in 1923 Jakob Jocz, together with two other young men from the *shtetl*, left Poland for a trip and ended up being in France for about eighteen months.[13] Jakob seems to have returned to Poland sometime in 1924, whereupon, according to the Jocz family website, he 'was drafted into the army stationed in Warsaw, and by the time of his discharge he held the rank of sergeant.'[14]

It was also during this period that Jakob was able to complete his studies. In 1924 he applied to CMJ for employment and wrote: 'It was made possible for me to take up my studies again, to a certain extent and I am now preparing

---

[10] Minutes 'Conference of Work Amongst Jews in Central Europe' Bodleian Library, Dept CMJ d.51/4.
[11] The BJS later became the Christian Witness to Israel (CWI) based at Eynsham, Oxfordshire. See also Glaser, p. 37. The Mildmay Mission had initially begun their work in Poland in 1905.
[12] For further information see Glaser, pp. 36-44.
[13] Myers, p. 5.
[14] *A Brief History*, p. 3.

to pass my examination of the 6th Gymnasium class.'[15] There were various communications between Warsaw and London during this period concerning the future of Jakob – Carpenter obviously saw great potential in Bazyli's son.

Finally in October 1924 CMJ's London Committee resolved that the training of Jakob should 'await the development of the Training Home.'[16] It seems that around this time, before or after his military service, Jakob had some brief involvement with the Herrnhut centre of the Moravian Christians in Saxony in Germany.[17] He was finally able to enrol in the CMJ Training Home in 1926.[18] Jakob, it would seem, was destined to follow an academic route.

Activities of Bazyli in Warsaw

As Jakob started his training his father, Bazyli, was continuing in his role of colporteur, distributing the Bible and other religious literature. Such work also included general evangelistic work. Concerning the general work of a colporteur at this time Rev. J. H. Adeney noted that: 'Visiting in the houses and shops, parks and markets, was diligently pursued, and literature sold and distributed.'[19]

Bazyli would invite Jewish people he met on the streets to visit him in the Bible Depot. He wrote in 1925:

> Two young men, workers in a Zionist organisation, who had been spoken to in the street, visited the Depot. One, a seeking soul, complained that his mother had snatched away and burnt the tract given him as he read it. He could not rest until he had another copy. Another young Jew invited me to go with him into a café. Here he related that he had been a Socialist, but an unsatisfied and unhappy one; since he had been acquainted with the Christian religion of Salvation his life had been better. He now bought from me several tracts with the remark that they were important, and should be read by every Jew.[20]

Apart from the work in Warsaw itself, Bazyli and the other evangelists would

[15] Jacob Jocz, *Curriculum Vitae.*
[16] CMJ General Committee 17 October 1924, Minute 1522.
[17] Jacob Jocz to Gill, 24 October 1925, Dept CMJ, File on Warsaw, d. 51.4.
[18] *A Brief History,* p. 3.
[19] Adeney, p. 82.
[20] CMJ Report 1925-26, p. 73.

occasionally travel to outlying areas. Abraham Ajzeman wrote that in 1923 they undertook two missionary journeys, 'each of twenty-five days… first in the south and the second in the north of the land.'[21] These visits were done by train until 1927, and thereafter by the car which the Society was able to procure. Adeney describes one such journey:

> As many as 120 towns and villages were reached in one journey… There was often opposition both in the city and on the journeys… In the country places, great crowds drawn by curiosity to see and hear missionaries for the first time, surrounded them and numbers came to their hotel to discuss the claims of Christ, often staying till late in the night. Sometimes their advent was warned against in the Jewish Press. This only had the effect of making the Jews the more curious and increasing the numbers.[22]

The re-opening of the work in Lemberg (1925)

Carpenter was very keen to re-open the key station at Lemberg, which was now known by its Polish name, Lwow. Permission was finally granted in August 1924.[23] Ajzeman was appointed to lead the work in this city of some 60,000 Jews and by June he was already able to procure a house.[24]

Many of the Jewish people living in Lwow were quite well established in the business world, including the press. Ajzeman began with meetings and Bible-readings, but when the Jewish press became aware of these meetings, they began to oppose the work. At one point pickets were even placed outside the Mission House to hinder Jews from entering.[25]

It was not long before Ajzeman began undertaking visits to outlying Jewish communities and distributing Messianic materials. On one such journey in 1926 he stated that he visited: 'Stryj with 15,000 Jews; Stanislawow with 27,000 ; Delatyn, with 200 Jewish families ; Kolomyja, with a Jewish population of 20,000 ; Truskawiec, also Jaremcze, summer resorts where many Jews come ; Skole, with 800 Jewish families ; Jaroslaw, where 70 per cent of the whole population are Jews ; Przemysl, containing 15,000 Jews.'[26]

[21] CMJ Report 1923-24, p. 68.
[22] Adeney, p. 83.
[23] CMJ General Committee, 1 August 1924, Minute 1355.
[24] CMJ General Committee, 26 June 1925, Minute 1838.
[25] CMJ Report 1926-27, p. 50.
[26] CMJ Report 1926-27, p. 51.

Some years later such places and numbers of Jewish people were being reported in a different context. In the 1940s they were part of reports from Nazi murder squads as to how many Jewish people had been shot in those villages and towns.

In his report of 1926 Ajzeman mentioned that there had been a 'great revival amongst the Greek Catholics' which had 'produced its fruits.' 'Many communities in the country', he continued, 'are faithful and converted and with their new life they get another opinion concerning the people of Israel. Their attitude towards the Jews has quite changed. They now try to win their Jewish neighbours for Jesus Christ…'[27]

This spiritual revival was quite significant as the Greek Catholic (Uniate) Church was very prominent in that region. More than likely these endeavours within the Greek Catholic Church were due to the efforts of Archbishop Andrei Sheptytsky. Sheptytsky had a very positive attitude towards the Jewish people. Rabbi David Kahane, one time Chief Rabbi of the Israeli Air Force, wrote of him, that he was one who 'had acquired a reputation as a friend of the Jews and who never concealed his positive attitude towards Judaism.'[28]

Additionally, in 1925 the Danish Missionary Society (DMS) had 'definitely decided to continue on with the work in Lemberg among the Jews there.'[29] This work was associated in the future with Pastor Henry Rasmussen. The Danish Society (DMS) and CMJ often co-operated in their work in Lwow.

Establishment of a new CMJ centre in Warsaw

On 18 May 1923 the CMJ General Committee authorized Carpenter to investigate 'the possible acquisition of land suitable for the erection of mission premises' in Warsaw.[30] Remarkably in 1924 he was able to locate and procure a large block adjacent to the university and the central post office in the very centre of the city.[31] After building permission was finally granted in July 1924

[27] CMJ Report 1926-27, p. 52. Adeney, p. 81.
[28] Kahane, D. *Lvov Ghetto Diary*, (Univ. of Massachusetts Press, 1990), p. 7.
[29] CMJ General Committee, 16 May 1925, Minute 1319.
[30] CMJ General Committee, 18 May 1923, Minute 867.
[31] CMJ General Committee, 25 April 1924, Minute 1284; 1 August 1925, Minute 1442. Carpenter's initial plans though were rejected by the Committee on 16 May 1924, Minute 1356.

fund-raising began in earnest in Britain.[32]

Despite numerous financial and other problems Carpenter was able to report that the first bricks were laid on 23 September 1926,[33] followed by the laying of the foundation stone for the new ministry centre on 19 November 1926. The new four-story building was opened on 7 November 1927. Rev. Adeney described the new centre:

> The building consisted of ground floor and three floors above. It had been planned to have shops on the ground floor and to let them to help with the expenses, but the numbers attending the English classes was so great that it was finally decided to use them as class rooms. On the first floor was the Church and the Mission Hall, divided by a partition and the Library-Reading Room. The floor above was occupied by Mr Carpenter and his family. On the third floor was the Training Home…[34]

The day of the opening witnessed the baptism of 'an earnest young Hebrew' and later four other Hebrew Christians were confirmed.[35] Within days the CMJ Emmanuel Church and Mission House (or the Emmanuel Centre) was a buzz of activity. Adeney describes these activities in brief:

> There were regular evangelistic meetings on Saturdays and Bible Readings and Discussion meetings. Smaller groups as well as individuals were dealt with in the Reading Room. English classes and club meetings were held. There were frequent discussions. There was also a Women's Sewing Meeting and a Sunday School. Each year there were a number of enquirers and a number of baptisms and, three times, services for Confirmation. The Hebrew Christian community continued to grow. The members came some to the English church service, others to a special service for them. After the arrival of Dr. Prentki, Polish was also taught, that being the language of the younger generation. Jews also attended these services.[36]

The completion of the new four-story building was a milestone in the work

---

[32] Carpenter to Gill, 23 July 1924, CMJ General Committee Minute 1475, 1 August 1924.

[33] CMJ General Committee, 15 October 1926. Minute 2412.

[34] Adeney, p. 82.

[35] CMJ Report 1927-28, p. 53.

[36] Adeney, p. 82.

of CMJ in Poland. With the arrival of Rev. Joseph Immanuel Landsman[37] in September 1927 to supervise the Training Home, and the addition of Dr Oscar Prentki to assist with the Polish services, CMJ's Emmanuel Centre, became a centre of Evangelical work in Warsaw. Bazyli and Anna Jocz and their sons were all part of this dynamic scene.

Dr Prentki had very high academic standards. Agnieszka Jagodzinska describes how, after one particular visit to Lwow in 1928, Prentki stated in his report to CMJ that he was disappointed with 'our missionary [...], for he is not intelligent and educated enough to deal with this kind of people.'[38] This was Ajzeman, who obviously did not attain to the standards that Prentki expected of a missionary!

Formation of the Hebrew Christian Alliance – Polish branch (1926)

As far back as 1813 a small association was formed in London named the *Benei Abraham* (Sons or Children of Abraham) to provide encouragement for the Jewish followers of Jesus. This association was reformed in 1866 and became the Hebrew Christian Alliance (HCA), and continued its work of offering support and encouragement to the ever-increasing number of Jewish or Hebrew Christians. A similar branch was formed in the USA in 1915.

At the HCA Conference in London in September 1925 delegates came from eighteen countries world-wide, but mostly from within Europe. At that Conference, and through the vision of Mark John Levy, it was decided to form the International Hebrew Christian Alliance (IHCA).[39]

---

[37] Lansman (1869-1931) came from a pious Jewish family near Kovno. He was introduced to Jesus by Pastor Meyerson, a Hebrew Christian who was associated with a Swedish mission society. Landsman later trained with the Lutheran Free Church of Sweden. About 1904 he began working with the Hebrew Christian Testimony to Israel (HCTI). In 1924 he went to the United States, and then returned in order to head up the new Training Centre in Warsaw. (See *The Hebrew Christian,* January 1932, p. 190.)

[38] Jagodzinska, A. *Duszozbawcy*, (Wydawnictwo Austeria: Krakow. Budapeszt, 2017), pp. 442-3. Jagodzinska was highlighting the not infrequent discrepancies between field reports and the subsequent published accounts in the CMJ publications. In the article in the *Jewish Missionary Intelligence* (*JMI*) of January 1929, no mention was made of the missionary who was 'not intelligent and educated enough.'

[39] *The Hebrew Christian*, (IHCA, Edinburgh), Volume 1, April 1928-January 1929, p. 9.

The new President of the International Hebrew Christian Alliance (IHCA) was Sir Leon Levison. Levison's biographer Frederick Levison wrote:

> The aim which the I.H.C.A set itself was to build up national Alliances which would be linked together in a universal fellowship of Hebrew Christians. Its purposes were to inculcate the loyalty of all members to the church of their adoption – with the exception of the Roman Catholic Church, for this was a purely Protestant movement; to enable Hebrew Christians to meet for fellowship and worship; to provide in every country an annual conference to consider the welfare of Hebrew Christians; and to inspire its members to seek and win for Christ their unconverted Jewish brethren.[40]

The designated President of the future Polish branch was Rev. Carpenter. In May 1926 he called for a meeting of the Polish Hebrew Christians in Warsaw at which the Polish branch of the IHCA was founded. Carpenter wrote:

> In May our community were much cheered by the presence and fellowship of the brethren from all parts of the country who gathered here in conference and prayer to inaugurate the founding of the Hebrew-Christian Alliance in Poland, and this fact will live long in the memory of every one who took part in this historical event.[41]

Both Bazyli and Anna were foundational members.[42]

Development of the Training Centre

The coming of Rev. Landsman enabled the Training Centre to further develop. Promising young Hebrew Christians could henceforth receive solid instruction in Poland. One graduate was Victor Buksbazen, who would later team up with Pawel Jocz and become a close friend of Jakob Jocz. He eventually headed up the work of the British Jews Society in Krakow.

One non-Polish student was Isaac Feinstein from Bucharest, who came with his Swiss-born wife Lydia (nee Spoerri). Isaac had become a follower of

[40] Levison, F. *Christian and Jew – Leon Levison,* (Edinburgh: The Pentland Press, 1989), p. 166.
[41] CMJ Report 1926-27, p. 54.
[42] Letter from Harcourt Samuel, President of the International Hebrew Christian Alliance, 13 January 1959, German File, p. 61.

Jesus through the work of CMJ in Bucharest, and Lydia had been a teacher at the CMJ School in Bucharest.[43] Feinstein would later head up the work of the Norwegian Mission to the Jews in Galatz and later in Jassy (Iasi), Romania, a work located on the CMJ property there. Feinstein would ultimately be murdered in the Holocaust.

Rev. Landsman was not just involved in the training, as he wrote shortly after his arrival:

> I have been preaching on Sundays at the Hebrew Christian Service, every Wednesday a Bible Reading with the Hebrew Christians and enquirers and every Saturday at the public meeting for Jews. In addition I have instructed the candidates for training every day excepting Saturday and Sunday. On Fridays I have conducted a Special Class for all the workers... Further, two enquirers have been coming twice a week for instruction in the New Testament and I have also published the first number of the Yiddish paper, *Der Weg*.[44]

This Yiddish language newspaper *Der Weg* ('The Way') soon had a wide distribution throughout the city and even the country.[45]

The IMC meeting of 1927

Warsaw was the venue in 1927 for a meeting arranged by the International Missionary Council (IMC). Among the delegates who attended was Moses Gitlin of the American Board of Missions to the Jews (ABMJ). Gitlin was appointed by ABMJ in November 1934 to establish a centre of operations in Warsaw.[46]

Another person attending that meeting was Pastor Leon Rosenberg, a Jewish Christian who had previously ministered in Odessa, but had been forced to leave there by the new Bolshevik regime. Rosenberg was interested in establishing a mission in Poland, and had mentioned this to Carpenter, Ajzeman

---

[43] Adeney, p. 129.

[44] CMJ Report, 1926-27, pp. 56-7.

[45] CMJ Report, 1927-28, p. 56.

[46] Glaser, 41. ABMJ – American Board of Mission to the Jews, today Chosen People Ministries. Sevener, H. *A Rabbi's Vision*, (Chosen People Ministries, 1994), p. 182.

and Bregman.[47]

Rosenberg was asked to speak at the conference where he presented his past work as well as his plans for the future.[48] His plans were endorsed and encouraged and in time Rosenberg and his family established the American European Bethel Mission in Lodz.

A number of Rosenberg's own family members would be murdered by the Nazis, including his daughter Helen, her husband Samuel Ostrer, Leon's brother Herman and his wife Esther. Additionally, as Leon's wife Fanny later wrote to him in 1945: 'Your sister Theophelia, with her husband, Br. Malcman, who were our faithful missionaries, were assassinated by the Nazis, with three of their five children.'[49] All of these family members were Jewish Christians.

The late 1920s

Throughout this time Bazyli continued with his routine of distributing Bibles and Biblical literature on the streets, entering into discussions with enquirers in the Bible Depot and going to outlying towns and cities. Of one place, Wlodna, he wrote that it was 'a small town of about one thousand Jewish inhabitants. Without any exaggeration one might describe it as a town thirsty for the Word of God.' The local Rabbi and several accompanying Chassids tried to disturb the gathering by proclaiming: "Jews, we are lost; the missionaries have come to baptise us!" But, Bazyli concluded, '… it was an advertisement for us, for in less than half an hour we had emptied our two bags which had been full of Bibles, New Testaments and tracts…'[50] Bazyli, however, was not able to continue with his work during much of 1929 having been laid up with sickness for nine months.[51]

The work of CMJ in Warsaw also reached a new height in 1929, as Carpenter highlights in an article in the *Jewish Missionary Intelligence* entitled 'An Epoch-making Event in Warsaw':

---

[47] Kuschnir, V. *Only One Life,* (American European Bethel Mission: Santa Barbara, 2000), p. 243.
[48] Kuschnir, p. 243.
[49] Mrs F. Rosenberg to L. Rosenberg, 10 August 1945, *The Bethel Witness*, Vol 9, No 4, 1945, p. 7. Br. Malcman is Alfred Malcman.
[50] CMJ Report 1927-28, p. 59.
[51] Adeney, p. 129.

> On the 6th of November we took a considerable step forward in the development of our Hebrew-Christian community in Warsaw. All the members of our Church, who are Polish citizens and therefore permanent residents, were summoned to a meeting to organize themselves into a proper parish. They elected a Church Council which is to take over parish responsibilities. Mr. Rosenfeld, who was a very valuable member of our Building Committee, was nominated as Vicar's Church Warden, Mr. Prentki, senior, was elected People's Warden, Miss Flora Prentki, as Secretary, and Mr Lypszic as her assistant, Mr A. Enholc, the director of the Bible Society's work in Poland, as Treasurer.
>
> There were nearly fifty persons present, all adults, which was a fairly good number... This then is a mile-stone in our history, and I believe unique in the Jewish mission field.[52]

The result of the CMJ operations and those of the other Evangelical societies was that by the end of the decade Jesus was being introduced as the Messiah of Israel to many Jewish people in Poland.

Rise once again of anti-Jewish sentiment

Ironically 1929, the year heralding the Great Depression, also witnessed a significant rise in anti-Jewish sentiment in Poland. There was a connection. Much of the economic morass in Poland stemmed from three sources, namely the disproportionate control of (1) a few large landowners; (2) the Roman Catholic Church, including over land control; and (3) a few large industrialists and business men (known as the Leviathan) over industry.

These entities were mostly responsible for the lack of economic development in Poland. Yet as has often happened in history, when there was a national catastrophe, as was the case with the Great Depression in Poland, scapegoats were sought. Thus in order to divert peasant and labour unrest away from themselves, these entities exploited deep-seated anti-Jewish sentiment to the fullest.[53] The Jewish people collectively became that scapegoat.

Sachar stated it best:

---

[52] *JMI,* 1930, p. 4.

[53] Sachar, *The Course,* p. 359.

> A collection of fascist paramilitary organizations, the most notorious of which were the *Endeks* and the *Naras*, mushroomed throughout the country, openly encouraged by Catholic propaganda, and subsidized secretly by the gentry and the Leviathan. Roaming the streets in uniforms, the rightist strong-arm gangs indiscriminately attacked Jews (were they not all Bolsheviks?), socialists, and liberals.[54]

The decade of the 1920s thus ended on somewhat of a negative note.

---

[54] Ibid., pp. 359-360.

Chapter 9

The 1930s – trouble is brewing

Many Jewish people become attached to the Roman Catholic Church

Despite the negative events of the late 1920s there seemed to be endless opportunities for introducing Jesus to the three million or so Jewish people living in Poland. During this period many Jews were joining the Roman Catholic Church. The *Jewish Missionary Intelligence* carried an article by Dr Prentki entitled, 'The Confessions of a Roman Catholic Jewish Christian in Poland'. It was based on a book in Polish entitled *Chrześcijańskiego żyda wspomnienia - łzy - i myśli* (*Reminiscences, Tears and Thoughts*) written by Gabriel Jehuda ibn Ezra, 'a prominent Jewish Christian belonging to the Roman Catholic Church.'[1]

Dr Prentki had written to the author, and noted in his article that both from the book and from their correspondence 'it appears that he is a true believer in Our Lord Jesus Christ. The importance of the book for the workers in Poland is that it is the first protest against the anti-Semitic spirit prevailing amongst the people and the Roman Church, made by a Christian Jew belonging to both….'[2] The article concluded:

> There must exist a large number of Jews in Poland who have joined the Roman Catholic Church, notably Jews belonging to the educated and wealthier classes. Nothing is ever heard of them, they never open their mouths to tell the world of their experiences as Christians, and no wonder, for their chief aim is that when they were baptized, to escape from the Jewish fold and become submerged in the mass of the Nation, avoiding by every means the slightest thing that would remind their neighbours of their Jewish descent.
>
> A few of them are active in the Press but they are known as outspoken anti-semites. A play is now being acted in the theatres by a poet who bears a name once very popular and highly respected amongst the Jews,

[1] *JMI* 1930, p. 139.
[2] Ibid.

> he being the grandson of a once famous Hebrew scholar and writer, but the tendency of the play is to make a laughing stock of the people from which he sprang.
>
> But it is quite different with the author of the book which is the subject of these articles. Here we have a noble and highly educated Jew who in his younger day joined the Church out of love, by "conviction and choice," as he himself says, and was the means of bringing at least his father and younger brother to Christ.'[3]

Jakob Jocz later wrote that this book 'is unique in its kind, for it is a frank confession of a truly converted Roman Catholic Jew, telling of the path of suffering and humiliation a Jew has to tread as a convert who wants to remain loyal to the Church but at the same time refuses to deny his Jewish descent. The Church expects the converted Jew to be merged in and disappear amongst the Gentile people, so that every trace of his "Jewishness" is wiped out of existence. This explains why so many Jews who have joined the Church of Rome have completely and tracelessly disappeared after a few generations.'[4]

Activities of Evangelical Christians

While the number of Jewish Catholics was increasing, there were also several significant developments in the Hebrew Christian movement. In early 1930 the Hebrew Christian Alliance was granted official recognition by the Polish Government. The IHCA journal *The Hebrew Christian* stated that such recognition would give them more freedom than previously. The journal also stated that 'our readers will be glad to know that a Hebrew Christian Church has been established in Warsaw which makes it the first place of worship of its kind in the land of Poland.'[5]

The Hebrew Christian Church referred to was the Emmanuel Church, where, Carpenter recorded, twelve Jewish people were baptised that year.[6] Landsman wrote an article entitled 'A Unique Church', in the *Jewish Missionary Intelligence* in 1930, stating:

---

[3] *JMI* 1930, p. 139.
[4] *The Hebrew Christian,* Volume XIV, 1941-1942, p. 62.
[5] *The Hebrew Christian,* Volume III, No. 1, 1928-1929, p. 9.
[6] *CMJ Report* 1930-31, p. 46.

> We have a Church with a seating capacity of about 125; adjoining there is a Mission Hall, and when the doors which separate the Church from the Hall are opened then we have a fine room seating some two hundred. Then we have a Reading Room, and a home for the training of missionaries. These new premises are used every day of the week and are especially filled on each Saturday and Sunday. If you visited our Church on a Saturday at four o'clock you would find it packed with Jews. In the winter we had to open the doors so as to enlarge the seating capacity of our Church.
>
> At this season, perhaps, there are fewer, but we always have between ninety and a hundred at our Evangelistic Meetings on Saturdays.
>
> On Sundays we have a Morning Service for the British Colony. In the evening our Jewish Christian Church assembles for Divine Worship. You must remember that we have in Warsaw a Jewish Christian Church, united with the Church of England... If you come in on the Sunday evening, you will see all Jewish faces. They had all heard the Gospel preached, and afterwards they were instructed for baptism, then they were baptized, and added to our Hebrew Christian Church because it consists entirely of Jewish Christians.
> ... We have over a hundred members in our Church of Jewish Christians.[7]

Bazyli, Anna and their sons (with the partial exception of Jakob who was away for some time studying) were all participants in this 'Church of Jewish Christians'. For some time in 1931 Bazyli was also away. He was relieved of his strenuous duties in Warsaw and went for a while to work in Plock and Minsk Mazowick.[8]

The activities of the other Protestant and Evangelical churches and societies, which included the Barbican Mission to the Jews, Mildmay Mission to the Jews, British Jews Society, the American European Bethel Mission, the American Board of Missions to the Jews, the Danish Mission to the Jews, the Swiss Friends of Israel (Basel Mission) and other agencies increased during this decade. It was almost as if they instinctively knew that something drastic lay ahead.

---

[7] *JMI* 1930, pp. 90-92. There was also a Yiddish language service on Saturday overseen by Rev. Dr Prentki.

[8] *JMI* 1931, pp. 111-12.

A cursory inspection of the journals, Minute Books and periodicals of these societies reveals tremendous activity in numerous locations, such as Warsaw, Bialystok, Lublin, Krakow, Lodz, Grodno, Rovno, Lwow, Brest-Litovsk and Vilna. Additionally these missionary societies sent workers out all over the country during the upcoming decade, speaking and distributing literature to many Jewish communities.[9]

One of these workers was Victor Buksbazen. After completing his studies at the CMJ Training Centre he then studied a further five years at the Warsaw University. In 1933 he was appointed as the BJS representative in Krakow.[10]

Idea for a Hebrew Christian colony

Despite all this activity and despite Jewish people becoming followers of Jesus, there still remained a serious problem - employment. Jewish people in general in Poland were under tremendous economic pressure at this time. That predicament was compounded when a Jew confessed faith in Jesus as Messiah. If they worked for a Jewish business they could very well lose their employment. The situation for Hebrew Christians therefore was doubly difficult, as they were often considered Jewish by the general Polish populace, and not considered Jewish by the general Jewish populace.

It was with this economic dilemma in mind that a suggestion was broached at the annual meeting of the Polish branch of the Hebrew Christian Alliance in November 1930 to establish an agricultural or industrial colony in order to provide employment for Hebrew Christians. The executive of the IHCA was sympathetic to the proposal but emphasised that the initiative needed to be taken up by the leading missionary societies in Poland.[11] Although there was considerable enthusiasm for such a project, and funds were even raised, ultimately the project did not succeed.[12]

---

[9] Although there was probably some 'literary license' in some of these reports, yet nevertheless there is little doubt that tremendous efforts were indeed being made to introduce Jesus as Messiah to as many Jewish people as possible throughout Poland.

[10] BJS - British Jews Society. See *Annual Review of the BJS,* 1933, p. 41; also Glaser, p. 45. Buksbazen moved to Britain in 1937, and then to the United States in 1941 to work for the ABMJ. In 1943 he was involved with the Friends of Israel Gospel and Relief Society.

[11] *The Hebrew Christian*, Volume III, 1930-31, pp. 152-53.

[12] When the Second World War broke out this plan was finally shelved. *The Hebrew Christian*, Volume XII, 1939-1940, p. 109.

Nazis on the move

By the 1930s many Jews in Poland were becoming aware of the unfolding events in neighbouring Germany. By 1930 the National Socialist party of Adolf Hitler was growing in numbers and exposure. Their agenda was not hidden, so any who read widely were familiar with their drastic message against the Jewish people. Few however ever thought that the Nazis could get into a position of authority and succeed in implementing their worldview.

That worldview, their *Weltanschauung* concerning the Jewish people, was not just that they did not belong to the German nation as they were outsiders. Rather, Nazi ideology considered the Jews an anti-race of sub-humans who possessed super powers that were the cause of every world evil. This radical ideology did have some overlap in traditional Christian anti-Judaism, but it went much further by claiming it was based on science and in particular, Social Darwinism.

In Nazism all German institutions were to convey this perspective, and the Church was an essential German institution. Thus if the Nazis ever came to political power, they would introduce their worldview through each and every state institution, including the Church.

One of the key components of the Nazi Party was the *Schutzstaffel*, or the SS. This was a paramilitary unit designated to be Hitler's private bodyguard and whose sole purpose was to carry out, more often to enforce, the dictates and agenda of the Nazi Party. It was composed of totally committed adherents to the Nazi ideology. From 1929 this ruthless organ of the Party was headed up by Heinrich Himmler. One heavily indoctrinated department within the SS was the special police, the Gestapo. Apart from Himmler, two other close intimates of Hitler who shared his worldview were Herman Göring and Joseph Goebbels.

The Nazi Party takes political control in Germany

On 30 January 1933 the unthinkable happened - the Nazi Party came to power. Within days Hitler's henchmen, especially the *Sturmabteilung* or SA, but also including the SS, began imposing their strong-arm tactics against political rivals such as the Social Democrats and Communists, and others – including the Jewish people.

Overt persecution of the Jews began on 1 April with a nationwide boycott of Jewish businesses, and then institutionally on 7 April 1933. On that day the Nazis began introducing anti-Jewish legislation, initially with the so-called 'Aryan Paragraph', which excluded Jewish people from the civil service.[13] This law was the official beginning point of the exclusion of Jews from German society, at first from the civil service, and later from the general work force.

The nationwide boycott and introduction of the 'Aryan Paragraph' law began Phase Two of the Nazi solution to 'the Jewish problem.' Until this point Phase One had been laying the foundations for the implementation of the Nazi programme. Phase Two, which I term the 'intimidation, exploitation and emigration' phase, witnessed the isolation of the Jewish people from the rest of German society.

Daniel Goldhagen states of this period: '… Germans inside and outside the government succeeded in making life for Jews in Germany – who suffered under a plethora of laws, measures, and assaults upon their livelihoods, social positions, and persons – all but unbearable.'[14] Methods tried and proven in Germany over the following years greatly assisted the Nazis when they occupied Austria and Czechoslovakia, and later Poland and other European countries.

These anti-Jewish developments in Germany provoked similar actions in Poland. Sachar stated: 'With the example of Hitler now before them, the *Endeks* and *Naras* grew steadily more brazen: advocating the total elimination of Jews from gainful employment; provoking riots, disturbances, synagogue and cemetery desecrations.'[15]

Bazyli and Anna move to Lwow and other family movements

In 1932 Bazyli and Anna were transferred to Lwow in order to assist Abraham Ajzeman. New premises had just been obtained so it was a time to expand the work, and larger premises were again necessary in 1934.[16] It might also have been a case of having Bazyli located in a slightly less stressful situation than Warsaw.

[13] The official title was the 'Law for the Restoration of the Professional Civil Service.'

[14] Goldhagen, D. *Hitler's Willing Executioners*, (Arnold Knopf, 1996), p. 91.

[15] Sachar, *The Course*, p. 360.

[16] CMJ General Committee, 18 May 1934, Minute 1644.

While their youngest son, Jan, accompanied them, the older Jocz sons did not. By this time Jakob had completed his studies at the CMJ Training Centre and was now studying at the 'Prediger-Seminar der Bischoflichen Methodistenkirche' (Theological Seminary of the Methodist Episcopal Church) in Frankfurt am Main in Germany. He graduated from there in 1934.[17]

The CMJ General Committee agreed in April 1934 that Jakob and Rudolph Brinker, another Jewish Christian, should go to Britain 'for a course of training in the doctrines of the Church of England.'[18] They were both enrolled at St. Aidan's College in Birkenhead in England.

Jerzy by this time was employed in the State Department of Agriculture in Warsaw. Pawel, so the Jocz family website states, 'graduated from secondary school in 1930 and went on to study at the Faculty of Theology at Warsaw University. He was ordained by the Polish Reformed Church.'[19]

Bazyli continued in his task as colporteur and evangelist.[20] That the work in Lwow was developing is testified to by Oscar Prentki, who wrote following his missionary trip in 1933: 'On our way to Stanislawow we passed Lemberg and I spoke to a very nice group of Hebrew Christians who gathered at our Mission station… On our way back to Warsaw we passed Lemberg again, and as it was Sunday I conducted a small service in the afternoon, and addressed a small group of Jews and Hebrew Christians at our Mission premises.'[21] One young Hebrew Christian who came to know Jesus during this period was named J. Ellenbogan.[22]

Overall, though, attempting to introduce Jewish people to Jesus in Lwow was, like in all other locations, often quite difficult. But in Poland after 1933 the difficulties increased, being affected by the broader geo-political develop-

---

[17] See *A Brief History,* p. 3.

[18] CMJ General Committee, 27 April 1933, Minute 1580, (Minute Book c.39).

[19] *A Brief History,* p. 3.

[20] Anna later testified that 'My husband was an active missionary, and dedicated himself to convert Jews to Christianity (Protestant Church). The organisation of which he was a member, and that transferred [to] him 600 Zloty every month, was called the Church's Missions to the Jews, headquartered at 16 Lincoln's Fields, London, W.C. 2.' Solemn declaration from Anna Jocz, German File, p. 55.

[21] *JMI* 1933, pp. 106-7.

[22] 'Joy and Sorrow,' *JMI*, April 1938, p. 45.

ments in the region – namely the rise of Nazism in Germany and the influence it had upon the German Church.

The influence of Nazism on the German Church

Even before the Nazi Party took over control there had been a conflict within the German Evangelical Church, between those who supported Nazism and those who did not. Once the Nazi Party formally gained power these tensions were exacerbated. During the 1930s the pro-Nazi element, known as the German Christians, gained the ascendancy and were determined to turn the Protestant (or Evangelical) Church into the Reich Church.

Most of those endeavouring to uphold Biblical teaching were associated with what became known as the Confessing Church. Many pastors and priests who openly opposed anti-Semitism and Nazi overt racism suffered significant consequences for their actions.

Those who suffered most from this dynamic were the Hebrew Christians who were progressively forced out of the German Church. To the Nazis the German Church was an institution whose task was to further spread German culture, as determined by the Nazi *Weltanschauung,* especially Nazi racial ideology. As such, there could be no place for Jewish people within it. To mitigate these measures many Jewish non-Aryan Christians formed what in time became known as the *Paulus-Bund* in order to assist each other.

The Hebrew Christian quarterly editorial in 1933 stated:

> For Hebrew Christians the position is a very cruel one. The Hebrew Christians in Germany have been treated in the same manner as their Jewish brethren, and we are glad that no distinction is made.[23]

Then to the dismay (and shock) of many, on 20 July 1933 the Vatican entered into an agreement, known as the Concordat, with Nazi Germany. Despite the reasons given by the Roman Catholic Church that this agreement would protect them from official interference, in the eyes of the Jewish people this was an endorsement of the Nazi *Weltanschauung* by the Roman Catholic Church. Bazyli wrote concerning the influence these dynamics were having in Poland:

---

[23] *The Hebrew Christian,* Volume VI, 1933-34, p. 91.

> It is obvious, that the anti-Semitic flood is coming from Germany [to] overflow Poland, filling the minds of [the] Jewish population with bitterness and hatred against everything connected with anti-Semitism thus even against Christianity.
>
> The Jewish world observes with utmost attentiveness the attitude of the Christian Churches to the burning questions of [the] present time.
>
> The Jew contemplates disappointedly but with a concealed inner satisfaction the position of the German Church and its passiveness regarding the Jewish question.[24]

Some overseas support for the beleaguered Hebrew Christians

With the growth of anti-Jewish sentiment in Germany, Jewish organisations both inside and outside Germany began to assist the Jewish people there as best they could. Often times, however, the Hebrew Christians and non-Aryan Christians would not be helped by these Jewish organisations. If there were few allies and supporters for the Jewish people from within the institutional German Church, from where would support come?

A number of overseas entities and individuals then became actively involved in assisting the Hebrew Christians in Germany. One was the Bishop of Chichester who was instrumental in obtaining visas for many Hebrew Christians to enter into Britain. Another was Sir Leon Levison in his capacity as President of the IHCA. Levison wrote in early 1934:

> The duty of looking after and listening to the cry of over a quarter of a million Hebrew Christians is no mean task. Our sorrows have been overwhelming, but we have also been able to rejoice in God for all that He has enabled us to do. We have helped doctors, divinity students, and professors to find new spheres of labour, and asylum for the time being where they can pursue their studies. We have relieved individuals in their distress in Germany itself, and some of the sixty thousand refugees who have fled from that country.[25]

[24] B. Jocz's Report for May and June 1934, Bodleian Library, Dept CMJ, c. 103, Monthly Correspondence.

[25] *The Hebrew Christian,* Volume VI, 1933-34, p. 149. Concerning Levison's stated number of Hebrew Christians in Germany, it could be that he is including the first four categories of non-Aryan Christians as outlined in the Introduction, as well as all those people who were full and part Jewish.

Shortly after Levison again wrote:

> The situation in Germany at present is as follows. From the German Government statistics it is now evident that there are some three million non-Aryan Christians in Germany. Of these it is estimated that, roughly speaking, half a million are either themselves Hebrew Christians or Christians of Jewish descent, who go back to the third or fourth generation.
>
> The I.H.C.A., however, realises that about half the above number of Christians of Jewish descent feel that they have been born in the Christian faith, and were not even aware that their ancestors were Jews. But we have to face the fact that about a quarter of a million of these people have taken their stand and come out into the light, acknowledging their Jewish origin, and glorying in their Christian faith. They have taken a firm stand...
>
> Nevertheless we are grieved to see that because of this attitude all our quarter of a million kinsmen who now belong to the Christian family seem to be wanted by neither side, for they are rejected by the Nazis on the one hand and the Jewish people on the other. The situation in Germany has not improved, but is getting worse every day. Persecution is becoming more refined, but it only means that these people are being morally murdered by degrees instead of being killed outright.
>
> Sixty thousands of these victims, of whom fifteen thousand are Hebrew Christians, have left Germany and taken refuge in other countries.[26]

Although many Jewish people and non-Aryan Christians were now being helped, the plight of all the Jews in Germany became progressively worse.

The Nuremberg Laws

The next major step backwards occurred with the issuing of the Nuremberg Laws in 1935. These Laws basically disenfranchised the Jewish people of Germany from being German citizens. It further defined 'who was a Jew.' Henceforth the basic categorisation was:

- One classified as fully Jewish had three or four Jewish grandparents.
- One classified as half Jewish (*Mischling* first degree) had two Jewish

[26] *The Hebrew Christian,* Volume VII, 1934-35, p. 5.

grandparents.

- One classified as quarter Jewish (*Mischling* second degree) had one Jewish grandparent.

These classifications would affect hundreds of thousands of people in Germany. If Nazism ever succeeded in spreading its influence beyond Germany then the numbers of people fitting those three categories would run into the many millions.

No distinction at all was made regarding faith. It did not matter at all if one was a confessing Orthodox Jew, a Reform Jew, a secular atheistic Jew, a Communist Jew – or a Jewish person who believed that Jesus was the Messiah and was part of the Lutheran or Roman Catholic Church. All were Jewish because the Nazi classification system was based on blood-line and not faith or belief.

The promulgation of these laws witnessed an increasing number of Jewish people leaving or attempting to leave Germany. One of those affected by this anti-Jewish legislation was Dr Gottfried Frohwein, the son of Dr Paul Frohwein, who could no longer work in Germany as a doctor.[27]

What made matters even worse for the devout Jewish Christians who were endeavouring to introduce other Jewish people to Jesus, was that the Nazis often used the anti-Jewish writings of the much revered Martin Luther at the Nazi rallies in Nuremberg in order to substantiate, even justify, their racial policies against the Jewish people.[28] These new circumstances were a challenge to Christian mission work to the Jewish people throughout Europe – and especially to Hebrew Christians reaching out to their own people.

They were also a challenge to Bible-believing Christians in Germany, to people such as Catholic priest Bernhard Lichtenberg, and Lutheran ministers Martin Niemoller and Dietrich Bonhoeffer. These men and many others courageously challenged the Nazi policies, both in the political sphere as well as within the Church. The theological divide between the German Christians aligned to the Nazi Party and those associated with the Confessing Church,

---

[27] *Annual Report BJS*, 1935, p. 6; BJS Minutes 14 February 1939, pp. 122-123.

[28] In 1543 Luther wrote a vitriolic anti-Jewish book entitled *Von den Juden und ihren Lugen* ('On the Jews and their Lies').

widened.[29]

All of the Jocz family – Bazyli, Anna, Jakob, Jerzy, Pawel and Jan were classified as full Jews under the Nuremberg Laws. But they were all 'safe' in Poland. Just how 'safe' though was now an open question. Even in Poland anti-Jewish sentiment was again on the increase. This is epitomised by a pastoral letter sent out in 1936 by Cardinal Hlond, the Primate of Poland, which, Sacher wrote, 'publicly urged a boycott of Jewish businesses.'[30]

The Frohweins in Vilna

In the 1930s the Frohwein connection returned to Vilna. Mrs Frohwein (the widow of Dr Paul Frohwein) had been working for many years in Danzig, and then in 1932 she returned to the city where her husband had worked for many years with the Lutheran Mission – and had been instrumental in the early faith lives of Bazyli and Anna. The British Jews Society (BJS) and Basel Mission were now carrying on the work there.

The BJS Annual Report stated in 1935: 'Mrs Frohwein's son, Dr. G. Frohwein, who was a sufferer from the non-Aryan regulations in Germany, is at present assisting in the work in Wilna.'[31] The medical work of the BJS was carried out together with the Basel Mission, in which Miss Frohwein, Gottfried's sister, was the head nurse. Mrs Frohwein stated in 1936: 'Never before did such masses of Jews hear and listen to the Gospel that is preached to them at the different mission stations.'[32]

Staff changes and growth in Lwow

Herman Carpenter retired in 1935 after more than twenty years of service for CMJ in Warsaw. He was replaced by Rev. Martin Parsons who arrived in January 1935. Writing some years later Parsons stated: 'In the short break after Easter I visited our work in Lwow, where Mr Ajzeman and his family entertained me, and I met Mr and Mrs Jocz, a dear couple. It is terrible to recall that Mr Jocz was shot by a Nazi firing squad for the crime of being Jewish. But what an influence that simple man of God has had when one recalls the

---

[29] Both Lichtenberg and Bonhoeffer were murdered by the Nazis and Niemoller was imprisoned for many years in a concentration camp.

[30] Sachar, *The Course*, p. 360.

[31] *Annual Report of the British Society*, 1935, p. 16.

[32] *Annual Report of the British Society*, 1936, p. 45.

subsequent career of Jakob and Paul, two of his sons.'[33]

In May 1935 Bazyli again succumbed to illness and asked Jakob to come and assist Ajzeman, which he did. But once he was well again Bazyli made up for lost time and again met with enquirers on a one to one basis, and also engaged with visitors to the Mission Hall.[34] The work expanded so much that by 1936 a larger hall had to be hired in order to accommodate the increased numbers attending the meetings.

Ajzeman himself was due to retire in 1936 and his place was taken by Rudolph Brinker,[35] who had previously travelled to Britain together with Jakob in order to receive his Anglican ordination. The CMJ General Committee had meanwhile resolved to expand the work in Lwow by adding a small medical work, to be headed up by Miss G. West, who was a Hebrew Christian.[36] Miss West arrived in Warsaw on 9 October 1936 and reached Lwow shortly afterwards.[37]

This small medical work grew and a local doctor came to work in the clinic. Medical equipment for the small surgery was donated, enabling them to furnish two rooms. Brinker wrote: 'But now, as more patients are coming we find that some special surgical instruments and drugs are required. Also, owing to the fact that about one-third of all the patients attended by the doctor are children, a special medical apparatus is required.'[38]

Being a Hebrew Christian Miss West was subject to a measure of intimidation from certain rabbis. This did not seem to deter her from her task in Lwow, as she also assisted with the English Classes, whose numbers by 1938 had grown to some 130 students.[39]

Now recovered from his illness, Bazyli continued with his work as colporteur and evangelist. In his report for 1936 he wrote of one older man who occa-

---

[33] Martin Parsons, *Autobiography*, Chapter 7, unpublished work, www.parsonsfamily.co.uk.
[34] *JMI* 1935, p. 139.
[35] CMJ General Committee, 19 July 1936, Minutes 2296 & 2297.
[36] Adeney, p. 128.
[37] CMJ General Committee, 16 October 1936, Minute 2758.
[38] 'Joy and Sorrow', *JMI*, April 1938, p. 44.
[39] 'Joy and Sorrow', *JMI*, April 1938, p. 44.

sionally visited the Mission, and who also visited the Evangelical Church. 'In reply to my question, as to why he would not officially join the Evangelical Church,' Bazyli wrote, 'he took off his hat & pointing to his white hair said "You see, it is now too late for me to be baptized but I will die in the Christian Faith."'[40] Bazyli's dedicated service obviously impressed the CMJ General Committee, for honorariums were bestowed on him (and on Victor Weisman from Warsaw) in June 1937.[41]

Bazyli and Anna continued being part of the small Hebrew Christian community in Lwow. Brinker wrote of this little community: 'We were praying for a harmonium for our little chapel and for a piano for our English Bible Class. Both prayers have been granted. It is a great joy to be able to have such hearty singing in our little chapel.'[42]

One occasional congregant was J. Ellenbogan. He had been working as a mechanic in a factory but when the factory closed he began to spend more time introducing other Jewish people to Jesus. Ellenbogan asked Brinker to come to his home, in a small village near to Brody, about one hundred kilometres north-east of Lwow, in order to baptise his three children. Brinker wrote of this occasion:

> Some weeks ago, I was invited by a Hebrew-Christian family in a neighbouring little town to come and baptize their three children. The man had been converted and baptized several years ago in our Mission. His wife is also a believer. I went to the little town called Brody. On the station I was met by the man. It was a very cold morning, nearly 25 degrees below freezing point, but the man had no overcoat on. After an hour's walk we arrived at his house. I entered a room damp and dark... With my head I nearly touched the ceiling. Two beds and a table and three chairs were all the furniture... In this room the family was living... I stayed in the house from 11 a.m. till 7 p.m... Soon, one after another – Jews, young and old – began to come to the room. They heard of my visit and came to talk with me.[43]

---

[40] Annual Reports. 1936 Lwow – Mr B Jocz, Bodleian Library, c.97.
[41] CMJ General Committee, 17 June 1937, Minute 2985.
[42] 'Joy and Sorrow', *JMI,* April 1938, p. 44.
[43] 'Joy and Sorrow', *JMI,* April 1938, p. 45.

Ellenbogan might have been poor, but he was a devout follower of Jesus, and his life was a testimony in the village. Brinker recorded that as a result of his life there were a 'number of enquirers and 3-4 definite conversions to Christ.' Ellenbogan later became involved with the Mildmay Mission to the Jews.[44]

In his 1938 yearly report – which was to be his last - Bazyli stated:

> Through God's grace I was able during the past year to regularly attend to my mission work.
>
> During the summer months from May to October I did colportage work in streets and parks. Never before have Jews listened so earnestly and eagerly to the Word of God as in the past year. Of course this does not mean that I had no adversaries at all, but even our opponents behaved kindlier than ever before.[45]

Many dangers there may well have been for the Jewish people at this time, but in the midst of those dangers many Jewish people were willing to hear more about Jesus of Nazareth.

---

[44] Tragically it seems that his family became victims of the Holocaust. *Trusting and Toiling on Israel's Behalf*, 1946, pp. 2-3.

[45] B. Jocz, Annual Report 1938, Bodleian Library, Dept CMJ, c.97.

Latvia
Lithuania
Vilna
Danzig
Germany
Minsk
Grodno
U.S.S.R
Bialystok
Germany
Berlin
Poland
Posen
Warsaw
Lodz
Breslau
Lublin
Rovno
Prague
Krakow
Lwow
Czechoslovakia
Austria
Vienna
Hungary
Romania

Poland 1938

Chapter 10

Jakob and Pawel begin work for CMJ

Jakob begins his association with CMJ

Jakob continued his studies through 1934 into 1935. But it was not all work and no play while he was in England. In 1934 he had been able to attend the annual Keswick Christian Conference in the Lake District of England where he met Joan Gapp.[1] Their relationship blossomed.

Jakob was ordained into the diaconate of the Anglican Church in April 1935. He then returned to Poland after the summer holiday to work in the Warsaw Emmanuel Centre for the next twelve months under Parsons' supervision.[2]

Parsons wrote that after the summer holiday 'Jakob Jocz arrived from England, a newly ordained Deacon and engaged to an English girl, Joan. [He was about my own age, very gifted as a theologian, and the sort of person that everybody loves…].'[3] Jakob would be an understudy to Parsons in order to prepare for being priested.

Jakob returned to England in 1936 where he was ordained a priest in the Anglican Church by the Bishop of Fulham on 2 August 1936 in St Luke's, Hampstead.[4] Joan wrote: 'Jakob was ordained a priest of the Ang [sic] Church for work in Warsaw & a few days later we were married in my parish church.'[5]

The newly-weds departed for Poland shortly after, arriving in Warsaw in September 1936. Jakob took over the responsibility for the Hebrew Christians from Rudolph Brinker, who had just been transferred to Lwow. Jakob was to develop a close working relationship with Parsons.

---

[1] *Joan Jocz Memoir*, Jocz Private Collection, pp. 1-2.
[2] CMJ General Committee, 12 April 1935, Minute 1943.
[3] Martin Parsons, *Autobiography*. [...] in the original. The General Committee made mention on 15 November 1935 of their future marriage. See Minute 2142.
[4] CMJ General Committee, 7 August 1936, Minute 2371.
[5] *Joan Jocz Memoir*, p. 2.

Parsons himself also married in 1936 – with the service conducted by Jakob! Parsons and his wife Emilie visited Gdynia in northern Poland on their honeymoon. He recalled that one evening 'we visited the Irish Presbyterian mission run by Prediger Rad… Paul Jocz, Jakob's brother, was there at the time and on another occasion we met up with him for a walk and a talk. He was truly converted at Prediger Rad's Enquirer's Home and his contribution to Jewish evangelism ever since has been great.'[6]

Joan Jocz meanwhile was settling into her new position in Warsaw. She became involved in the English Language classes, and later stated that one of the students at the classes was a young Jewish man named Rachmiel Frydland.[7] Frydland became a follower of Jesus, and some years later survived numerous attempts by the Germans to murder him.

Another new teacher at the English school was Elisabeth Singer, who began her work there in September 1936.[8] Elisabeth (whose Polish name was Elzbieta) was the daughter of Herbert and Fredericke Singer, who were involved with the ministry of the Irish Presbyterian Mission to the Jews in Hamburg, a work synonymous with Dr Arnold Frank (1859-1965).[9] Herbert Singer assisted Dr Frank in Hamburg until 1937 when the Singers left for the United States.[10] Dr Frank was regarded as one of the patriarchs of the Hebrew Christian movement in Europe, and succeeded Sir Leon Levison as the President of the International Hebrew Christian Alliance.[11]

Two newly married young couples and a new young woman teacher (who would one day be another Mrs Jocz) meant that there was plenty of youth and zeal at Number 3 Sewerynow Street in Warsaw. There needed to be, as the

---

6 Martin Parsons, *Autobiography*.

7 *Joan Jocz Memoir,* p. 3. After the War Frydland moved to the United States. Joan was surprised to meet him in Toronto many years later.

8 Bodleian Library, Dept CMJ, c. 98. Missionary Reports.

9 CMJ also had a work in Hamburg. This work began in 1825 but closed in 1840, and only re-started in 1855. In 1896 the work was headed up by Rev. D. H. Dolman, and then by his son Rev. George Dolman until 1934. Ultimately the work was forced to close by the Nazi authorities.

10 Bodleian Library, Dept CMJ, d. 91. 1-16, Staff lists 1935-37. Herbert was a Hebrew Christian while Fredericke was a Gentile background follower of Jesus. 11 For further information on the work of Dr Frank I refer you to Allen, R. *Arnold Frank of Hamburg*, (James Clarke & Co Ltd, London, no date).

amount of activities occurring there was considerable. Some years later Joan Jocz wrote concerning the Christmas event in 1936:

> A very special party was held for our H.C. [Hebrew Christian] friends... It is a very poignant memory, because of the large group of people present that evening, only 3 or 4 survived the Holocaust.[12]

Paul begins his association with CMJ

On 10 August 1936, after arriving back from his honeymoon, Parsons sent a letter to CMJ 'regarding arrangements for the training of Mr Paul Jocz for missionary work.' The Committee stated they would give it their consideration.[13]

By October 1936 Pawel (Paul) was already in Britain[14] and on 20 November, the Committee reported: '... that Mr Paul Jocz had arrived and entered the Glasgow Bible Institute in order to begin his missionary training.'[15] Study obviously suited Pawel. On 17 June 1937 the General Committee recorded 'with pleasure that Mr Paul Jocz had headed the list at the recent examination at the Glasgow Bible College, and that when he finishes his Course there he be appointed to the Warsaw Mission as a "student-missionary" in Local Connexion.'[16] Parsons would arrange for his further instruction in Warsaw.

Pawel returned to Warsaw and began his work in CMJ's Emmanuel Centre in 1938. Parsons wrote: 'Blessing is attending the colportage work, and the two new workers, Messrs Paul Jocz and N. Szuman, are doing this work with great zeal. In this way the word of God is getting into the homes of the Jews more than formerly.'[17]

During the 1930s a number of Polish-born Jewish Christians were involved with CMJ, including Joseph Sommer (also spelt Zomer), M. Wolfin,[18] Natan

---

[12] *Joan Jocz Memoir,* p. 5.

[13] CMJ General Committee, 16 October 1936, Minute 2397.

[14] CMJ General Committee, 16 October 1936, Minute 2371 and 2397, Minute Book 1930-1940, Dept CMJ, c. 39.

[15] CMJ General Committee, 20 November 1936, Minute 2444.

[16] CMJ General Committee, 17 June 1937, Minute 2985.

[17] JMI, November 1938, p. 138.

[18] Mitch Glaser states that 'In January 1932 in Warsaw, M. Wolfen was appointed missionary representative of the Hebrew Christian Alliance of America (HCAA).' Glaser, p. 45.

Szuman, John Enis and Victor Weisman, while many others were associated with the Emmanuel congregation. In addition there were many other Polish-born and other Jewish Christians endeavouring to introduce Jesus to the Jewish people in Warsaw and elsewhere.

Significant IMC meeting in Vienna – 1937

In 1937 the 'International Missionary Council on the Christian Approach to the Jews' held a meeting in Vienna. The Chairman of this body was Dr Conrad Hoffman, a man who was doing his utmost to alleviate the suffering of the Hebrew Christians in Germany. Parsons delivered a message at the meeting relating primarily to Warsaw. He stated:

> The American Board of Missions[19] has a center in Warsaw on the east of the river. They have room for some inquirers, in addition to general evangelistic work. The Mildmay Mission[20] has a hall in the Jewish quarter in Warsaw and their work mainly touches poorer Jews. The American European Fellowship is in Warsaw and works particularly among children. They have a villa at Radoso, which is used in the Summer for children's work. The Bethel Mission[21] in Lodz has an evangelistic center and a colony. In addition, in Poland there is one Pentecostal evangelist, one member of the Open Brethren, one member of the Closed Brethren and a few private evangelists living by faith. The four missions in Warsaw work together in close cooperation. The shape of this is in the form of monthly-united prayer meetings and monthly evangelistic meetings. In Lvov there is active cooperation between the Church Mission to the Jews (CMJ) and the Danish Mission (DIM) with their joint monthly evangelistic meeting.[22]

In addition to the above there was also the work of the Barbican Mission to the Jews (BMJ), led by Rev. Piotr (Peter) Gorodishz which was centred in Bialystok, but which had operations throughout the land. Gorodishz would ultimately suffer a similar fate to Bazyli, as too would Nathan Sendyk, the

[19] Chosen People Ministries today.
[20] Later became the Messianic Testimony.
[21] American European Bethel Mission.
[22] IMCCAJ Vienna Conference 1937, cited in Glaser, *Heroes of the Holocaust: Messianic Jews in Warsaw Ghetto,* 27th Annual Pre-Trib Study Group, Sheraton Grand Hotel Dallas/Ft. Worth, December 3–5, 2018, no page numbers.

one-time leader of the Mildmay work in Poland.

A further rise in anti-Jewish sentiment

Although there were many opportunities to share the message of Jesus, this decade also witnessed a steady increase of anti-Jewish sentiment in Poland. This situation is illustrated by Sachar, who described, concerning the spring of 1936, how in the town of Przytyk 'Jewish students who sought to resist the assaults of anti-Semitic thugs were thrown in prison by the government magistrates. By the end of 1936 dictator Smigly-Rydz, who had succeeded Pilsudski on the latter's death, now deemed it politically expedient to compromise with fascist anti-Semitism whenever possible.'[23]

Sachar also recorded a 1938 speech of Smigly-Rydz who stated: "[The Jews] have separate national aims," he declared. "They weaken Polish national forces. They interfere with national evolution."[24] Rudolph Brinker derscribed the situation in Lwow in 1938:

> The situation is growing more desperate from day to day. Jew-baiting is becoming a noble sport of all and especially for the University students. It is no longer safe for the Jewish students to enter the University. One of the Mission friends was seriously wounded when entering a lecture hall. A gang of "Christian" students with sticks, etc., got hold of him. He soon lay wounded at their feet crying for help, but none came… A professor who was informed by a friend of the incident, replied that he had no time to come. The government tries sometimes to suppress the riots, but they seem powerless.[25]

In the national election that year the Jewish people of Poland were on edge, fearing that a more extreme right wing majority would get into power. Thankfully Smigly-Rydz was denied a majority in the Parliament (Sejm), and the Jewish population let out a huge sigh of relief. But alas, it was not the end of their travails, but only the beginning.

Tensions there were in the country, and soon there would be crises in the neighbouring lands. Yet the work of introducing Jesus to the Jewish people

---

[23] Sachar, *The Course*, p. 360.
[24] Sachar, *The Course*, p. 361.
[25] *JMI* April 1938, p. 44.

continued unabated. The *JMI* recorded that Easter 1938 was 'a very joyful occasion in the Warsaw Mission, seven people were baptized and later on in April two more while in May the Bishop paid a visit and confirmed twenty-three candidates at Warsaw and fifteen in Lwow.'[26] The Hebrew Christian congregation welcomed over one hundred people on a regular basis.

Conflict and tensions in the region

Meanwhile the situation for the Jews in Germany continued to deteriorate. The non-Aryan Christians continued to experience the unpleasant pressure of being caught in the middle. Even the *Paulus-Bund* encountered internal friction, between the Jews classified as full-Jews from those classified as *Mischling* first degree and *Mischling* second degree.[27] The Confessing Church endeavoured to assist these beleaguered Jewish Christians and non-Aryan Christians by setting up a bueau in 1938 headed by Pastor Heinrich Grüber.

But further more ominous events then impacted the region. On 12 March 1938 German troops crossed the border into Austria and orchestrated the *Anschluss* – unification (annexation). Austria ceased to exist as a sovereign nation and was integrated into the German Reich. This was a fulfilment of the vision of Hitler and others associated with the 'pan-German' movement.

Within days persecution against the Jewish people became much more severe. The Nazis pressured the Jews to leave Austria. The Nazi official entrusted with facilitating this was Adolf Eichmann. The desperate plight of these Jewish refugees caused concern among the Western leaders and a conference was convened in the French town of Evian between 6-16 July 1938 to discuss the issue. Unfortunately little was done practically to help these desperate Jewish refugees. The Nazis meanwhile took note of the apparent disinclination of the Western powers to offer much assistance to the Jewish people.

The situation in Austria also affected the non-Aryan Christians, most of whom were Jewish, and most of whom were associated with the Roman Catholic Church. But there were also many Jewish Protestants as well. Several key Protestant works were based in Vienna and they did their utmost to

---

[26] *JMI*, February 1940, p. 15.

[27] For further information see Werner Cohn, 'Bearers of a Common Fate ? The "Non-Aryan Christian Fate-Comrades" of the Paulus Bund, 1933-1939', in *Leo Baeck Institute Yearbook,* Vol. XXXIII, 1988, pp. 327-366.

alleviate the suffering of the Hebrew Christian community. Foremost among the Protestant entities in Vienna were the Institutum Judaicum Delitzschianum; the British Jews Society; the American Board of Missions to the Jews; Christ Church (the Anglican chapel of the British Embassy); and especially the Swedish Israel Mission.[28]

The ordeal of the Jews in Austria, including the Hebrew Christians, was soon to be replicated in a part of western Czechoslovakia named the Sudetenland where many ethnic Germans lived. Hitler demanded this region be annexed to Germany, and in order to avoid conflict the political leaders of Germany, Britain, France and Italy met in Munich between 28-30 September 1938. Hitler's demands were granted by the so-called 'Munich Pact' – and war was avoided. German troops then occupied the region. Jewish people throughout Europe watched in trepidation, while Winston Churchill looked on in unbelief at the naivety of the British and French leaders.

Germany demands Danzig

Shortly afterwards, on 24 October 1938, Germany's Foreign Minister, Joachim von Ribbentrop, presented the Polish Government, via Ambassador Jozef Lipski, with a very serious demand. This was the return to Germany of the former German port city of Danzig (today Gdansk), and permission for Germany to establish a highway across the Polish Corridor connecting Germany with Danzig and East Prussia. One very important condition attached to this German 'request' was that Germany also wanted Poland to join in the Anti-Comintern Pact against the Soviet Union.[29]

Danzig was a former German city but the League of Nations had given it special status as a 'free city' under the League's political supervision, and it was controlled economically by Poland. In order to provide Poland with access to the sea, the League had separated East Prussia from the remainder of Germany, creating what became known as the Polish Corridor.

On orders from his Government the Polish foreign minister, Jozef Beck,

[28] Glaser, pp. 286-307.

[29] Conversation between Foreign Minister Ribbentrop and Ambassador Lipski, Berchtesgaden, 24 October 1938 in *Documents on German Foreign Policy*, Series D, Vol. V, Doc. 81, p. 104. Shirer, W. *The Rise and Fall of the Third Reich*, p. 455. The Anti-Cominterm Pact was aimed against the Communist International (mostly the Soviet Union), signed initially between Germany and Japan on 25 November 1936.

refused most of these German demands on 31 October 1938,[30] but Lipski was only able to communicate these instructions to von Ribbentrop on 19 November.[31] Hitler then sent an order to the commanders of the German armed forces[32] on 24 November to prepare a plan for the seizure of Danzig. Most Poles were by now apprehensive about German intentions.[33]

When it became clear that Poland was not going to accept the German terms, the German authorities expelled some 17,000 Polish Jews living in Germany. This expulsion on many occasions was quite brutal. One Jewish family expelled in such a brutal way was the Grynszpan family.

Kristallnacht – Night of Broken Glass (9-10 November 1938)

One member of the Grynszpan family, Herschel, was living in Paris. Herschel was so affected by the plight of his family that he decided to bring this despicable situation to the attention of the world. On 7 November he shot a German Embassy official in Paris.

The shooting and subsequent death of this official gave the Nazis a prime opportunity to enact collective revenge upon the German Jewish population. On the night of 9 November and throughout the following day Jewish people and property were attacked throughout the German Reich. It was a state-orchestrated pogrom, known as *Kristallnacht*, which resulted in the destruction of hundreds of synagogues and other Jewish institutions and property, and the murder of almost one hundred Jews.

Many thousands of Jewish men were quickly bussed off to the three new concentration camps of Dachau, Buchenwald and Sachsenhausen, as well as other holding places. The vast majority of these were beaten and intimidated, and released only on condition that they leave the country. This was all part of Phase Two of the Nazi solution to 'the Jewish problem' - to rid the Reich (the region now controlled by Nazi Germany) of the Jewish people.

---

[30] Shirer, p. 455.

[31] Memorandum by the Foreign Minister, 19 November 1938, in *Documents on German Foreign Policy,* Series D, Vol. V, Doc. 101, p. 127.

[32] *Oberkommando Wehrmacht* (OKW) – Army, Airforce and Navy.

[33] Shirer, p. 456.

Chapter 11

The lead up to war

The beginning of 1939

The year began on a high note for the Hebrew Christian community in Warsaw. Jakob wrote in his annual report:

> We began 1939 in a remarkable way.
> At about 9 o'clock at New Year's Eve a crowd of our Jewish friends gathered in our Mission Hall. Many of our Hebrew Christians & friends of the other two missions in Warsaw were also present. We arranged a social evening & were expecting over a hundred people, but in the end we had well over 200 guests.
>
> … At about 11.30 we all moved to the adjoining Church… After midnight our Service developed into an evangelistic meeting. An appeal was made that those who would make their decision at the beginning of this N. Year & give their lives to Christ should come up to the Communion rails and confess Him in prayer before the whole Congregation. Between 20-30 came forward. Some of them were amongst those who later confessed Christ in Holy Baptism & were confirmed by the Bishop at Easter.
>
> Such was the beginning of 1939. There was a wonderful spirit of enquiry & a unique opening for the Gospel message. We all had reason to expect great things from the ensuing year.[1]

It seems likely that a similar event would have taken place in the smaller Hebrew Christian and Evangelical community in Lwow.

Hitler's speech in the Reichstag – 30 January

It wasn't long, however, before international events began to cast a shadow over the future of the vibrant Jewish-Hebrew Christian communities in Poland. On 30 January 1939 Hitler gave a speech in the Reichstag commemo-

[1] Jakob Jocz, Report for 1939, Bodleian Library, Dept CMJ, c. 99.

rating the Nazi accession to power, in which he stated:

> If the international Jewish financiers in and outside Europe should succeed in plunging the nations once more into a world war, then the result will not be the Bolshevization of the earth and thus the victory of Jewry, but the annihilation of the Jewish race in Europe![2]

This speech re-emphasised Hitler's fantasy that Bolshevism was foundationally associated with the Jews, and also introduced very clearly his goal of ridding Europe of the Jewish people. At this point the key issue was determining exactly what he meant by the word annihilation. Did he mean evicting the Jewish people from Europe, or did he even at that point have something more sinister in mind?

The German takeover of Czechoslovakia – 15 March

Outright German aggression in the region intensified on 15 March 1939 when German troops occupied the remainder of Czechoslovakia, thereby violating the Munich Pact. The Germans then established the Protectorate of Bohemia and Moravia (which included Prague), which was now effectively controlled by Germany. The remainder of the country, mostly Slovakia, became independent, but was closely aligned with Nazi Germany.

As in other regions occupied by the Nazi German regime, persecution broke out almost immediately against the Jewish people – and the Hebrew Christians for the most part were not exempt.[3] Wherever possible Jews emigrated, but now entry into other nations was becoming more and more difficult.

---

[2] www.yadvashem.org/docs/extract-from-hitler-speech.html. Numerous endeavours were made to provide safe havens for these Jewish people in the Reich. One such endeavour was to settle them in the Kimberley region of Western Australia.

[3] Apart from the Czech national Church (the Czech Brethren), other mission agencies involved with the Jewish people included the United Free Church of Scotland (UFCS) and the Barbican Mission to the Jews (BMJ). Glaser, pp. 206-212. A number of Jewish Christians associated with the Barbican Mission were murdered, including Mr Fontheim, who died in Buchenwald, and K. Lohs, a journalist who was taken to Izbica in 1942. *Immanuel's Witness*, April 1945 – March 1946, p. 71. 'Also Mr. and Mrs. Huppert, the Fuchs family with their children were sent to Poland. So far there is no news of them, it is possible that they are all dead.' *Immanuel's Witness*, April 1945 – March 1946, p. 86.

Hitler's intimidation of Poland – 21 March

Hitler had an overall objective – to bluff and bully the surrounding nations into capitulating to Nazi Germany's objectives. One of these objectives was to bring all 'historic' German territory and ethnic German people under the direct control of the Reich. Another was to bring all the surrounding nations into a common front against the Soviet Union, as part of the Anti-Comintern Pact. Next on his hit list was Poland.

Poland had rejected Germany's initiative to draw her into such an alliance against the Soviet Union as Poland desired to maintain equanimity in her political relationship with both Germany and the Soviet Union. Additionally the German 'request' of 1938 was coupled with the desire to reintegrate Danzig back into the German Reich. On both of these points Poland could not accept Hitler's 'requests' – which were in reality, demands. The Poles then began to seek fresh alliances with the western democracies, and discussions began with the British and French.

If anything was becoming clear by now it was that Hitler hated being rebuffed. He met the Polish foreign minister, Beck, on 5 January 1939, and reiterated his desire to re-incorporate Danzig into the German Reich, and to build a highway and railroad through the Corridor which would connect East Prussia with the remainder of the German Reich.[4] Hitler had also intimidated Lithuania into surrendering the port city of Memel, in which there was a sizeable German minority.

Then on 21 March von Ribbentrop threatened the Polish ambassador, Jozef Lipski, declaring that Poland needed to decide if she was going to accept Hitler's ultimatum concerning Danzig and the Corridor or not. Von Ribbentrop stated: 'I told Ambassador Lipski once again that Danzig would certainly return to the Reich sooner or later.'[5] Germany was not allowing Poland any middle ground. To prove that Germany would tolerate no ambiguity, on 23 March she annexed the district of Memel from Lithuania.

The Polish government nevertheless refused to be intimidated by Hitler and on 26 March Lipski presented an official Memorandum on this matter to

---

[4] Shirer, p. 461.

[5] *Documents on German Foreign Policy*, Series D, Vol. VI, March – 3 Sept 1939, Doc. 61, p. 70.

von Ribbentrop.[6] Von Ribbentrop informed Lipski that the Polish response would not please Hitler. It didn't. Tensions then mounted in both countries, as reports in the German Foreign Office documents testify. With Germany demanding the return of Danzig and Poland refusing, war was inevitable.

Britain offers Poland unilateral support – and the ramifications
Britain and France thereupon offered security guarantees to Poland to try to deter a German attack. Britain's commitment was revealed in a speech in the House of Commons by Prime Minister Neville Chamberlain on 31 March, in which he stated that Britain (and France) would fully support Poland.[7] Then on 6 April a 'temporary pact of mutual assistance' was signed in London between the British and the Poles.[8]

However, Britain had left the Soviet Union out of any impending alliance against German aggression. Both Germany and the Soviet Union recognised this omission. In an effort to draw closer to Germany, Stalin dismissed his Foreign Minister Maxim Litinov, who was more pro-British and pro-French (as well as being Jewish), and replaced him with Vyacheslav Molotov – who was more acceptable to the Germans. Thereafter relations between Germany and the Soviet Union slowly warmed.

On 3 April Hitler made his future intentions clear to his associates concerning Poland.[9] Then on 11 April he issued what was termed *Operation White*, a directive for the upcoming invasion of Poland. In it he stated:

> German relations with Poland continue to be based on the principles of avoiding any disturbances. Should Poland, however, change her policy towards Germany, which so far has been based on the same principles as our own, and adopt a threatening attitude towards Germany, a final settlement might become necessary in spite of the Treaty with Poland.
>
> The aim will then be to destroy Polish military strength, and create in the East a situation which satisfies the requirements of national defence. The Free State of Danzig will be proclaimed a part of the Reich territory at the

6 *Documents on German Foreign Policy,* ibid, Doc. 101, p. 121.
7 Shirer, p. 454.
8 Ibid., p. 469.
9 Ibid., p. 468.

outbreak of hostilities, at the latest.

The political leaders considered their task in this case to isolate Poland if possible, that is to say, to limit the war to Poland only.[10]

Further expulsion of Poles from Germany - May

Tensions between Germany and Poland continued to mount. In May 1939 the Nazi authorities decided to expel all remaining residents with Polish citizenship. The majority of these unfortunate people found themselves at the border, and worse, were caught in no-man's land as the Polish Government did not want to receive them back again.

One of those at the border at this time was Leon Rosenberg who was on his way back to Poland from the US. He wrote: 'The frontier was blocked with thousands of exiles – Jews, Polish citizens from Germany: men, women and children were suddenly forced to leave without means and deprived of everything. They came unsuspected to the borders, which was a surprise to the Polish Government. ...I witnessed scenes of utter despair among those destitute.' He managed to save a woman and her two small children.[11]

The Mildmay Mission assisted these destitute people as best they could, as did the other Evangelical societies, including CMJ. Rachmiel Frydland wrote: '... an exodus of German Jews started, and those who were born outside of Germany had to return to their own countries. Thousands of refugees began to swell the Jewish community in Warsaw. All day they searched for work in the city. In the evening they needed a place where they would be welcome. At the Mission they found an open door and if they were hungry they would also find some relief. They were not opposed to faith in Messiah but wanted to understand and to have it explained. We had a full house every evening.'[12]

The Pact of Steel and Hitler's long-term plans – 22-23 May

Throughout the previous years Hitler had been cultivating Benito Mussolini of Italy. An agreement between the two dictatorial nations was signed in Berlin on 22 May 1939 and named the 'Pact of Steel'. According to the Pact both

[10] 'Directive by the Fuhrer: Operation White', in *Documents on German Foreign Policy*, Series D, Vol. VI, Doc. 185, p. 224.

[11] *The Bethel Witness*, April – June 1939, p. 3.

[12] Frydland, *Joy Cometh in the Morning*, (Rachmiel Frydland, Cincinnati: No date), p. 26. Frydland's book was later republished as *When Being Jewish Was a Crime*.

nations were united and 'resolved to act side by side and with united force to secure their living space.'[13]

Now Hitler could further plan for his next objective, to bring Danzig back into the Reich. At a high level meeting with Hermann Göring and his military leaders on 23 May Hitler outlined his plan, which went much further than just Danzig. It included the taking of all of Poland. The destiny of Germany demanded that they have more living space, and resources, and a labour market (the Polish people) who could be exploited.

Prit Buttar in his book *Battleground Prussia* quoted Hitler informing his subordinates that '… Danzig is not the subject of the dispute at all. It is a question of expanding our living space in the East and of securing our food supplies, of the settlement of the Baltic problem…' Hitler also indicated that his ultimate concern was Russia, but that Poland first had to be subdued: 'The Polish problem is inseparable from conflict with the West. Poland's internal power of resistance to Bolshevism is doubtful. Thus Poland is of doubtful value as a barrier against Russia. It is questionable whether military success in the West can be achieved by a quick decision, questionable too is the attitude of Poland. The Polish government will not resist pressure from Russia. Poland sees danger in a German victory in the West, and will attempt to rob us of the victory. There is therefore no question of sparing Poland, and we are left with the decision: To attack Poland at the first suitable opportunity.'[14]

At this meeting Hitler also admitted that Britain would be an obstacle to Germany achieving its goals. A further problem would be if Britain, France and the Soviet Union all joined together against Germany.

Various staff movements and activities

Despite all these diplomatic manoeuvrings the Jocz family continued with their daily lives. Pawel continued his work as a colporteur as well as being a 'student-missionary' under the tutelage of Parsons in Warsaw, although from May Parsons was absent in Britain on sick-leave. Upon Pawel's return to Warsaw he was re-acquainted with Elzbieta (Elisabeth) Singer, and a romance began to blossom.

---

[13] Shirer, p. 483.

[14] Buttar, P. *Battleground Prussia,* (Bloomsbury Publishing. Kindle Edition), p. 8.

In March Jakob and Joan went to Britain for deputation work (a speaking tour). While there Joan realised she was pregnant and wanted to stay and have their child in Britain. Following a family holiday after the deputation tour, Jakob returned to Poland on his own at the beginning of July.[15] He again took up his responsibilities as the pastor of the Hebrew Christian congregation - as well as his duties as the vice-President of the Polish branch of the IHCA.

Meanwhile changes were afoot in Lwow. Rudolph Brinker was being transferred to London, and Rev. Roger Allison, a recently ordained clergyman, was being sent out from Britain to replace him.[16] Meanwhile Bazyli was continuing with his work in Lwow, making the most of every opportunity to introduce Jewish people to Jesus. Judging from the various journal reports, the same could be said of all of the Evangelical workers throughout Poland at this time.

Allison arrived in Warsaw in May 1939 and initially covered for Parsons while he was on sick leave in Britain.[17] Allison received a rapid introduction to ministry among the Jewish people, and wrote shortly afterwards about one aspect of this work, the night classes:

> Through the medium of evening English classes, as has been the custom in other countries, closer personal friendships were being formed with Jewish people of all ages. Whatever may have been the religious persuasions of students who have come to us for some practical help, they have always, in my experience, been open to the use of the Bible, including the New Testament, as a text-book, with its interesting and illustrative stories. After all, the Jews are also a 'people of the Book.'[18]

With the rise of tensions in Germany and the recent events in the region, many young Jewish people desired to leave – to Palestine if they were more Zionist in leaning. For the non-Zionists it was to any country which would

[15] *Joan Jocz Memoir,* p. 5.

[16] CMJ General Committee, 17 March 1939, Minute 3243, Minute Book c. 39. Upon the suggestion of the Bishop of Fulham, and endorsed by the General Committee, it was deemed wise that 'he obtain a License to act as British Chaplain at Lwow.'

[17] Allison, R. *Journey to Jerusalem*, (Fastprint & Design: St Leonards-on-Sea, 1988), p. 9.

[18] Ibid., p. 12.

accept them. Unfortunately, following the relatively ineffectual Evian Conference of 1938 there seemed little chance of Jewish people being accepted elsewhere. Nevertheless many clung to the hope of being able to leave, and they felt it was imperative to have a grasp of the English language.

Political and military preparations being made

During this tense period Winston Churchill encouraged Chamberlain and his government to enter into an alliance with the Soviet Union in order to ensure that Hitler would stop any further acts of aggression in the East. Finally, on 27 May, the British and French envoys in Moscow showed a draft version of a proposed pact to Foreign Minister Molotov.

From 1 June two separate entities were vying for a new relationship with the communist Soviet Union - the Anglo-French democracies and Nazi Germany. The fate of Europe and of the Jewish people depended upon whom the Soviets would ultimately align themselves with. Meanwhile, during this very same period, Hitler and his staff were fine tuning their plans for destroying Poland via *Operation White.* (Sometimes also referred to as 'Case White'.)

Hitler was planning for total war, and several million German soldiers would be mobilised. This would place a huge strain on local manpower, and plans were now being made to utilise inmates from concentration camps and Polish citizens to assist with the war effort. This marks the beginning point of the slave labour force which would become more apparent in time.

As tensions concerning the Polish Corridor and the region around Danzig mounted, negotiations between the Soviets and Germans recommenced on 22 July. Then just the next day, 23 July the British and French 'finally agreed to Russia's proposal that military-staff talks be held at once to draw up a military convention which would spell out specifically how Hitler's armies were to be met by the three nations.'[19]

Complications for the Frohwein's

The international situation between Germany and Poland made it very complicated for the Frohwein family, who were German by nationality. The Minutes of the British Jews Society stated on 14 February 1939: 'The work was proceeding in Wilno, but as a German, and a non-Aryan, Dr Frohwein was

[19] Shirer, p. 502.

finding it none too easy.'[20]

Gottfried Frohwein was looking forward to a visit to Britain, which occurred in May, in order to speak to the BJS Committee. He was desirous to migrate to Britain, together with his wife and children, but it seems his application was unsuccessful. By July he had returned to Vilna.[21] One could but imagine the pressure all the Frohwein family was under, being Germans in Poland, and being Jewish Christians at the same time.

Summer in Poland

When the summer arrived Roger Allison joined the local evangelists (Victor Weisman, M. Wolfin and Pawel Jocz) on the annual summer evangelistic trip. He wrote: 'During part of June and July I joined the missionaries on two of their journeys, visiting in the Mission car towns and villages in other parts of Poland.'[22] On another occasion he wrote, 'one of the Polish evangelists invited me to join him on one of his regular tours of the countryside, visiting small groups of believers and in some way spreading the Gospel. .. endemic anti-semitism was to be found in the population as a whole…'[23]

'Our travels', Allison continued, 'took us in my companion's car along the typically long, straight, dusty roads, stretching many miles without so much as a single bend.' Jakob also joined them on this same missionary journey and wrote: 'The Rev. R. Allison, Brothers Weisman, Wolfin and Paul Jocz took part in this journey & we had a happy time together. None of us realised that this was the last time of our being together… It was a special joy to me to be able to see my parents while on our visit to Lwow.'[24]

This visit to Lwow was in fact the last time that Jakob saw his father Bazyli.

---

[20] Minute Book of BJS, 14 February 1939.

[21] Minute Book of BJS, 18 April 1939, 16 May 1939, 11 July 1939.

[22] Roger Allison, 'Warsaw on the Eve', *JMI,* February 1940, p. 22.

[23] Allison, *Journey*, p. 12.

[24] Jakob Jocz, Report for 1939, Bodleian Library, Dept CMJ, c. 99. Both Weisman and Wolfin would later be incarcerated in the Warsaw Ghetto and perished, either in the Ghetto or in the Treblinka death camp.

Chapter 12

August 1939

The Jocz family in August

At the conclusion of the missionary journey Jakob left Poland, and later wrote:

> At the beginning of August I came back to England by invitation of CMS to speak for the Society at the Malvern Summer School. I came to this country with a return ticket in my pocket & all my worldly belongings in Warsaw.[1]

While Jakob was speaking at meetings in Britain, Allison remained with the Jocz family near Lwow, and recorded that: 'In August I enjoyed a most happy and memorable holiday with two of our young workers, Paul Jocz and Elisabeth Singer, and with Paul's parents and younger brother.'[2] Of that time he later recalled: 'We were to spend a few weeks in the cottage home of Paul's parents in a small village called Brzuchovice, only a few miles from Lvov (Lemberg), where a new Mission Centre was hopefully to be established.'[3]

Allison remembered it as a particularly peaceful time:

> In the sunshine, which smiled on us so much, we played Ludo and other games, read books and papers, or simply lay and basked: a rather lazy but very refreshing holiday. One day towards the end of August, as we sat in an open space on a ski-ing hill, we were thrilled at the sight of about a thousand storks in the distance, circling in preparation for the great migration: then, having chosen their leaders, they flew off in flocks in intervals, almost over our heads. They felt, as we did, the approach of

[1] Jakob Jocz, Report for 1939, Bodleian Library, Dept CMJ, c. 99. CMS – Church Missionary Society, an Evangelical Anglican society which had been founded in 1799.

[2] Roger Allison, 'Warsaw on the Eve', *JMI*, February 1940, p. 22. Allison used both the English spelling of Elisabeth and the American spelling of Elizabeth.

[3] Allison, *Journey*, p. 12.

colder weather, and one wonders whether they had, besides, a premonition of that bitter conflict and its horrors which was so soon to devastate the land.[4]

Meanwhile the negotiations between Britain, France and the Soviets were progressing slowly and tediously. The main sticking point was Poland. Poland (and Romania) refused to allow Soviet troops to enter their territory as they didn't trust they would leave. The Soviets contended that they couldn't realistically assist the Poles if Soviet troops were not able to enter Polish territory and confront the Germans. But the Polish Government, on 20 August, formally rejected this possibility. The die had been cast.

Significant meetings

While Allison, Pawel and Elzbieta were enjoying a summer holiday and having relaxing social meetings at the cottage of Bazyli and Anna near Lwow, and while Jakob was speaking at the CMS meeting in England, other more sinister meetings were being held in Berlin and Moscow.

The lack of a clear and decisive understanding between the British, French and Soviets had allowed Hitler to determine what he was prepared to agree with the Soviets. Finally, on 14 August, he instructed von Ribbentrop to inform Molotov of German willingness to establish an agreement with the Soviets. Within the German instructions was the strong hint of Germany and the Soviets dividing up Eastern Europe. This was inducement enough for Stalin to consider entering into such an agreement with Hitler.

So confident was Hitler that Stalin would enter into an agreement, that on the same day, 14 August, he summoned his military leaders to a meeting to outline the final preparations for a surprise invasion of Poland.

Serious negotiations between the two totalitarian regimes began on 15 August. There was a definite urgency from the German side to complete a non-aggression pact with the Soviets. Not only was *Operation White*, the proposed invasion of Poland, ready to begin on 1 September, but German battleships and submarines were ready to depart German waters in order to be in certain key locations in the Atlantic Ocean by that date. The Soviets, however, were determined to ensure they would receive some definite concessions from the

---

[4] Roger Allison, 'Warsaw on the Eve', *JMI*, p. 22.

Germans before agreeing to von Ribbentrop flying to Moscow.

Hitler outlines his plans to his generals – 22 August

On 22 August 1939 Hitler held a planning meeting with his leading generals. The overall German plan was for Poland to be conquered and divided into three regions:

- The western region bordering Germany would be annexed and become part of the German Reich.
- The eastern region bordering the Soviet Union would be given over to the control of the Soviet Union.
- The large region in between would be under direct German administration and named the General Governorate for the Occupied Polish Region (usually referred to as the General Government).

At this meeting Hitler gave full vent to his hatred of the Poles, and to his desire for the destruction of Poland.[5] In what was codenamed *Operation Tannenberg* Himmler had drawn up plans for the destruction of 'the upper levels of society.'[6]

This ruthless plan was to be entrusted to specialised SS murder units named *Einsatzgruppen der Sicherheitspolizei* (special task forces of the Security Police - *Sicherheitsdienst* or SD) but regular *Wehrmacht* soldiers were also to be employed.[7] The initial priority was to destroy the Polish intelligentsia in the western region of Poland, the region designated to be annexed to the German Reich.[8] Himmler's deputy, Reinhard Heydrich would have responsibility over the operations of the *Einsatzgruppen*.

The German-Soviet Non-Aggression Pact – 23 August

Meanwhile, following a communication from Hitler to Stalin, consent for an agreement was given on 21 August and it was announced that Foreign Minister von Ribbentrop would be going to Moscow to conclude a non-aggression

---

[5] Browning, C. (with contribution from Jurgen Matthaus), *The Origins of the Final Solution*, (Arrow Books: London, 2005), p. 15. Henceforth *Origins*.

[6] Snyder, T. *Bloodlands: Europe Between Hitler and Stalin*, (Basic Books, 2010), p.126. (Henceforth *Bloodlands*.)

[7] *Wehrmacht* - 'defence force' was the name adopted in 1935 for Germany's regular armed forces, the *Heer* (Army), *Luftwaffe* (Airforce) and *Kriegsmarine* (Navy).

[8] Browning, *Origins*, p. 16.

pact. As Stalin later told Churchill, what choice did the Soviet Union have?

Then on 23 August Molotov, the Soviet Foreign Secretary, and von Ribbentrop signed the German-Soviet Non-Aggression Pact in Moscow (also known as the Molotov-Ribbentrop Agreement). It was a secret agreement permitting Poland to be divided between Germany and the Soviet Union roughly along the line of the Narew, Vistula and San Rivers, ending at the northern frontier with Lithuania.

Additionally Finland and the Baltic states of Estonia and Latvia would all come within the Soviet orbit, as too would the region of Bessarabia (mostly present day Moldavia), which the Soviets had lost to Romania in 1919. Aside from these territorial conditions, the agreement also stated that neither party would attack the other, and that neither party would enter into an agreement with a third party.[9]

On 25 August formal discussions between the Soviets and the British and French delegations ended without any agreement. There was now no turning back. The Polish people, and especially the Jewish citizens, were soon to experience a combined Nazi German and Communist Soviet onslaught. The atmosphere over Poland during these last days of summer was changing, and changing drastically.

The impressions of Roger Allison concerning the stork migration were becoming more relevant each day. On another occasion he wrote:

> The migration that year in Poland was, in fact, earlier than customary and we later wondered whether, by some uncanny sense, those birds felt something abnormal in the air, with war bringing in its train disruption of animal as well as human plans.'[10]

Pawel and Elzbieta marry and then return to Lwow

With just a few days of August left, Pawel, Elzbieta and Allison made their way back to Warsaw. It was there on 27 August that Pawel and Elzbieta were married in the Polish Evangelical Church.[11] Allison wrote that they all then

---

[9] Shirer, pp. 540-541.

[10] Allison, *Journey*, p. 13.

[11] Protestant Church in Warsaw, Marriage License, Nr 168/1939, 28 December 1945, German File, p. 118. CMJ General Committee, 15 September 1939, Minute 3391.

returned to Lwow where he was determined to stay:

> I felt it my duty to remain at my new station, even though war should come. And the clouds were quickly gathering. That first, and last, week in Lwow was a very busy one, with war-time precautions to take and stores of food to be laid up. We were almost daily at our Mission Hall, but the usual work had hardly begun to function again.[12]

Jakob stranded in London

Despite the growing tension and threat of conflict, Jakob was nevertheless preparing to return to Warsaw, while Joan would remain in Britain at her parents' home for the birth of their first child. Jakob wrote of this time: 'I was to leave England at the end of August in order to resume my work in Warsaw.'[13]

But this was not to be. He was informed that there were no more trains as all forms of public transport to the Continent had been cancelled. Joan would later write: 'I still have his return ticket, some Polish money & the keys to the big gate & the door of our [Warsaw] flat.'[14] Neither Joan nor Jakob, nor anyone else in fact, would ever use those keys again.

Nearing the end of Phase Two

The imminence of war also meant that Phase Two in the lead up to the final solution of 'the Jewish problem' in Europe, was about to end. Until this point Phase Two, which began on 30 January 1933, had as a major goal the expulsion of Jewish people, initially from Germany, and then ultimately from the expanded German Reich.

The imminence of war would mean the closing of international borders, and henceforth it would become more difficult for Jewish people to be able to leave the confines of the German Reich. Conversely, the imminent war with Poland would then bring the German Reich into contact with more than three million Jewish people, over two million of whom were destined to come under her ultimate control if she defeated Poland.

---

[12] Roger Allison, 'Warsaw on the Eve,' p. 22.

[13] Jakob Jocz, Report for 1939, Dep CMJ, c.99, Bodleian Library.

[14] *Memoirs of Joan Jocz*, p. 7. [Warsaw] added by the author.

Jochanan Don

Jerzy (George) Jocz

Standing: Pawel (Paul), Jan (John)
Sitting: Bazyli, Anna, Jakob (Jacob)
(Jocz Collection)

Warsaw staff. Standing L - R: J. Berkowicz, P. Weiss, B. Jocz, V. Weisman. Sitting; D. Pankhurst, H. Carpenter, A. Aizeman, M. Bregman. (CMJ Archives, Bodleian Library, Oxford)

Plans for CMJ Emmanuel Church and Mission House, 3 Sewerynow St, Warsaw. (CMJ Archives, Bodleian Library)

CMJ
Emmanuel Church
and Mission House,
1930s.
(Glass Slide Collection,
Schick Library
Collection, Christ
Church, Jerusalem)

Emmanuel Church. (Schick Library)

In the market of a Jewish village. Young and old listen to the message. (Schick Library)

CMJ staff in and around the new CMJ open roof car. (Schick Library)

Scene in Lwow. (Schick Library)

Lwow - English Class, Christmas 1937. (Schick Library)

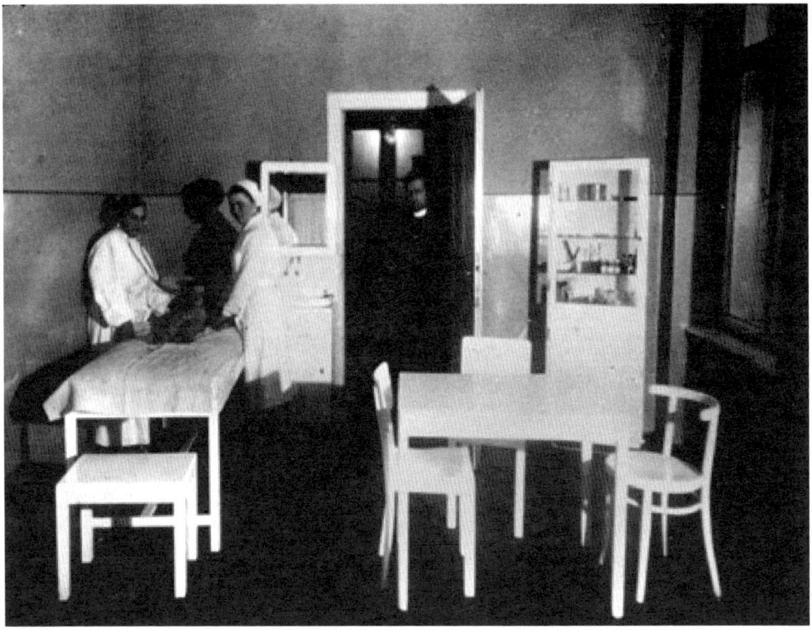

Medical work in Lwow. (Schick Library)

Lwow - June 1938. Probably students from the English Class (Schick Library)

Group of Hebrew Christians in Warsaw circa 1938.
(Parsons Album, Schick Library)

Top: Jakob at his desk in the Emmanuel Centre. (Schick Library)

Right: Jakob and Joan and another person, Warsaw. (Jocz Collection)

Street meeting, including M. Wolfin, Rudolph Brinker and Martin Parsons. (Schick Library)

Warsaw staff at a picnic, circa 1938. Possibly only three people from this group survived the Holocaust. (Schick Library)

Victor Weisman and his wife and son, circa 1938. All three perished in the Holocaust. (Schick Library)

Anna Jocz

Bazyli Jocz

Keys to 3 Sewerynow Street - Emmanuel Centre. (Jocz Collection)

Roma Piotroska. (Jocz Collection)

Below: Report of Bazyli's death by the CMJ General Committee, 16 November 1945. (Bodleian Library)

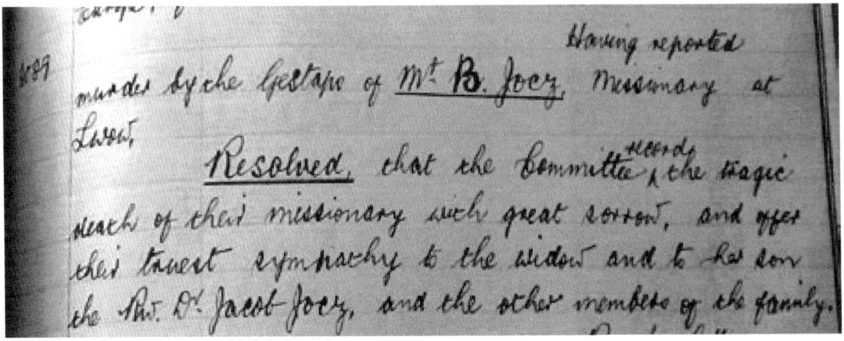

Having reported

489 murder by the Gestapo of Mr B. Jocz, missionary at Lwow,

Resolved, that the Committee records the tragic death of their missionary with great sorrow, and offer their truest sympathy to the widow and to her son the Rev. Dr. Jacob Jocz, and the other members of the family.

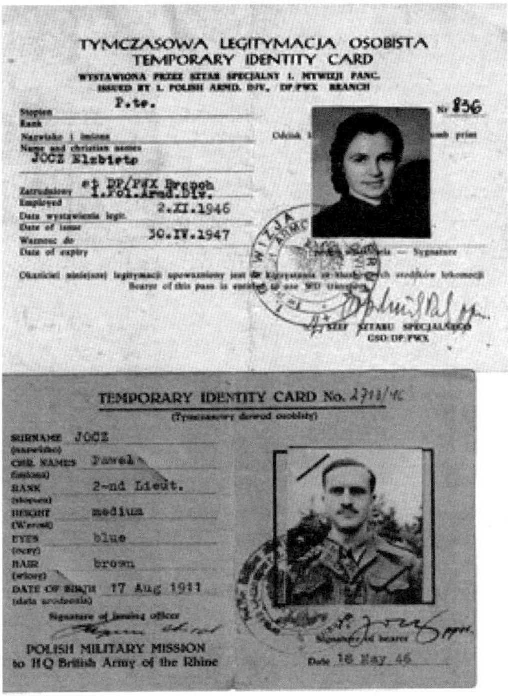
TYMCZASOWA LEGITYMACJA OSOBISTA
TEMPORARY IDENTITY CARD
WYSTAWIONA PRZEZ SZTAB SPECJALNY 1. DYWIZJI PANC.
ISSUED BY 1. POLISH ARMD. DIV., DP/PWX BRANCH

Nr 836

Stopień / Rank: P.te.
Nazwisko i imiona / Name and christian names: JOCZ Elzbieta
Zatrudniony / Employed: #1 DP/PWX Branch 1.Pol.Armd.Div.
Data wystawienia legit. / Date of issue: 2.XI.1946
Ważność do / Date of expiry: 30.IV.1947

Sygnature

Bearer of this pass is entitled to use WD transport.

SZEF SZTABU SPECJALNEGO
OSD DP/PWX

TEMPORARY IDENTITY CARD No. 2713/46

SURNAME: JOCZ
CHR. NAMES: Pawel
RANK: 2-nd Lieut.
HEIGHT: medium
EYES: blue
HAIR: brown
DATE OF BIRTH: 17 Aug 1911

Signature of issuing officer

POLISH MILITARY MISSION
to HQ British Army of the Rhine

Signature of bearer

Date 18 May 46

Elzbieta (Elizabeth) and
Pawel's (Paul's)
Polish Army
I.D. Cards.
(Jocz Collection)

Pawel (Paul) and Elzbieta (Elizabeth), 1948.
(Jocz Collection)

L-R: Paul and Elizabeth Yates (Jocz), Joan and Jakob Jocz, Lydia and Victor Buksbazen. (Jocz Collection)

Anna with one of the grandchildren. (Jocz Collection)

Chapter 13

The Jocz family in the midst of the War

The outbreak of war

When the German *Wehrmacht* attacked Poland on 1 September it was a *blitzkrieg* or 'lightning war' the likes of which the world had never witnessed before. No one and no place was exempt. Civilian and military locations were both ruthlessly attacked.

Jakob wrote of this time:

> None of us in Poland suspected the war to come so soon, although we all felt that war was inevitable.
>
> But before the month elapsed the frontiers were closed and at the 1st Sept war was declared.
>
> By the providence of God I was to remain in England for the duration of the war, & so to be spared the suffering & anguish which is the lot of our missionaries & friends in Poland.[1]

In line with Hitler's overall order to show no mercy, and Himmler's specific targeting in *Operation Tannenberg* of the upper levels of society, thousands of innocent Polish people were executed. On many occasions innocent Jewish people were also murdered – for no reason except that they were Jewish.

While fierce fighting was taking place all over the country, Warsaw, the capital city was the focal point of particularly intensive German bombing. On one of the early days four German bombs fell directly on the CMJ Emmanuel Centre at 3 Sewerynow Street. The magnificent four story building was completely destroyed. CMJ reported in the *Jewish Missionary Intelligence*, 'During the siege of Warsaw four bombs fell upon our new Mission House and within a few minutes some 20,000 pounds of damage was done. We thank God the

[1] Jakob Jocz, Report for 1939, Dep CMJ, c.99, Bodleian Library.

agents escaped with their lives, though some of their relatives perished.'[2]

Another city to receive the full brunt of the German assault was Lodz. The Helenowek orphanage, operated by the Bethel Mission which lay outside the city, drew the attention of German bombers due to its proximity to a railroad. Leon Rosenberg of the Bethel Mission wrote: 'Our buildings quaked from the air pressure of the frequent explosions. We were all, young and old, in constant prayer, which the Lord graciously honoured.'[3]

As the German land forces attacked from the west and south-west, many civilians fled Warsaw, heading east and north-east, towards such locations as Lwow and Vilna.

One young Hebrew Christian named Israel Melzak, from the congregation pastored by Jakob Jocz, managed to get out of Warsaw. He wrote later to Jakob that had he left Warsaw on 7 September and cycled to Lwow where he met Paul and Elisabeth and then went on in the direction of Vilna. On the way his bicycle was stolen and he had to continue on foot from place to place, finally arriving in Vilna in the middle of December. He was in a sorry state: 'By the time I reached Vilno I was in rags, hungry, worn out physically and mentally, dirty and full of vermin, as my underwear remained unwashed for these three months. In Vilno I expected to find my father and the Szumans, but was disappointed. I found some relatives who gave me a roof over my head and some food.'[4]

As difficult as life was in Vilna and Lithuania for those who managed to get there, at least they could correspond with the outside world. The Hebrew Christian Alliance (IHCA) could also send some support for Jewish Christians who were now refugees in that country. In their quarterly *The Hebrew Christian* they wrote: 'No further news has reached us from Poland, but we have been able to send additional sums for the relief of Hebrew Christians who have escaped into Lithuania. Letters received tell of very great distress on all hands.'[5]

---

[2] *Bread Cast Upon The Waters,* 1939-40, p. 7.

[3] Kuschnir, V. *Only One Life,* p. 272.

[4] Melzak to Jakob Jocz, *JMI*, February 1940, p. 18. Like many others Melzak, presumably, later became a victim of the Nazi genocide when Germany took control over this region after 22 June 1941.

[5] *The Hebrew Christian*, Volume XII, July 1940, p. 44.

In Warsaw matters became progressively desperate for the local CMJ staff and the Hebrew Christians associated with the Emmanuel Church. The CMJ Secretary, Rev. C. H. Gill, recorded that it had thereafter been 'impossible to send our faithful staff any real help. The British authorities have proved to their own satisfaction that not even parcels of food are allowed to remain in the hands of the addressees, and they have absolutely forbidden any attempt to send money, clothing or food.'[6]

Providentially, about a month before war broke out the Hebrew Christian Alliance 'was led to make a grant of money to our Hebrew Christian Alliance in Poland for the relief of the poverty-stricken Jewish Christians during the coming winter.' This money arrived before hostilities broke out, and could therefore be distributed. In view of the present situation, though, the Alliance recognised the need for further help.[7]

The situation in Lwow

Roger Allison, alongside Pawel, Elzbieta, Bazyli, Anna and Jan, remained in Lwow. Allison recalled that they tried to keep going as normal, stating '… we were very glad to be able to hold a Service for our fellow Christians on September 3rd, and gather them together again on the following Wednesday for a short social gathering.'[8] Lwow at that point was quite a cosmopolitan city. Within its population in 1939 of 312,231, there were 157,490 Poles, 99,595 Jews, and 49,747 Ukrainians.[9]

The outbreak of war presented Allison with a dilemma. His plan, with Pawel and Elzbieta, had been to settle into new premises in Lwow and continue with the work. 'In accordance with official advice,' he wrote, 'we were making some preparation against gas warfare even before war was declared. With its outbreak British citizens were advised to leave. Instinctively I rebelled strongly against the thought of leaving so soon after arriving in the country where I had expected to spend many years of service.'[10] Allison wrote further: 'For

---

[6] Report of Rev. C. H. Gill 1939-1940, Bodleian Library, Dept CMJ, Missionaries Reports, c.99.

[7] *The Hebrew Christian*, Volume XII, p. 101.

[8] Roger Allison, 'Warsaw on the Eve,' p. 22.

[9] Mick, C. Incompatible Experiences: Poles, Ukrainians and Jews in Lviv under Soviet and German Occupation, 1939-44, *Journal of Contemporary History*, 46(2), (2011), pp. 336-363.

[10] Allison, *Journey*, p. 13.

ten days I resisted repeated appeals of the Consul who warned that I would stay entirely at my own risk.'[11]

The Soviets had remained out of the conflict during the early stages, but, on 17 September their forces moved in from the east and north-east, as Allison recorded: 'The Russian and German armies were by then engaged in a pincer movement, as they made their way from both directions into Poland, squeezing Lemberg into an ever decreasing area of freedom.'[12]

Allison leaves and the Jocz family remain

Faced with such a difficult decision, Allison thought long and hard about whether to stay or leave. He later recorded:

> I was coming to realise that the alternative to departure would certainly be internment as an enemy alien, if not worse, and what use would I then be to the people I had come to serve? So, when the consul rang me up to say that he was offering me a last chance of getting out, I conferred rapidly with Paul and Elizabeth and we agreed that it would be right for me to go. The 'offer' was actually made by a member of the British Council in Warsaw, who had just arrived in Lemberg in his private car with one lady passenger and had room for one more plus minimum luggage. I was given two hours to make final preparations for that journey, 'en-route' to Roumania, the only escape corridor left open.[13]

Allison managed to escape at a time when both Soviet and German troops were in the vicinity of Lwow. Several days later he arrived in Bucharest and found shelter at the CMJ base there. The Poles formally surrendered Lwow to the Soviets on 22 September.

Life in Soviet-held Lwow

It took some time before Allison was able to receive word about how the Jocz family and other Hebrew Christians were coping in Soviet-held Lwow. Towards the end of November he finally received a letter from Pawel, who wrote: 'It is impossible to describe the panic and horrors we experienced, but

---

11 Ibid., p. 13.

12 Ibid., p. 13.

13 Allison, *Journey*, p. 13. The remainder of Allison's journey is described in *Journey to Jerusalem*.

the Good Shepherd kept us alive protecting us from all dangers, I suppose for further service.'[14]

Pawel also informed Allison that he had moved to a smaller flat 'as he could no longer afford to pay for the other. Services are not being held as the congregation is scattered.' One quite troubling episode involved Elzbieta: 'On one occasion while he was absent from home his wife was arrested as a spy,' wrote Allison, 'but later she was released.'[15] This is perhaps not surprising considering her German background and involvement with a British society.

The CMJ General Committee recorded on 15 December 1939 in relation to Pawel's letter: 'Having read letter from Mr Paul Jocz received at Bucharest by the Rev. R Allison … and forwarded to London, stating that he and his wife (nee Singer) were safe and well in Lwow, though they had suffered a great deal and were in need of help.'[16]

The CMJ Secretary, Rev. Gill, summarised the situation: 'Lwow in the Russian sphere of Poland is perhaps slightly better situated, but the Russian authorities will not recognise that there is any destitution or hardship in Russia, and we cannot be sure that help sent reaches the sufferers and there is very real fear that drastic steps will be taken against those to whom aid is sent from outside. It is certain that discrimination is exercised against active Christians, especially missionaries and their families. While however we cannot now send much, our supporters will be glad to know that [the] Committee is laying aside money for salaries to be paid when the country opens again, for it is practically certain that their possessions will be swallowed up by that time.'[17]

The defeat and division of Poland

It was a depressing situation in Poland. Ludwik Hirszfeld, an assimilated Jewish scientist (mentioned in Chapter 7), and a member of the Roman Catholic Church, wrote that only 'for a few days did a certain degree of optimism prevail in Poland. ...When we realized that our army had been knocked off the battlefield as swiftly as it had been placed there, a strange sobering-up took place. A few days later, we heard on the radio that the government was

[14] 'Poland', *JMI*, 1940, p. 15.
[15] 'Poland', *JMI,* 1940, p. 15.
[16] CMJ General Committee, 15 December 1939, Minute 3503. 17 17 Report of Rev. C. H. Gill 1939-1940, Bodleian Library, Dept CMJ, Missionaries Reports, c.99.

leaving the capital and going into exile.'[18]

After relentless bombing, Warsaw finally surrendered to the Germans on 27 September and fighting throughout Poland ended on 6 October. With the end of hostilities the Germans and Soviets put into operation the terms of the Molotov-Ribbentrop Agreement – and divided Poland between them. Poland now, as planned, became three separate entities:

- The eastern region, including Lwow, came under Soviet control.
- The western region bordering Germany including Danzig was annexed and became part of the Reich (joining Austria and the Sudetenland). Lodz became part of this region. Many Poles and all Jewish people were to be deported from there and replaced by ethnic Germans from the Baltic states and other areas of the Soviet Union.
- The large area between the annexed German territory and the Soviet region was to be called 'General Government for the Occupied Polish Region' (General Government). The General Governor (referred to as 'Governor') was Dr Hans Frank who was appointed on 12 October, ruling from Krakow Castle.

Frydland leaves Warsaw

Following the surrender Rachmiel Frydland of the Mildmay Mission decided to leave Warsaw and head north to Plock to work on a farm. As he was leaving the city he was stopped by a German SS soldier who asked him, "Bist du Jude" [Are you a Jew?]. Frydland stated that this 'was the first time I was addressed in such a way. It had not occurred to me that being Jewish might be a crime!'

Sensing danger Frydland, instead of answering, showed the soldier his baptismal certificate 'from the German Baptist Church.' The soldier responded "Ja, aber du bist doch Jude" [Yes, but you are a Jew for all that]. The soldier then hit Frydland hard with a shovel forcing him to fall into a ditch 'where a few other Jews were already working burying dead horses.'

'Hungry and humiliated', Frydland recalled, 'my tears began to run. The other Jewish people tried to comfort me. It was not that I was concerned for the beating, but for the very fact that I belonged to a Church which was

[18] Hirszfeld, L. *The Story of One Life,* (Kindle), location 5160.

identified with these people. In this Church I had learned to appreciate the Protestant and Baptist Christianity that came to us in Poland via the German people, and that these very people should behave in such a cruel way was too much for me at this moment.'[19]

This incident and Frydland's reaction had already been the experience of the Jewish followers of Jesus in Germany, Austria and Czechoslovakia. It was the harsh reality that being a Jewish Christian with a baptismal certificate meant little to the atheistic, nihilist ideology of Nazi Germany. If you had at least one Jewish grandparent then you were technically a non-Aryan Christian, but for the Nazis you were, in practice, simply 'just a Jew.' Countless thousands of non-Aryan Christians in Poland were to have the same experience during the following years.

Beginning of Phase Three – the Lublin and Ghettoization Plan

Within the General Government area of Poland there was a further sub-division. All the Jewish people initially from the western or annexed region of Poland, as well as from other regions within the Reich, were to be deported to this General Government area and placed in a specified region in the vicinity of Lublin, south-east of Warsaw.

Associated with this Lublin proposal was an order from Himmler issued on 21 September 'authorising the ghettoization of Polish Jewry.'[20] Reinhard Heydrich then declared: 'The first preliminary measure for achieving the final goal is the concentration of the Jews from the countryside in the larger cities. It must be speedily implemented.'[21]

On 27 September Himmler formed a special SS branch for dealing with Jewish affairs. It was named the Reich Main Security Office (*Reichssicherheitshauptamt* or RSHA) and came under the control of Heydrich. The task of relocating these Jewish people was entrusted to the RSHA.

Browning makes it clear that these moves were sanctioned from higher up. On 29 September Hitler informed Alfred Rosenberg (a major adherent of Nazi ideology) that 'all Jews, including those from the Reich, would be settled

---

[19] Frydland, p. 28.
[20] Goldhagen, p. 145.
[21] Nur. Doc. 3363-PS, quoted in Nazism, p. 1051, cited in Goldhagen, p. 145.

in this newly acquired territory between the Vistula and the Bug Rivers.'[22] This was the region of Lublin.

This Lublin proposal, together with the ghettoization decision, were part of Phase Three of the German solution for 'the Jewish problem'. At that point the Nazis may not have understood exactly what their final solution to 'the Jewish problem' would be, but this dual plan was their present position. Incidentally, the ghettoization plan did not move quite as quickly as Himmler and Heydrich had initially anticipated.

Of the Lublin Plan CMJ's journal, the *Jewish Missionary Intelligence*, stated under the title 'A New Ghetto', and sub-title, 'Lublin':

> This town and its environment to the extent of about 4,300 square miles, that is considerably less than Yorkshire, has been set apart as a Jewish Ghetto. It will be exclusively Jewish and the Jews will be strictly confined to it. It is calculated that 2,000,000 of these unfortunates will be domiciled in this area. This might not seem an over-dense population relatively to that of our own country, but as the only occupations in which they are to be permitted to engage are medicine and agriculture and the land is said to be poor in quality, it is difficult to see how they can live.[23]

Very shortly after the Nazis began implementing the Lublin Plan, the RSHA was already transporting Jewish people there from elsewhere in the Reich. Adolf Eichmann had been designated the task of transferring Jewish people out of the new Reich-controlled region, and on 12 October Eichmann also deported some 4,000 Austrian and Czech Jews to the Lublin reservation area.

The International Missionary Council presented a report about the Lublin Reservation in December 1939, stating:

> The district chosen for the "Reservation" is situated in the South of the Lublin area. Its frontiers and its size have not yet been definitely fixed. Its boundaries are probably the rivers San and Vistula in the West, and the new Russian frontier in the East. The place Nisko on the San must be situated at the Southern entrance of the Reservation since many transports from

[22] Browning, *Origins*, p. 27.
[23] *JMI*, February 1940, p. 1.

> Vienna and Moravia have ended there. An official map of the district is going to be issued; the Reservation, it is said, will be called "Judea". The district is one of the most remote parts of Poland and consists mainly of marshy country and woods. The inhabitants are the poorest Jews and Poles, the latter being evacuated to give room to the new-comers… The number of Jews who have already been sent there by the Nazis is not known…
>
> When the transports arrive near Nisko they are unloaded on the open country and the Jews are compelled to walk about 6 miles carrying their luggage. Then the younger men are compelled to build hutcamps, to clean forests, etc… Roughly speaking the whole Reservation is nothing else than a huge concentration camp with conditions of life still worse than those of Dachau or Buchenwald.[24]

The IMC report then described how the deportations of Jews to the Lublin 'Reservation' was to be carried out. It would be implemented in four stages:

1. From the areas being incorporated into the Reich, i.e., western Poland.
2. The Jewish people from Vienna, of whom, the report states, there were about '10,000 Non-Aryan Christians.' Some 5,000 had already been sent to Nisko. If they could emigrate, then all the better, but if they couldn't, then they would be sent to the 'Reservation.'
3. After the deportations from Austria, Jews would be deported from the Protectorate (former Czechoslovakia). A beginning had already been made, the report stated, with Jewish people being deported from Mahrisch-Ostrau in early October. As usual, the report continued, 'no difference is made between Jews and Non-Aryan Christians.'
4. From the *Altreich*, old Germany.[25]

The report was deeply disturbing and it was clear that the situation was becoming desperate. In general the Hebrew Christians were not exempt from the harsh conditions being imposed upon Jewish people throughout the regions now under German control.

---

[24] 'The Jewish Reservation near Lublin and the situation of the Jews and Non-Aryans in Germany and in the territories under German control.' December 1939, International Missionary Council Archives, 1910-1961, Call number: Fiche Ms85, Yale University, Part I, H-10.002, 26.12.01.

[25] Ibid.

The Helenowek orphanage of the Bethel Mission in Lodz was in territory now annexed to the Reich. The property was commandeered by the German Army early in the War and the occupants removed. The editor of the Bethel Mission journal, *The Bethel Witness*, wrote: 'The children, with the matron and other workers were forcibly shifted to the new reservation about 100 miles distant.'[26] The majority of these children and young adults, as well as the majority of the Hebrew Christian staff, never survived the coming genocide.

The situation for the Jocz family

While in Bucharest Allison received numerous communications from the Jocz family in Lwow, and life had clearly become extremely difficult under the Soviet regime. It is unclear where Jerzy was, but Jan at this stage was still with them. Pawel later testified of this time:

> … soon after the entry of the Soviet troops into the city of Lwow (Lemberg) Poland in 1939, the mission in which my father (Basili Jocz) was working, was closed by the Soviet Russian authorities and my father exposed to retributions due to his religious work he was engaged in. The situation was still more aggravated due to the fact that I, his son, was the minister of the only Evangelical Church in the city.[27]

We know from later evidence that Anna was living in Lwow on Lwowskich Dzieci Street in 1941, so there is a chance that with the closure of the CMJ operations, both Bazyli and Anna and possibly Jan were forced to relocate from the village of Brzuchovice due to limited finances. As for Pawel the Jocz family history records: 'A certificate dated July 30 1944 from the Board of the Polish Evangelical Church in Lwow attests to his service as pastor there for the years 1940-1941.'[28]

The CMJ General Committee sought ways to get financial assistance to the CMJ workers in Europe. However, when it was apparent that these workers were locked behind enemy lines, the General Committee stated on 16 February 1940 that, following advice from the Solicitors, the Secretary was to write

---

[26] Kuschnir, p. 284 and *The Bethel Witness,* October- December 1940, p. 12. In late 1939, Rosenberg managed to get out of Poland and went to the US in order to raise financial support for the work.

[27] Attestation by Paul Yates (Pawel Jocz), 3 March 1960, original in Jocz Private Collection.

[28] *A Brief History,* p. 9.

to all foreign agents in lands at war, stating 'that their engagement with the Society shall come to an end in the event of hostilities breaking out in the lands where they work.'[29]

Despite this legal position, CMJ did still endeavour to send support. One of the main avenues of getting support to the Jocz family members in Lwow was via the Red Cross. Among the documents in the Jocz Private Collection is a brief message from the Red Cross dated 14 May 1940 with these words inscribed in German:

> "My dear, received money 209 Rubl [roubles] and your letter, thank you. A joy to hear from you. Our health is as always. No word from George. Regards, Anna, Johann, B. Jocz."[30]

Presumably the letter and money were sent from Britain, either from CMJ or more likely from Jakob. At the beginning of the War Jakob and Joan were living with Joan's parents, where their first child, Anne, was born.

Life under German occupation

For the Jewish people living under German occupation life was becoming progressively more difficult, and, as usual, the same was true for the Jewish Christians.

Already, before the final fighting between Polish and German forces had ended and 'official' partition had begun, the Germans had begun implementing their anti-Jewish plans, especially in Warsaw. On 3-4 October they ordered Adam Czerniakow, a former member of the Polish Senate, to form a Jewish Community Council (the *Judenrat*) of which he was to assume the leadership.[31]

As head of this Warsaw *Judenrat* Czerniakow had an enormous task to perform. Not only was he entrusted with representing the 300,000 or so Jewish residents of Warsaw to the Nazi leaders, he also had to deal with the complexities within this community. One of those complexities included the existence of a large number of Jewish non-Aryan Christians. Prior to taking

---

29 CMJ General Committee, 16 February 1940, Minute 3552.

30 Jocz Private Collection. Also *A Brief History*, p. 8. Interestingly here Jan is named Johann and Jerzy is named George.

31 Czerniakow, A. *The Warsaw Diary of Adam Czerniakow*, (Elephant Paperbacks, Chicago: 1999), p. 78.

up this position Czerniakow most probably would have had little contact with this particular group of people. They were now under his jurisdiction.

In his diary Czerniakow recorded on 6 October an upcoming meeting (which did not take place), at which one of the items on the agenda was to be '*Taufe* [baptism]'.[32] Then on 24 October he wrote out the agenda for a meeting with the SS commander he had to report to. Under item 11, he wrote: 'The problem of converts [baptized Jews].'[33]

Another problem which Czerniakow had to deal with was the influx of Jewish refugees into the city. The expulsion of Jewish people out of the new Reich regions of western Poland had now increased in tempo. This was in order to accommodate the numbers of Baltic Germans being brought into that region.

Czerniakow and the *Judenrat* were then faced with a new dynamic when on 26 October a measure was introduced in order to separate the Jewish people from the remainder of the Polish people. Henceforth Jewish people over the age of ten were required to wear a Yellow Star insignia.[34]

Despite this frightening experience, until November the Jewish community, although under duress, was still able to move wherever they wanted in Warsaw. But on 4 November Czerniakow and the *Judenrat* were ordered to move all the Jewish people of Warsaw to a particular area within three days, essentially forming a Jewish ghetto.

To his relief, Czerniakow was able to persuade the military commandant, General Neumann-Neurode, to postpone such a move for several months. But the Germans did, nevertheless, establish a quarantine area, or *Seuchengebiet,* mostly in the Jewish area of the city.

The German authorities meanwhile continued making their plans for the formation of just such a ghetto. It was, of course, only seen as a temporary solution – ultimately all the Jewish people were to be deported to the Lublin region.

---

[32] Ibid., p. 79.
[33] Ibid., p. 83.
[34] Pileggi, D. *A Narrow Bridge,* (Jerusalem 2018), p. 48.

A further development as part of the Lublin Plan occurred with a memo prepared on 19 December 1939 by Heydrich's RSHA office, which included a section on the "Final Solution of the German Jewish problem." It centred on the need to deport Jewish people from Germany. Thereafter Heydrich employed Adolf Eichmann as his "special advisor" in order to implement this plan for the deportation of German Jews.[35] The deportation of Jewish people from the *Altreich* (Old Reich), however, was temporarily suspended at the beginning of 1940.

But the movement of Jews out of the newly annexed territory of Poland continued. The first actual ghetto for Jewish people was at Lodz, created in order to accommodate many of these people being relocated out of the annexed area. Construction began on 8 February 1940 and was completed by April 1940. Following this, ghettos were then established in other areas into which smaller Jewish communities were also relocated. Life was becoming increasingly intolerable for most of the Jewish people in the German occupied regions of Poland.

The situation in 1940

Stranded in Britain Jakob continued to speak on behalf of CMJ, and was able to establish contact with other exiles from Europe. He wrote: 'Going about the country I met with German Refugees, mostly Jews, to whom I could act as a messenger of the Gospel.'[36]

Although being physically spared from the carnage of Poland and particularly in Warsaw he was not spared the mental anguish of concern for his family, friends and congregants who were trapped in Poland. At the CMJ Annual Meeting in 1940, Jakob spoke movingly:

> A year ago when I stood before you Poland was an independent country. I was the Pastor of a Hebrew Christian community in Warsaw. My parents, my brother [sic], and my friends were in that country. To-day everything has changed. Poland, as in other times in her history, lies in ruins once again; the Hebrew Christian community is scattered. My parents, my friends, my co-workers are in distress.[37]

---

[35] Browning, *Origins*, p. 52.

[36] Jakob Jocz, Report for 1939, Dep CMJ, c.99, Bodleian Library.

[37] Missionary Returns, Bodleian Library, Dept CMJ, c. 99.

One Hebrew Christian who survived the initial carnage of the War and who was later able to write about life in Warsaw at that time was Rachmiel Frydland, Joan Jocz's student in 1936 and later involved with the Mildmay Mission to the Jews (MMJ). He managed to get into the Jewish area (initially the *Seuchengebiet* and later the actual walled Ghetto) and testified that the majority of the Hebrew Christians there had not managed to get out of the city at the time of the German capture and remained stranded there. The vast majority of these, as Joan Jocz would recall in her memoir, did not survive the upcoming genocide.[38]

One former member of Jakob's congregation who did manage to escape from Warsaw was Leon Machlis. He wrote to Parsons (and Jakob Jocz and 'Miss Zinger') from Vilnius on 29 January 1940:

> In a short time Poland was occupied by the enemy. I as resident of Warsaw was compelled just as hundreds of thousands other men – evacuate Warsaw. We had a dreadful way, dangerous adventures. Many of us were killed. At last after many weeks of wanderings - – reached Lithuania.
>
> There is no reason to go at present back to Warsaw... because there govern now Germans, there is no use for me to go back. I am a Jew and you know that they persecute Jews in the most impityable way. To stay here in Lithuania is also impossible, as it is too small country to absorb such a big number of refugees (about 25,000). So, we can think only about emigration.[39]

As much as Parsons and Jakob would have desired to have Leon and other survivors of the Hebrew Christian community come to Britain, in reality there was virtually no chance that this would happen.

One other Jewish Christian who was in Vilnius was Dr Gottfried Frohwein, and indeed all of the Frohwein family. The British Jews Society initially had no news of their fate, but on 10 October 1939 they reported that Dr Froh-

---

[38] *Joan Jocz Memoir*, p. 5.

[39] Leon Machlis to Martin Parsons (Messrs Jotch or Miss Zinger), 29 January 1940, Jocz Private Collection, in envelope 'Cries for Help from Hebrew Christians in Poland'. Others also reached Vilnius, which the Russians had given over to Lithuania. The vast majority of these Jewish refugees were later murdered when the Germans invaded Lithuania during *Operation Barbarossa* in June 1941.

wein managed to escape to Danzig. At this stage the plight of a Jewish Christian in Germany was less extreme than that of a Jewish Christian in Poland. It was hoped that he could secure some work in Danzig.[40]

The BJS Committee then heard in April 1940 that Dr Frohwein had managed to secure a medical practice in East Prussia.[41] Little news came from the Frohwein family after this, and there was constant apprehension about their safety.

Life for the Jewish people of Poland, including the Jewish Christians, deteriorated during the first months of 1940. This despite the realisation by German officials that the Lublin Plan was going to be much more difficult to implement than originally expected. However, they still wanted to move Jewish people out of certain areas.

While most of these deported Jews were being crowded into ghettos all over Poland, the German authorities were lacking an over-arching policy to solve their 'Jewish problem'. Forthcoming events, however, would potentially provide the Germans with a new solution to their so-called 'Jewish problem'.

---

[40] Minutes of BJS, 10 October 1939, p. 159.
[41] Minutes of BJS, 9 April 1940, p. 186.

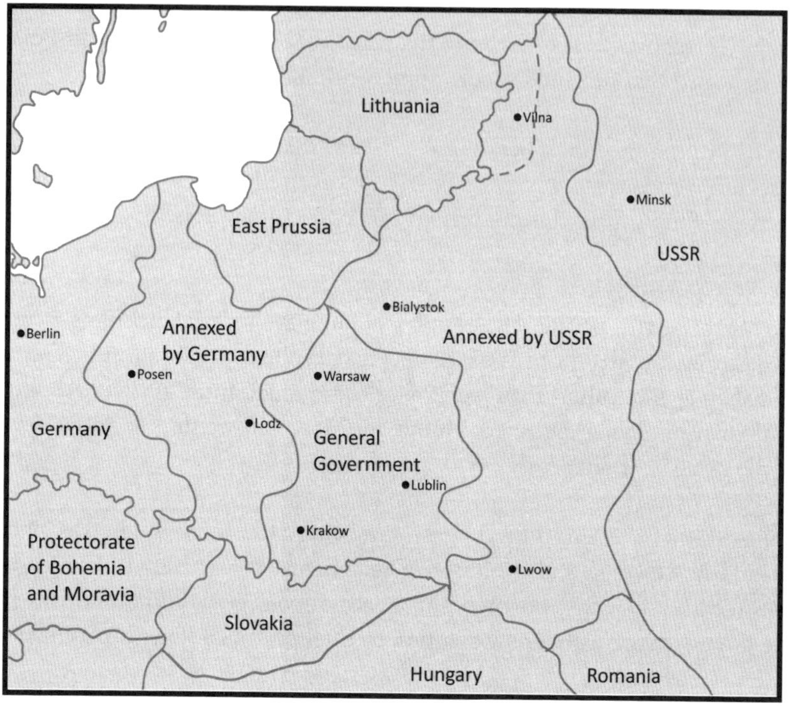

Poland - October 1939

Chapter 14

Invasion of the West & the Madagascar Plan

Germany invades the West

Hitler wanted to subjugate the West before turning his eyes further East. On 9 April 1940 German armed forces invaded Denmark and Norway as part of *Operation Weserubung*. Denmark capitulated quickly, while Norway managed to hold out until 10 June.

These invasions were followed by a *blitzkrieg* offensive against the Netherlands, Belgium and France beginning on 10 May 1940. Following a ruthless bombing of the centre of Rotterdam, the Netherlands surrendered on 15 May. The conquest of Belgium took longer, as a combined British and French force entered Belgium on the day of the German attack and temporarily thwarted this German *blitzkrieg*.

Simultaneously and unbeknown to the Allies a large German assault force had also penetrated through the forested Ardennes region and crossed into France on 14 May. It broke through the French defensive line and began moving steadily towards the Atlantic coast. Their objective was to block any possibility of British, French and Belgian forces retreating into central France.

The combined German force then manoeuvred the bulk of the Allied (mostly British) forces into the port of Dunkirk. This was Winston Churchill's first major challenge since becoming Britain's new prime minister. The majority of these troops were then miraculously rescued from the beaches of Dunkirk between 28 May and 4 June.

Broaching the Madagascar Plan – 3 June

This new onslaught now brought some 220,000 Jewish people under German control in the Netherlands and Belgium, and potentially another 330,000 or so in France. The fate of all these Jews in Western Europe was at that very time being discussed by the Nazi leadership. On 3 June Franz Rademacher, head of the *Judenreferat* (Jewish desk) at the German Foreign Ministry, wrote a memorandum to his superior, Undersecretary Martin Luther, to ensure that the Jewish question was not left out of the upcoming armistice discussions with France.[1]

In his memorandum, Rademacher proposed the idea of separating the eastern from the western Jews. The eastern Jews would remain around the Lublin region, while the western Jews would be transported overseas, perhaps to Madagascar - a French administered colony off the coast of East Africa.[2]

Rademacher's memorandum came at an opportune time. By mid-1940 the policy of establishing a Jewish reservation in and around Lublin had proved somewhat impractical. Now, with the invasion of Western Europe, Germany had inherited over half a million more Jews and an overarching Jewish policy was clearly required.

Undersecretary Luther mentioned Rademacher's proposal to Foreign Minister von Ribbentrop, who in turn mentioned it to Hitler. Due to his positive military situation Hitler was very sympathetic to the general proposal.[3]

That Hitler was interested is evident from the reference to the Plan when he and von Ribbentrop met with Mussolini and the Italian Foreign Minister, Galeazzo Ciano, on 18 June. Ciano recorded in his diary that von Ribbentrop stated: 'that there is a German project to round up and send the Jews to Madagascar.'[4] Hitler then mentioned the proposal to Admiral Raeder, the head of the *Kriegsmarine*, the German Navy, two days later on 20 June.[5]

Defeat of France

There were, however, important criteria upon which this proposal hinged - the defeat of France and a treaty with Britain. A French defeat would ensure that the island of Madagascar was available, and a treaty with Britain would mean the seas would be open, thus enabling the transportation of the Jewish people to take place. The outworking of the first part of the equation, the defeat of France, was already in progress.

---

[1] Browning, *Origins,* pp. 82-3, n. 168.
[2] Ibid.
[3] Ibid., p. 83.
[4] Ciano, Galeazzo, *The Ciano Diaries 1939-43,* (Simon Publications, Florida: 2001), pp. 265-66. See also Browning, *Origins*, p. 83.
[5] Browning, *Origins*, p. 83.

Following the defeat and evacuation of the Allied forces from northern France the German forces quickly moved south. Paris surrendered on 14 June. France capitulated shortly after, and the Armistice was signed on 22 June 1940. France was then divided, into a region under direct German rule, and an area under a French government based in the city of Vichy. Both entities in time began to implement anti-Jewish policies.

Heydrich takes over the Madagascar Plan and gives it to Eichmann

Reinhard Heydrich of the SS, who had been given jurisdiction over Jewish emigration within Europe in January 1939, became aware of the Madagascar Plan on 24 June. He wrote to von Ribbentrop on the same day reminding the foreign minister that such matters fell under his own jurisdiction.

At this point Rademacher was informed that von Ribbentrop had accepted in principle the expulsion of European Jewry, and that the implementation of this policy was to be conducted in conjunction with the SS.[6] Heydrich entrusted the bulk of the responsibility for planning this mass expulsion to Madagascar to Adolf Eichmann, head of the RSHA Sub-Department which was dedicated to Jewish migration affairs. Eichmann and his colleague, SS Captain Theodor Danneker, ultimately drafted a very detailed and precise plan.[7]

News of the plan spreads

News of the Madagascar proposal quickly spread. Hans Frank, Governor of the General Government, was aware of it at the beginning of July. Frank had always doubted the viability of the Lublin Plan. On 1 July Adam Czerniakow, head of the *Judenrat* in the Warsaw Ghetto, wrote in his diary that 'Mende (Gerhard Mende of the SD[8]) declared that the war would be over in a month and that we would all leave for Madagascar.'[9]

Such news was especially welcome within the General Government, as it meant that deportations of German Jews into their territory would now cease, which they did on 10 July. It also meant that in the future even the Polish Jews in the region of the General Government would also be deported

---

[6] Ibid.

[7] A full version of this plan is found in the file of Martin Luther at the Wannsee House Museum, entitled *Reichssicherheitshauptamt: Madagaskar Projekt.*

[8] SD, Sicherheitsdienst – Security Service of the SS.

[9] Czerniakow, p. 169.

to Madagascar.

One tangible result of this new development was that the planned construction of the ghetto in Warsaw was stopped. Christopher Browning quoted from one official statement which said that construction was halted because 'according to the plan of the Fuhrer, the Jews of Europe were to be sent to Madagascar at the end of the war and thus ghetto building was to all practical purposes illusory.'[10]

Deportation of the Jewish people to Madagascar, however, was contingent upon one further major event - a peace treaty with Britain, which had not yet been achieved.

The Germans begin to implement Phase Four – the Madagascar Plan

Eichmann's plan called for the deportation of four million Jewish people to Madagascar to be implemented over four years – one million a year. Rademacher wrote in early July: 'The imminent victory gives Germany the possibility and, in my opinion, also the obligation to solve the Jewish question in Europe,... The desirable solution is: All Jews out of Europe.'[11]

Rademacher continued: 'The Madagascar solution means, as seen from the German point of view, the creation of a superghetto. Only the Security Police has the necessary experience in this area.'[12] Rademacher then went on to describe the mechanics of how this Jewish 'colony' would be administered.[13]

All that was now required was to ensure that the British Navy would not hinder the implementation of this Plan. In the meantime, though, a beginning could be made. On 1 July 1940 Jewish people from the annexed region of Alsace and Lorraine were deported into France.[14] Then on 22 October some 6,500 Jews from the western part of Germany began to be deported to detention camps in the south of France in readiness for their deportation to

---

[10] Browning, *Origins,* p. 84, n. 175.

[11] Ibid., p. 85, citing footnote 179.

[12] Ibid.

[13] Much of the information about the Madagascar Plan is found in the file of Martin Luther, located in the Wannsee House Museum, Wannsee, near Berlin.

[14] The contested region of Alsace-Lorraine was ceded to Germany in the 1940 Armistice with France.

Madagascar.[15] Hitler's objective of creating a *judenrein* Europe was, seemingly, coming closer to implementation.

Among these Jewish deportees were many non-Aryan Christians. The main camp where they were sent was at Gurs at the foot of the Pyrenees, where many participated incongregations for both Jewish Protestants and Jewish Catholics. One Jewish Christian was Otto Samuel, who was associated with the American Board of Missions to the Jews (ABMJ), and who had worked in Hamburg with the Jerusalem Church (Irish Mission) before escaping to Belgium.[16] It was in Belgium that he was picked up by the Nazis, and deported, first to the detention camp at Riversales and then to Gurs.[17]

Operation Sea Lion

Complete implementation of the Madagascar Plan would require the subjugation of Great Britain. Although there had been some thought given to a German landing in Great Britain, Hitler only issued his Directive No. 16 outlining just such an invasion on 16 July. He did so when he realised that Brita n was not going to capitulate as he expected they would. The proposed landing was code-named *Operation Sea Lion*, and scheduled to take place in September.

The first and most important phase of this operation was a period of concentrated aerial bombing of Britain, intended to destroy strategic locations as well as weaken the resolve of the people and the government. When this strategy did not succeed, the *Luftwaffe* resorted to 'terror' bombings of civilian targets. Hitler eventually had to postpone the landing scheduled for September, although the aerial bombardments continued unabated.[18]

---

15 More information about the Madagascar Plan and the camp at Gurs will be provided in the forthcoming publication *They Suffered Like Other Jewish People.*

16 The Jerusalem Church was part of the work associated with Arnold Frank and was where Elzbieta Jocz's father Herbert Singer had worked.

17 On a research trip in 2019 I visited Gurs and found evidence of both a Protestant and a Roman Catholic congregation. Samuel was the pastor of the Jewish Protestant congregation for a short period. He stated: 'Among the 12,000 prisoners at Gurs there were about 500 Protestants, and I became their minister, assisting a French pastor.' *The Hebrew Christian*, Volume xviii, 1945-1946, pp 17-18. The ABMJ managed to get Samuel to the US, but his health had suffered from the experiences of the previous years.

18 Shirer, pp. 758ff.

The Jocz family under the bombs in Britain – and surviving in Lwow

In London Jakob, Joan and baby Anne were experiencing the German aerial bombardment first hand. In 1940, sometime after Anne's birth, the Jocz family moved out of Joan's parents' house. Joan recalled: '… we were offered the use of a rectory in N. London & a friend sent us a truck load of furniture & necessities to put in it.'[19]

Then came the bombing. Joan wrote again: 'It wasn't an easy time as the bombing of London began & we were very vulnerable as we were next to a large power station.'[20] After some months they were able to rent a small house in Surrey, but, life was still hazardous, as, Joan continued, 'we were in the path of the doodle-bugs & other horrors Hitler sent against London.'[21] Jakob meanwhile continued his work of speaking throughout the country on behalf of CMJ.

The events in France and Britain had little immediate effect upon the Jewish people in Eastern Europe, including the Jocz family, who were 'safe' under Soviet control. While in Bucharest Allison continued to receive notifications from Pawel and Elzbieta, and then forwarded this information to London. Allison wrote later concerning that period: 'Paul and Elizabeth settled down, as I learnt later, to a new way of life. With no continuing financial support from the Mission, they began to earn their living as costermongers, selling fruit and vegetables from their barrow on the streets.' At the time when he wrote his memoirs Allison wasn't quite sure of the chronology of events, and continued: 'Or was it Elizabeth only who did this later, after the arrival of the Germans?'[22]

The CMJ journal, the *Jewish Missionary Intelligence*, reported in 1941:

> It is gratifying to know that we are able to send a little money to our missionaries in Lwow (Soviet Russia). Paul Jocz has recently sent the following cable:- "Money received. Parents very grateful for help because difficult for me to provide for all. Greetings Paul Jocz. From Lwow.[23]

---

[19] *Memoir of Joan Jocz*, p. 7.
[20] Ibid., pp. 7-8.
[21] Ibid., p. 8.
[22] Allison, *Journey*, p. 14.
[23] *JMI*, 1941, p. 47.

Despite various deprivations, in June 1941 Bazyli, Anna, Jan, Pawel and Elzbieta were surviving under Soviet rule in Lwow. But this was soon to change. The very survival of the Jocz family and all other Jewish people living in the Soviet controlled part of Poland, was soon to be severely imperilled.

The fate of other Jewish non-Aryan Christians in Poland

The fate of all Jewish people, inclusive of the non-Aryan Christians, in the regions of Poland either annexed by Germany or under direct German administration continued to deteriorate throughout 1940 and into 1941.

Towards the end of 1940 re-settlement was again in progress. The vast majority of the Jews were being relocated to the many ghettos now dotted all over Poland. The largest were at Warsaw and Lodz. Additionally, many were being sent to vast labour camps.

Those in the ghettos endured steadily deteriorating conditions, and hunger became a huge problem. Thousands succumbed to death in this manner, as well as by direct German brutality. Most of the staff and congregation associated with the American European Bethel Mission were in the Lodz ghetto – and few ultimately survived.[24]

In the Warsaw Ghetto there was a large number of Jewish Catholics, including the esteemed medical scientist Dr Ludwik Hirszfeld. Hirszfeld was representative of the many assimilated Jewish Catholics who thought they were sufficiently assimilated so as to be 'safe'. Emmanuel Ringelblum, an historian who documented events in the ghetto until his death in 1944, wrote on February 28 1941: 'Among the converts who have moved into the Ghetto are Professor Hirszfeld, who has a European reputation in the field of bacteriology…'[25]

The actual story of how Hirszfeld ended up in the ghetto is illustrative of the fate now befalling all non-Aryan Christians, even those who were seemingly highly assimilated. Hirszfeld described the time when he was summarily or-

---

[24] Leon Rosenberg was in the United States continuing to raise financial support, especially for the orphanage. The work was being led by his wife Fanny.

[25] Ringelblum, E. *Notes from the Warsaw Ghetto,* (ibooks, New York: 2006), p. 129. Hirszfeld was included on a list, known as Ronikiers list, which had the names of all of the assimilated often well-established Jewish Catholics in Warsaw. The Nazis obtained this list by deceit.

dered to leave his comfortable home in 'Gentile' Warsaw and relocate to the Jewish Ghetto:

> The soldier on guard ordered us to place our suitcases on the muddy pavement and open them. He took everything he liked... In one suitcase he came across my book published by the Mannheim Academy when I was an assistant in Heidelberg. He asked what it was. I told him that I had written the book when I was an employee of the German State. His answer was "Jetzt bist du aber nur ein Jude" (Now you are only a Jew) and he went on stealing.[26]

Hirszfeld, like thousands of others, was not 'safe' living on the Gentile side, for he, like the others, fell into the category of being Jewish based on the Nazi race laws.

Their predicament is borne out by Israeli scholar Havi Ben-Sasson, who stated in her article relating to 'Jewish converts to Christianity' in the Warsaw Ghetto:

> It is a basic Jewish principle that even a sinful Jew still remains a Jew. Thus, a Jew remains affiliated with the Jewish community at large (for better or worse) irrespective of his/her actions. During World War II, this tenet of the faith took on practical significance. With the occupation of Warsaw, obviously, the Jews of the city and its surroundings fell into the clutches of the Nazis. However, some 2,000 converts to Christianity who, despite their non-Jewish way of life were perceived by the Nazis as full-fledged Jews based on a racial definition of a Jew, were also at risk.[27]

In his book *Christians in the Warsaw Ghetto*, a leading expert on Jewish Catholics in the Warsaw Ghetto, Peter Dembowski, quoted a Catholic priest, Reverend Zdzislaw Krol, who had accessed all available source material of the time. According to Krol: "There were 5,200 Christians in the ghetto, most of them Roman Catholic."[28]

[26] Hirszfeld, L. *The Story of One Life,* (Kindle, University of Rochester), p. 289.

[27] Havi Ben-Sasson, 'Christians in the Ghetto: All Saints' Church, Birth of the Holy Virgin Mary Church, and the Jews of the Warsaw Ghetto', in *Yad Vashem Studies* XXXI, edited by David Silberland, (Yad Vashem Jerusalem, 2003), pp. 153-54.

[28] Dembowski, P. *Christians in the Warsaw Ghetto*, (University of Notre Dame: Indiana, 2005), p. 66.

Chapter 15

Hitler's *Generalplan Ost*

Initial planning for invading the Soviet Union

Despite his Non-Aggression Pact with Stalin Hitler had long envisioned invading the Soviet Union, as part of what was called the *Generalplan Ost.* The goal of this Plan was the subjugation of the Slav and non-Aryan peoples of the East to German dominance. This would involve the colonisation of the fertile regions especially of the Ukraine, by German farmers, and where necessary, the starvation of huge numbers of Soviet citizens.[1] This region, Germany's real *lebensraum*, would then be turned into a 'Garden of Eden.'

In *Mein Kampf* Hitler ruled out Germany seeking overseas colonial acquisitions, stating that 'the only possibility for carrying out a healthy territorial policy lay in the acquisition of new land in Europe itself.'[2] 'If land was desired in Europe' he continued 'it could be obtained by and large at the expense of Russia.'[3] He further stated: 'If we speak of soil in Europe today, we can primarily have in mind only Russia and her vassal border states.'[4]

When writing about Russia he referred to the travesty which occurred when it was taken over by the Bolsheviks. Bolshevism for Hitler was the embodiment of an evil political regime – and it was controlled by and synonymous with the Jews. 'In Russian Bolshevism' he observed 'we must see the attempt undertaken by the Jews in the twentieth century to achieve world domination.'[5]

Although these were ideas expressed in the 1920s, they had not changed in 1939-41. Hitler had two objectives when considering Russia. First was the need to obtain territory for Germany in Europe, *lebensraum*. Second was the

---

[1] Snyder, *Bloodlands*, pp. 161, 172, 187-88, 213, 254, 294. Much of this policy was recorded in the Hunger Plan released on 23 May 1941.

[2] Hitler, *Mein Kampf*, p. 128.

[3] Ibid.

[4] Ibid., p. 598.

[5] Ibid., p. 604.

need to eradicate a form of government based upon an ideology which he believed was controlled by the Jews.

The Soviets make moves in the Baltic States and Eastern Europe
Although Hitler had his ambitions for conquering the Soviet Union, he knew he had to first defeat France and Britain as he did not want to wage war on two fronts. France had been subdued by June 1940 but Britain had not. Despite this major negative factor it was at this time that he began formulating his plans for the invasion of the Soviet Union. Why did he do so?

It might be that the Soviets provoked him into action. On 15 June 1940 Soviet troops entered Lithuania and during the following days they also entered Latvia and Estonia.[6] These three regions were part of the Soviet sphere of interest according to the German-Soviet Non-Aggression Pact of August 1939.

Another area designated as part of the Soviet sphere of interest was Bessarabia.[7] This strategic region bordered Romania and the Soviet Union and the Soviets had lost it to Romania after the First World War. The Soviets wanted it back. But they also coveted another region, northern Bucovina, adjacent to Bessarabia. On 26 June the Soviets 'delivered an ultimatum to Rumania demanding the ceding to it of Bessarabia and northern Bucovina.'[8]

Such Soviet requests greatly concerned the Germans, as it would bring the Soviets nearer to the oil fields in Romania which Germany desperately needed. Nevertheless, Germany persuaded Romania to accede, in order to stop the Soviets conquering all of Romania.

These moves by the Soviets seem to have shaken Hitler into action. On 31 July 1940, while planning was still taking place for *Operation Sea Lion* in the West, Hitler presented his initial outline for the invasion of the Soviet Union.[9] According to German General Franz Halder, Hitler believed that a quick victory over the Soviet Union would compel Britain to surrender.[10]

[6] Shirer, p. 794.
[7] Today most of Bessarabia is in Moldavia and the remainder in Ukraine.
[8] Shirer, p. 795.
[9] Shirer, p. 798.
[10] General Halder's report from meeting of 29 July, Halder's diary July 31 1940, cited in Shirer, p. 798.

Perhaps further Soviet moves then further influenced Hitler's thinking. In early August 1940 Lithuania, Latvia and Estonia were officially incorporated into the Soviet Union. During the same period Hungary was agitating to recover Transylvania from Romania, which she had lost after the First World War. In this atmosphere Hitler ordered a meeting in Vienna between von Ribbentrop, Ciano and the foreign ministers of Hungary and Romania. Hitler informed Ciano on 28 August that the only thing he 'has at heart is that peace is preserved there, and that Rumanian oil continue to flow into his reservoirs.'[11]

On 29 August von Ribbentrop and Ciano informed the Hungarians and Romanians of their decision to arbitrate in Hungary's favour. While Hungary was elated by the acquisition of much of Transylvania, Romania was deflated. It was obvious she was being squeezed – and being prepared either to be taken over by the Soviets, or to bow to German hegemony.

The pro-Nazi Marshal Ion Antonescu then engineered a *coup d'etat* on 4 September, which coincided with the abdication of King Carol.[12] The Romanian government, led by Antonescu and supported by an extreme anti-Jewish right wing group, the Iron Guard, then officially joined the Axis alliance in November 1940. Anti-Jewish measures then began to be legislated. In January 1941 the Iron Guard attempted a coup against Antonescu – during which the Iron Guard also carried out a deadly pogrom against Jewish people, sadistically murdering about 125 of them. The attempted coup failed and many members of the Iron Guard were subsequently imprisoned, but this proved to be temporary.[13] Both Hungary and Romania were coming under increasing Nazi German influence and even control.

Plans for *Operation Barbarossa*

Meanwhile Hitler had been fine-tuning his thoughts and on 18 December 1940 he issued his Directive No. 21. This Directive instructed his military commanders to develop their plans for the invasion of the Soviet Union, which were to be complete by 15 May 1941.[14] All such plans were certain to impact the lives of the Jocz family in Lwow.

[11] Ciano, p. 288.
[12] Ciano, pp. 288-290.
[13] It was during this period of turmoil that Roger Allison was forced to leave Romania, arriving ultimately in Palestine.
[14] Shirer, p. 810.

Concerning the matter of Britain Hitler stated: 'The German Armed Forces must be prepared, even before the conclusion of the war against England, to crush Soviet Russia in a rapid campaign.'[15] At the time when he presented his initial plan for the invasion of the Soviet Union Britain had still not been subdued. Hitler was either optimistic that Britain would yet submit and enter into an agreement with Germany, or that she would be confined to her island fortress and not cause any trouble for Germany.

The military plan for the Soviet attack, codenamed *Operation Barbarossa,* was to be a surprise invasion. The military objective was to move quickly and capture Moscow and Leningrad and obtain the surrender of the Soviet Union well before the onset of winter. There were to be four major thrusts:

- Army Group North: from East Prussia through the Baltic states with Leningrad as a major objective. Finnish troops would simultaneously attack Leningrad from the north.
- Army Group Central: through Belarus with Smolensk and Moscow as major objectives.
- Army Group South: through Ukraine, with Kiev and ultimately Rostov and the Caucasus region as objectives. Lwow lay directly in the path of this huge force.
- A mostly Romanian and German force, with some Hungarian troops further south, whose objectives were Odessa and the Crimea and the Black Sea. Ultimately they, together with Army Group South, would capture the region of the Donets Basin where much Soviet industry was located.[16]

Apart from large numbers of Finnish and Romanian forces and some Hungarians, the Germans had other allies also: *Deutschvolke* (people of German descent) and many disgruntled locals, especially Lithuanians and Ukrainians and others (Belarusians, Estonians and Latvians) who were opposed to the Soviet Communist regime. Many of these very same allies were also vehemently anti-Jewish.

---

[15] Hitler's Directive No. 21, 18 December 1941, cited in *Documents on German Foreign Policy* (1918-1945), Series D, Vol. XI, Document No. 532.

[16] Churchill, W. *The Grand Alliance*, (Houghton Mifflin; Boston, 1950), pp. 377-8, 389 (map). Shirer, p. 811.

Introduction of ideological factors

Initially Hitler's thinking and planning, as presented to his commanders, was along military and geo-political lines. But by February 1941 planning began to include more economic and ideological factors. In short: in order for the Soviet Union to be effectively captured and subjugated and its economic resources utilised, the prevailing political system, Communism (Bolshevism), would need to be totally destroyed.[17]

A draft of the military plans for the invasion of the Soviet Union was presented to Hitler on 3 March 1941 by the chiefs of the three armed services.[18] Hitler instructed Alfred Jodl, the Chief of the Operations Staff of the OKW,[19] to revise these plans in accordance with his sentiments, as follows:

> This imminent campaign is more than just a battle of weapons; it also entails a conflict between two worldviews ... The Jewish-Bolshevik intelligentsia, the "suppressor" of these peoples until now, must be removed... Moreover we must avoid under all circumstances that in place of a Bolshevik now a nationalist Russia is allowed to emerge, which as history proves will in the end again be hostile to Germany. It is our task to construct as quickly as possible with a minimum of German military power socialist state forms that are dependent upon us. These tasks are so difficult that one can not burden the army with them.[20]

The new plans would therefore be drawn up in accordance with Hitler's declared desire for the 'Jewish-Bolshevik intelligentsia' to be 'removed.' The revised draft was ready by 13 March, within which these ideological factors had been addressed. The operational zone of the military was to be very shallow and SS units would operate together with the Army. This meant there would need to be close co-operation between the Army and the SS, and a memorandum of understanding between the two entities was concluded by 28 April. Additionally the Army would not establish military administration over conquered areas, but would hand over administration of these regions to a *Reichsfuhrer SS*.[21]

[17] Browning, *Origins,* p. 215.

[18] Shirer, p. 830.

[19] OKW – *Oberkommando Wehrmacht* – Germany's armed forces, including Army, Airforce and Navy. Not to be confused with OKH – which was the supreme command of the *Heer* - Army.

[20] KTB OKW, 1: 341-42, March 3, 1941, cited in Browning, p. 216.

When the *Wehrmacht* had invaded Poland most of the killing of Polish intelligentsia in the region to be annexed to the Reich was carried out by SS related units, especially the *Einsatzgruppen*. Now, however, the military were to be much more actively involved in eradicating the Bolshevik intelligentsia – although the bulk of the killing was still to be carried out by the SS-related groups especially the *Einsatzgruppen* and ordinary German Police Battalions.[22]

Four specialised *Einsatz* units were formed, one attached to each Army Group. Each *Einsatzgruppe* was composed of hard-core members of the SS, supplemented with some *Waffen-SS* soldiers (the military branch of the SS). The Reserve Police Battalion 9 was also spread between the *Einsatzgruppen*.[23] Later a fifth *Einsatz* unit was formed.[24]

On 30 March Hitler met with some 200 leading military officers and once again reiterated his appeal, as General Franz Halder, the Army Chief of Staff recorded, that this was 'a war of destruction' and called for the 'Extermination of the Bolshevik Commissars and the communist intelligentsia.'[25]

The planned invasion involved harsh economic measures. On 23 May the Hunger Plan was formulated. Snyder outlines this plan thus: '...during and after the war on the USSR, the Germans intended to feed German soldiers and German (and west European) civilians by starving the Soviet citizens they would conquer, especially those in the big cities. Food from Ukraine would now be sent not north to feed Russia and the rest of the Soviet Union but rather west to nourish Germany and the rest of Europe.'[26]

The impending invasion of the Soviet Union was threatening to be a brutal destructive affair for all of the Soviet citizenry – but especially so for the Jewish people. The Jocz family as well as all the Jewish Christians spread throughout the Soviet Union, but especially in those regions to the west of Leningrad,

---

[21] Browning, *Origins*, p. 216.

[22] Browning, C. *Police Battalion 101*, (Harper Collins; New York, 1992), p. 10.

[23] Police Battalions were heavily involved in the murder of tens of thousands of Jewish people in Poland in 1942. Interestingly, the members of the Police Battalions, although under Himmler's overall authority, were not always ardent Nazis.

[24] Browning, *Police Battalion 101*, p. 10.

[25] Halder, Kriegstagebuch 2: 336-37 (entry for March 30, 1941), cited in Browning, *Origins*, p. 218 and footnote 18.

[26] Snyder, p. 162.

Moscow and Stalingrad, would not be exempt from this impending onslaught. On 4 June a statement was given to Army divisional leaders, to be read out to the troops at the beginning of the invasion. It began:

> Bolshevism is the deadly enemy of the national socialist German people. This disintegrative worldview and its carriers must be combatted by Germany. This struggle demands ruthless and energetic measures against bolshevist agitators, guerrillas, saboteurs, Jews, and complete elimination of any active or passive resistance.[27]

Here 'Jews' are mentioned alongside other groups against whom 'ruthless and energetic measures' were to be taken. Interestingly, as Browning points out, 'the officer corps accepted the equation of Bolshevism with the Jews.'[28]

Daniel Goldhagen contends in his book *Hitler's Willing Executioners* that it was the Nazi intention from the very outset of *Operation Barbarossa* to murder the Soviet Jews. This would begin slowly and together with aid from local sympathisers, with limited executions and mostly of men, and then in time the level of murders would increase.[29] As events unfolded, some local Lithuanians, Latvians and Ukrainians were often only too eager to assist with this policy of what was essentially genocide. Many more Romanians were involved in the killing of Jews as the Romanian government actually endorsed such killings.

The final 'Commissar Order' – 6 June

Hitler laid out his final plans for the invasion of the Soviet Union on 6 June with the publication of his Commissar Order. In it he gave open license to the German Army to execute all captured Soviet officers and Soviet Commissars. The Commissars were the ideological conduit between the Communist Party leadership and the ordinary soldiers, and the Nazi leaders did not want any to end up in captivity and in a position to influence their captors.

Hitler's sentiments as expressed in the Commissar Order were later attested to by two leading Generals, General Franz Halder, Chief of Staff of the

---

[27] Doc. Nr. 11: Richtlinien fur das Verhaltender Truppe in Russland, June 4, 1941 [Nbg. Doc. NOKW-1692], cited in Jacobsen, "Kommissarbefehl," pp. 223-24, cited in Browning, *Origins,* pp. 222-23, n.40.

[28] Browning, *Origins*, p. 224.

[29] Goldhagen, pp. 148-152.

Army (OKH), and Field Marshal Wilhelm Keitel, Chief of Staff of the German Armed Forces (OKW). General Keitel would later testify: 'Hitler's main theme was that this was the decisive battle between two ideologies and that this fact made it impossible to use in this war [with Russia] methods, as we soldiers knew them, which were considered to be the only correct ones under international law.'[30]

The essence of the Commissar Order was that German soldiers would not be tried by a military court martial for the killing of Soviet prisoners of war and civilians. Although a number of generals were seemingly unhappy with this authorisation for murder, the die had now been cast. Despite some protestations, the German military forces would be co-labourers with the specialised murder squads in the forthcoming invasion of the Soviet Union.

Briefings with the *Einsatzgruppen* – 17 June

The SS meanwhile had been fine-tuning exactly which groups of Soviet citizens would be murdered. The *Einsatzgruppen* had been undergoing specific training and on 17 June Himmler held a planning meeting with the officers in Berlin, and then later addressed them at their camp in Pretzsch.[31]

A matter of great importance was the exact content of these briefings: were these officers given limited instructions concerning the killing of Jewish males of a certain age-group, or were they given instructions for the all-out murder of Soviet Jews?[32]

One *Einsatz* commander who was present, Walter Blume, later testified: "Heydrich himself explained that the Russian campaign was imminent, that partisan war was to be expected, and that in this region many Jews lived who had to be exterminated through liquidation… He explained further that Eastern Jewry, as the breeding ground [Keimzelle] of World Jewry, was to be annihilated. There was no mistaking it that all Jews were supposed to be exterminated, without regard to age or sex."[33]

---

[30] Nuremberg Documents, Part XI, p. 16, cited in Winston Churchill, *The Grand Alliance,* (Houghton Mifflin, Boston: 1950), p. 368. Churchill records this meeting as 14 June. [with Russia] is in Churchill's book.

[31] Browning, *Origins*, p. 226.

[32] Goldhagen, p. 149.

The basic outline for the Eastern Plan – Phase Five

It had become quite clear to the Nazi leaders by early 1941 that, as Snyder points out, like their previous 'solutions' for dealing with 'the Jewish problem' of Europe the Madagascar Plan was now basically obsolete.[34] A new solution was required.

The revised plans for *Operation Barbarossa* introduce what I see as Phase Five of the Nazi solution for 'the Jewish problem' – the 'Eastern Plan.' Phase Five basically had two components:

First, according to basic Nazi ideology, one of the greatest threats to 'civilisation' was Bolshevism, which was viewed for the most part as a Jewish dominated and driven ideology. The aim therefore was to destroy the Communist-Bolshevik leadership (the Commissars) and other potential dangerous elements. This included Jewish men, who were seen as potential future Bol shevik leaders. But it would appear that this grouping of Jewish males was just the beginning of a more systematic murder of all Soviet Jewish people.

The second component of this Eastern Plan was that once regions in the Soviet Union had been captured, that is primarily Belarus and Ukraine, as well as the Baltic states of Lithuania, Latvia and Estonia, then Jewish people from the remainder of Europe would be transferred or deported to these regions. This was to be the first stage in their ultimate deportation 'further east,' out of Europe proper – so that Europe could be *judenrein*. At this point there did not appear to be an official plan for the systematic murder of all European Jews.

Bazyli, Anna, Pawel, Elzbieta and Jan Jocz were about to become victims of this brutal Nazi inspired anti-Jewish worldview.

---

[33] Walter Blume, ZStL 207 AR-Z 15/58, vol. 4, p. 981, cited in Goldhagen, p. 149 and footnote 58. The matter of when specific orders were given for the systematic murder of all Soviet Jews is a contested one. Although Blume stated this order was given by Heydrich before the invasion, several other Einsatz commanders maintain that it was only given in mid-August, while several maintain that they never even received such an order. For more on this matter see Browning, *Origins*, pp. 226-227; Goldhagen, pp. 148-150.

[34] Snyder, p. 160.

Jakob's insightful article

It was about this very time that Jakob was compiling a very insightful article entitled 'Hebrew Christianity in Poland' which was later published in the October 1941 edition of *The Hebrew Christian.* Jakob highlighted the history of the Jewish people in Poland, and the attitude of the Roman Catholic Church towards them. He also highlighted the pioneering role played by the foreign missions in endeavouring to present Jesus to the Jewish people in Poland. He concluded with these sobering words:

> The sudden and relentless onslaught of Nazi Germany on Poland put an abrupt stop to missionary work and to Hebrew Christian activity. From what we know of conditions in Poland at the present moment, the lot of the Jewish-Christian believers must be even worse than that of the Jews. The Nazis, who condemn every Jew as a pariah, irrespective of creed, have probably driven the Hebrew Christians back into the Jewish ghetto. But within the ghetto the Hebrew-Christian is again a *pariah,* this time in the eyes of the Jews. He can scarcely expect any help or sympathy from the Jewish community. His plight must be terrible.
>
> Thus the young Hebrew Christian groups in Poland are going through a time of testing and great trial.... Their temptation to deny or renounce Christ must be great. Some of them will probably lapse. We pray that many may endure and remain faithful. History has often proved the truth of the old saying that the blood of the martyrs is the seed of the Church. It may be, by the grace of God, that the suffering of the Hebrew Christians in the midst of their Jewish brethren will be the seed of a nationwide movement Christward.[35]

[35] *The Hebrew Christian,* Volume XIV, 1941-1942, p. 65.

Chapter 16

Operation Barbarossa begins

The invasion begins on 22 June 1941 – and early warning signs

Life for the Jocz family in Lwow, and every Jewish person in the Soviet Union changed once and for all on 22 June 1941. On that day the Germans launched *Operation Barbarossa*, the invasion of the Soviet Union and the biggest land invasion in world history.

The North, Central and South Army Groups and the composite Romanian-German Group, set out to achieve their military objectives with incredible speed and ferocity. This *blitzkrieg* far surpassed those of September 1939 and May 1940. Following the *Wehrmacht* were the killing units, especially the *Einsatzgruppen.*

From the outset the Commissar Order was operational. Already on 22 June at Garsden (Gargzdai) near the German-Lithuanian border the Germans separated out the Jewish population. Two days later two hundred Jewish males and one Jewish female were executed on trumped up charges.[1]

Further killings took place in Lithuania, at Kaunas and Vilnius, after they were captured on 24 June. Soon after the arrival of German troops local Lithuanians began killing Jewish people in these locations and elsewhere in pogroms in which German soldiers played a supporting role. At Bialystok on 27 June, various German units murdered some 2,000 Jews, almost entirely men. Bialystok was the centre of the operations of the Barbican Mission and it seems likely that some Jewish Christian members of the St Peter's Church were caught up in these events. Rev. Peter Gorodishz had been forced to leave Bialystok by the Soviet regime and at this time was residing in Vilnius.

By the end of June there had already been considerable killing of Jewish people, mostly those fitting the narrow criteria of the Commissar Order. There were, however, various pogroms in which locals were involved, and in these

[1] Jurgen Matthias, *Origins,* p. 254.

settings all ages and both men and women were affected. One such event occurred in Romania.

Isaiah Feinstein is murdered

The southern offensive of *Operation Barbarossa* was carried out mostly by the Romanian Army together with some German divisions. Considerable numbers of Jewish people lived in the border region between Romania and the Soviet Union in June 1941. Marshal Antonescu saw them as a potential fifth column who would operate against the Axis forces. On 22 June the fighting began in the region of Jassy (Iasi) in this disputed area, and on that same day all of the Iron Guard prisoners were released from prison. They were to play the leading role in upcoming persecutions of the Jewish people.

Lydia Feinstein recalled how also on that day her husband Isaac, a former student at the CMJ Training Centre in Warsaw, and who was then pastor of a congregation of Jewish Christians at Jassy, held his last service. Lydia wrote: 'He spoke as though he knew that this was the very last time and put his whole heart into his words.' He concluded with the words of Psalm 46: 1-2.[2] The words of the Psalmist were appropriate: 'God is our refuge and strength, an ever-present help in trouble. Therefore we will not fear, though the earth give way and the mountains fall into the heart of the sea.'

The situation grew progressively worse for the Jews. During the following week, as the conflict between the Axis and Soviet forces intensified, Jassy was subject to constant bombardment from the Soviet forces. Unfortunately rumours began to spread that Jewish people were signalling to the Soviet planes.

For Lydia Feinstein the night of 29 June 'was the most fearful night of all.' 'Soon after 10 p.m.' she wrote 'a dreadful shooting commenced.' Isaac and the deaconess Sister Olga 'dismounted our large sign at the building front "Missiunea Norwegiana Israel." (Norwegian Mission for Israel). They had recognized the danger.'[3]

The danger soon became more apparent when a friend came that night and urged Isaac to hide, telling him that, 'It had been plotted to arrest or kill all

---

[2] Lydia Feinstein, 'That My Children May Remember', in *The Chosen People,* November 1947, p. 12.
[3] Ibid., p. 13.

Jews.'[4] During that night thousands of Jews were murdered by an anti-Jewish force of Romanians, including Iron Guard members. The following day many more were rounded-up and taken to the local police station. The local population, aided and abetted by the police, then began to massacre them at this location. Isaac did not hide, but was taken away to the police station.

Lydia later met some men who were with Isaac and they stated that he had been a strong witness for God and had encouraged many others during that difficult time.[5]

Those who survived the massacre, some 4,000, were then herded on to railroad wagons and the train moved off. Isaac was one of those. One survivor later informed Lydia that they were crammed into a cattle car: 'Perhaps your husband did not have to suffer long. He soon started to recite Psalms with a loud voice and his face was like that of an angel. He begged the other victims to make their peace with God, and to seek Salvation through the blood of Christ before it was too late. And some did so. Then he dropped to the floor, and fell asleep never to wake up again.'[6] Some 2,650 or so ultimately died on the so-called 'death train.'[7]

Another Jewish Christian, Richard Wurmbrandt, who was associated with the CMJ work in Bucharest, later wrote: 'Not a single man from the Jewish Christian congregation in Jassy survived; all were killed in the pogrom.'[8] Some 13,000 Jewish people were murdered altogether in the Jassy pogrom.

Unfortunately atrocities against the Jewish people continued, perpetrated by local sympathisers and Romanian as well as German troops. Such activities were also being carried out further north.

The Germans arrive in Lwow – 30 June 1941

The Germans captured Lwow on 30 June. Christopher Mick wrote that by that time the Jewish population had swelled to more than 150,000 with many

---

4 Ibid., p. 13.

5 Lydia Feinstein, 'Days of Terror in Jassy', *The Hebrew Christian,* Volume XXI, 1948-1949, p. 14.

6 Ibid., p. 18.

7 www.yadvashem.org. www.ushmm.org.

8 Wurmbrandt, R. *Christ on the Jewish Road,* (Hodder and Stoughton, London, 1970), p. 33.

having previously fled there from the region of the General Government.[9] The following day, 1 July 1941, an outbreak of violence broke out aimed primarily against the Jewish people. 'This was the Lviv pogrom of 1 July 1941,' wrote Patrick Cockburn 'when thousands of Jews were dragged from their homes, beaten and executed by either German troops or their Ukrainian helpers.... Ukrainian militiamen and mobs of supporters carried out the pogrom, though the Germans oversaw it and committed many of the murders.'[10] The first step which led to this outrageous crime was when the Germans forced Jews to dig up the bodies of people previously executed by the Soviets in the three prisons of Lwow.

This terrible massacre, Cockburn stated, was carried out primarily by 'the militia of the Organisation of Ukrainian Nationalists (OUN) acting under German auspices.'[11] It happened quickly after the German occupation because, as John-Paul Himka wrote, the OUN wanted to show 'the Germans that it shared their anti-Jewish perspectives and that it was worthy to be entrusted with the formation of a Ukrainian state.'[12]

One of those who witnessed this pogrom was Rabbi David Kahane, later the Chief Rabbi of the Israeli Air Force. Like many others Kahane hid in his cellar during the days of the pogrom. Kahane later wrote his reminiscences in a book, *Lvov Ghetto Diary*.

Between 4-6,000 Jewish people were violently murdered in this pogrom. The remaining Jewish population now lived in a constant state of fear and anxiety. Their fears heightened shortly after, as Kahane explained in his diary:

> On July 15, announcements were posted on the walls throughout the city with the "armband" (opaska in Polish) decree. Every Jew, including

---

[9] Mick, C. (2011). Incompatible Experiences: Poles, Ukrainians and Jews in Lviv under Soviet and German Occupation, 1939-44. *Journal of Contemporary History*, 46(2), pp. 336-363. One source states 220,000. See 'Russian troops seize Lwow from Nazis, find the Jews gone', *Haaretz*, 5 May 2020, www.haaretz.com

[10] Patrick Cockburn, 'To look at what Ukraine's future might be, just look at Lviv's shameful past.' *Independent*, 9 March 2014.

[11] Ibid.

[12] John-Paul Himka, The Lviv Pogrom of 1941: The Germans, Ukrainian Nationalists, and the Carnival Crowd, in *Canadian Slavonic Papers/Revue Canadienne des slavistes*, Vol. LIII, Nos. 2–3–4, June-September-December 2011, p. 234.

> Catholics whose Jewish ancestry could be traced back to the third generation, was required to wear a "Jewish armband" on the right sleeve – a Star of David painted blue on a piece of white fabric. From that moment on each Jew was branded with an identifying mark. The armband singled out its owner like an animal and whoever wanted to was allowed to beat or murder him with impunity.[13]

Here was clear evidence that any Jewish Christian, by whatever name they called themselves, was not exempt. No matter how assimilated they were or thought they were, to the Nazi occupying force, they were like all other Jews.

Shortly after the issuing of this decree another violent pogrom broke out in Lwow in late July, known now as the Petliura Days, in which a further 2,000 or so Jewish people were murdered.[14]

New administration at Lwow

By the end of July the German military had penetrated further eastwards pursuing the Soviet forces. At a high level meeting on 16 July Hitler implemented new administrative measures. The front line would be under the North, Central and South Army Groups. Those regions already conquered would be placed under a civil administration. These would be classified as the *Reichskommissariat Ostland* (which included Estonia, Latvia, Lithuania and Belarussia) and the *Reichskommissariat Ukraine.*

The Galicia region of western Ukraine, which included Lwow, Stanislawow and Tarnopol, would be incorporated into the General Government, ruled from Krakow. This change was implemented on 1 August 1941. Henceforth the status and well-being of the Jewish community in Galicia would be determined by the decisions emanating from Krakow, and in time from Lublin, which became the seat of power of the SS. For now the region of Galicia was preserved from the policy of overall genocide being implemented in the regions governed by the *Reichskommissariat.*

Part of the new administration for Lwow also included the formation of a Jewish Community Council or *Judenrat*, whose chairman was Dr. Yosef Par-

---

[13] Kahane, D. *Lvov Ghetto Diary,* p. 9.
[14] United States Holocaust Memorial Museum (USHMM) and Kahane, pp. 12-13.

nas. The *Judenrat*, as in all the ghettos created in other parts of Poland, was merely there in order to carry out the German, or more precisely, the SS and Gestapo directives. Each ghetto became a 'state-within-a state', with a police department, labour department, sanitation department, economic department, housing department, and so on.[15] The Jews of Lwow were gradually forced to relocate to the localised Jewish part of the city, which would become the ghetto.

Life for the Jocz family

The Jocz family managed to survive the initial period of terror but now it became clear just how cheap and expendable Jewish lives were. With the constantly changing Nazi policy concerning the Jews, no Jewish person anywhere in Poland or Europe could feel safe – even if they were totally assimilated and highly involved in the Church.

It was at this time that some Christian clergy began to give serious consideration to the Jewish predicament. One such person was Andrei Sheptytsky, the Metropolitan Archbishop for the Greek Catholic, or Uniate Church, in Lwow, who took the bold step of writing a letter to Himmler regarding the hostile Nazi attitude towards the Jewish people.[16] There was another, whose name we do not know, who played a heroic role for the Jocz family. Anna later recalled:

> When the German troops occupied our city of Lemberg, soon after the start of the German-Russian war in the year 1941, we lived in Lwowskich Dzieci Street. (I cannot remember the number of the house.) Even though we were both Christians, we knew that according to the Nuremberg Laws we were counted as Jews and felt under threat. My husband looked unmistakably Jewish, while I do not look Jewish. A member of our church offered to hide my husband and we decided that he should go into hiding while I stayed at our apartment. Should anyone ask, I would conceal my Jewish origin. My husband's friend hid him in the room where the wood was stored, and I stayed in the apartment by myself. After the occupation the army needed apartments, not only for soldiers but also for administrators. My apartment was requisitioned as well. The soldiers that

[15] Kahane, pp. 14-25.

[16] Himmler ordered the arrest of the aging Archbishop, but was advised against it owing to his popularity in western Galicia. See Kahane, pp. 124, 141.

were assigned to my home left the kitchen for me, since I functioned as their servant. They did not know that I was of Jewish origin, because I only had Polish friends and only spoke Polish. They used me to attend to all the domestic chores.[17]

Forced labour camps

With the new administration came another new development: labour camps and other institutions which utilised forced labour, mostly forced Jewish labour. Although there would soon be numerous such labour camps in the vicinity of Lwow, Poles were also transported elsewhere.

It is unclear what became of Jan after the German invasion but he is not mentioned by name in any future reference. According to his nephew Philip Jocz, 'At some point John [Jan] left the family and survived the war somewhere in Europe. I remember a story that suggested he spent some time in a German munitions factory where he sabotaged bombs intended for England.'[18]

Rabbi Kahane mentions how the Gestapo took over a farm near Sokolniki and turned it into a forced labour camp.[19] Then, he continued, 'In early September, when the front lines had moved eastward a great distance from Lvov, various German military institutions serving the front installed themselves in the city and its environs. Their demand for forced labor knew no bounds. Private German companies working for the army also operated in the city. They, too, looked for workers.'[20] One such industrial complex near Lwow was known as the Suchowola estate.

Pawel Jocz the Evangelical pastor

It appears that Pawel Jocz survived this period because of his position as an Evangelical pastor. A reference to him is found in the autobiography of

[17] Statutory Declaration of Anna Jocz, Toronto, 8 January 1959, Jocz Private Collection, German File, p. 55. Jakob later wrote: 'When the Germans began the systematic extermination of the Jews, my f father who looked Jewish, went into hiding. My mother did not look Jewish and so survived the holocaust.' Memorandum regarding reparation from the German Government of Mrs. Anna Jocz, deceased. By Jacob Jocz. No date., German File, p. 1.

[18] Email from Philip Jocz to the author, 11 June 2020.

[19] Kahane, p. 27. A terrible massacre of some of the forced labourers occurred here on the first day.

[20] Kahane, pp. 29-30.

Roman Frister, a Jewish Holocaust survivor who grew up in Lwow.[21] Frister was a young boy when the Soviets took control in 1939. As the Germans were approaching in June 1941, he recalls the Bolsheviks departing 'without a shot' and even offering to take the Frister family with them, an offer which was declined.[22]

Sometime afterwards Roman and his parents found themselves ensconced on the Suchowola estate near Lwow. He explained how this happened:

> The Suchowola estate was part of a leatherworking business expropriated by the Nazis after the occupation of Lvov and put under the management of the SS logistics corps. The German military had established a wide network of profitable enterprises that enriched its coffers over and above what it received from the state budget. Our estate, which was one link in a huge syndicate, grew saxifrage for the tanneries in Lvov. A Protestant minister named Paul Jocz had put my mother in touch with Kurt Brinker, a high SS officer and the syndicate's director. Unlike most of his colleagues, Brinker was religious and took the priest's opinions seriously.[23]

Roman then continued:

> My parents had met Jocz shortly before the Russians left Lvov. He knew we were Jews. "So what? Jesus was a Jew too," was all he said. I liked the man. There was nothing condescending or unfair about him. Lies and hypocrisy were foreign to his nature. Yet in introducing my mother to Brinker, he had vouched without a qualm for her pure Aryan background. Brinker was looking for a German-speaking secretary, and Pastor Jocz promised that he would find no better one. All he asked in return for this service was my baptism into the Christian faith. He was interested only in me, he said, because my parents' souls were beyond salvation. Even if circumstances forced them to the baptismal font, they would be living a lie. He had no desire to make them sin like that. I, however, might yet see the light and pure truth of the faith of Martin Luther.[24]

[21] Frister, R. *The Cap*, (New York: Grove Press, 1993). *Der Spiegel* called Frister's account 'The most important book on the Holocaust written in the last ten years.' (Blurb on back cover.)

[22] Ibid., p. 180.

[23] Ibid., p. 182.

[24] Ibid., p. 182.

It is somewhat difficult accepting what Frister wrote of Pawel seemingly offering some kind of 'spiritual bribery'. This seems to be completely out of character for Pawel, as it was not how Jocz or other CMJ missionaries operated. There is little doubt though that Roman felt comfortable with Pawel and saw him as a man of integrity. The outcome of this trust is that the Frister family, although Jewish, was safe – at least for the time being.

But at some time afterwards their Jewish identity was about to be exposed, and the Frister family had to make a very quick exit from Lwow, and finally made their way to Krakow.

Janowska labour camp and establishment of the Ghetto

In September 1941 the SS established a factory on Janowska Street in Lwow to produce weapons for the German war effort. Many of the Jews in the city were sent there as slave labourers. This camp, or factory, was just one of numerous such enterprises that the SS operated in the area.[25]

Two months later in November 1941, a ghetto was formally established in the north-east section of the city. Some 150,000 Jewish people were crammed into this small area. The Lwow Ghetto was sealed on 15 December 1941 and many of those who were now enclosed in the Ghetto were sent to work daily in the Janowska Camp.

Life in Lwow during this period was one of daily cruelty, especially during the period when the notorious '*Aktion* under the bridge' occurred. During this period many hundreds of Jews were ruthlessly murdered. The daily challenge was how to remain out of harm's way and to survive.

The establishment of the Lwow Ghetto was part of the broader new direction now adopted by the Nazi hierarchy relating to the Jewish people.

---

[25] Kahane, p. 33.

Chapter 17

The beginnings of Genocide

Moving into Phase Six

During the first months of *Operation Barbarossa* countless Jewish people had been murdered. But in those early months the majority of these had died in localised pogroms, or were men who 'fitted' the narrow criteria of the Commissar Order. But this was about to change, as Jurgen Matthaus describes:

> In June 1941 a solution to the Jewish question was still envisioned by the German leadership in terms of forced settlement that, though inherently destructive, did not amount to the systematic mass murder of all Jewish men, women, and children. Precedents set in the early weeks of the Barbarossa campaign would prove crucial in the turn to systematic and total mass murder.[1]

By the end of July 1941 the number of Jewish women, children and older men being executed had dramatically increased. Then, as Timothy Snyder states, 'On 31 July 1941 Heydrich secured the formal authority from Göring to formulate the Final Solution.'[2] Christopher Browning confirms this sinister development, stating, 'At the end of the month [July], Göring had authorized Heydrich to prepare "a total solution of the Jewish question in the German sphere of influence in Europe."'[3]

William Shirer presents the text of the message from Göring to Heydrich:

> I herewith commission you [...]to carry out all preparations with regard to ... a *total solution* of the Jewish question in those territories of Europe which are under German influence...
>
> I furthermore charge you to submit to me as soon as possible a draft

---

[1] Jurgen Matthaus, 'Operation Barbarossa and the onset of the Holocaust', in Browning, *Origins*, p. 253.
[2] Snyder, p. 188.
[3] Browning, *Origins*, p. 277. [July] added by the author for clarification.

> showing the ... measures already taken for the execution of the intended *final solution* of the Jewish question.[4]

There was a definite change in the field thereafter, as revealed by Jurgen Matthaus: 'August 15, 1941, marks a caesura in the history of the Holocaust... For on that day and the following, EK 3 in Lithuania for the first time reported the incorporation of children in mass executions.'[5] A line was being crossed and Nazi Germany's solution to 'the Jewish problem' was shifting into Phase Six – systematic genocide.

The horrible reality of Phase Six was further revealed in the Ukrainian capital, Kiev, shortly after it was captured by German forces on 19 September. Between 29-30 September *Einsatz* and other German units, along with local Ukrainian collaborators, executed some 34,000 Jewish people at a place named Babi Yar. The man responsible was SS commander Paul Blobel.[6]

This was most definitely not just Jewish men of a certain age group, but Jewish males of all ages, as well as Jewish women of all ages - and children. It may well have been part of the Hunger Plan policy – but it was not the Gentile residents being executed, just the Jewish residents, and they weren't being starved to death, but shot.

This event indicates clearly that Phase Six, the plan to totally destroy the Jewish population in the Soviet Union - and elsewhere – had begun. In the conquered regions of the Soviet Union, the *Einsatzgruppen*, Police Battalions and other components of the murder squads at this point visited hundreds of villages where Jewish people lived. They either shot the Jewish people in the town itself (usually at the Jewish cemetery), or in most instances took them into the nearby forest and executed them there.

Father Patrick Desbois, a Roman Catholic priest and professor honoured for his documentation of the Holocaust, carried out extensive research in Ukraine and located hundreds of execution locations where over a million Ukrainian Jews had been murdered. There were more who were executed by

---

[4] Shirer, p. 964, citing NCA, pp. 525-26 (ND, 710, PS.) Italics in Shirer.
[5] Jurgen Matthaus, p. 283. EK 3 = *Eintsatzkommando* 3, from *Einsatzgruppe* A.
[6] Desbois, F. *The Holocaust by Bullets*, (St. Martin's Griffin, New York: 2008), p. 153.

shooting in Belarus, Russia and other former Soviet republics.[7]

Further implementation of Phase Six

Germany's initial decisive victories in the Soviet Union gave rise to new possibilities concerning the Jewish people. On one hand more and more indiscriminate murders of Jews were taking place, and on the other hand there was now a greater opportunity for deporting Jewish people from the Reich to the East.

By August Heydrich and Goebbels were pressuring Hitler to officially permit the deportation of Jewish people from Germany.[8] At first Hitler withheld deportation permission. However, during meetings in Berlin on 16-17 September, which coincided with decisive victories in the Soviet Union, Hitler altered his position and agreed to begin deporting German Jews to the East.[9] Himmler stated in a letter to Arthur Greiser, a senior SS leader, who was then in Lodz, that Hitler's desire was 'that the Old Reich and Protectorate be emptied and freed of Jews from west to east as quickly as possible.' Himmler explained to Greiser that this was the first step 'in order to deport them yet further to the east next spring.'[10]

At this very time the marking decree was enacted. From 19 September Jews in Germany were required to wear the Star of David armband, thereby marking them out from the rest of the German population. Goldhagen stated of such an edict: 'The effects of this were obvious... wearing such a visible target among such a hostile populace also caused Jews to feel acute insecurity, and ... Jews, especially Jewish children, suffered increased verbal and physical assaults.'[11]

The situation for the German Jews deteriorated further when, on 6 October 1941, Hitler himself stated: 'All Jews have to be removed from the Protec-

---

[7] Ibid. Paul A Shapiro states in the Foreword of *The Holocaust by Bullets,* p. vii, that 'over 1.5 million had already been murdered by the Germans and their Axis allies and local collaborators in the towns and villages of Ukraine, Belarus, Russia, and other republics of the USSR.'

[8] Browning, *Origins*, p. 318.

[9] Ibid., p. 325.

[10] Himmler to Greiser, 18 September 1941, cited in Browning, *Origins*, pp. 325-6, n. 63.

[11] Goldhagen, p. 138.

torate not only to the General Government, but straight on to the east.'[12] Those Jews being deported were to be sent to Lodz, Minsk (Belarus) and Riga (Estonia). These were supposedly mere holding stations until the time was right to deport them 'further east'.

The first deportation trains left from Vienna on 15 October and from Prague on 16 October. These initial trains went to Lodz. The deportees were to be held there over the winter before being deported further East the following spring. Other transports of approximately 1,000 people each were sent to Minsk (Belarus) from 11 November onwards and to Riga (Latvia) from 19 November.[13] Following some military objections the anticipated number of these transports was decreased.

In the midst of all these developments Himmler, on 18 October 1941, informed Heydrich that henceforth there would be: "No emigration by Jews to overseas."[14] On 23 October the emigration of Jewish people from Europe officially ended. There was now no escape whatsoever for the Jews under Nazi German control. Their fate had been sealed.

Mass murder also in the General Government region

While Jewish people from the Reich were being moved to the East, mass murder of Soviet Jews continued. In October such murders began in the regions of the General Government.

David Kahane recorded how he was alerted to just such a massacre at Stanislawow, only 130 kilometres south of Lwow, by a woman who had managed to escape from there. She related that: 'Almost all Jews in the town were shot. Once Stanislawow ghetto had been practically emptied of its residents, the Germans started bringing Jews in from the surrounding townships and villages until there were no Jews left in the entire district. The Jewish graveyard in Stanislawow turned into one huge mass grave.'[15] Some 10,000 Jewish people were murdered in this 'Bloody Sunday' massacre of 12 October 1941 - a harbinger of things to come.

---

12 Browning, *Origins,* p. 328, n. 73.
13 Browning, *Origins,* pp. 332-3.
14 Himmler to Heydrich, 18 October 1941, cited in Browning, *Origins,* p. 369, citing footnote 278.
15 Kahane, p. 41.

Developing more 'humane' ways to murder Jewish people

Heinrich Himmler visited the 'killing fields' of the East in the summer of 1941, and on 15 August observed an execution of Jewish men and partisans near Minsk in Belarus. Following this execution Himmler spoke with several Nazi commanders 'about the possibility of killing methods other than shooting.'[16] Shockingly, part of the reasoning behind this request was connected to the mental well-being of the German executioners!

One major method pursued thereafter was the use of gas, and involved utilising the expertise of those participating in the T-4 euthanasia programme. This programme involved the murder of various types of physically and mentally incapacitated people in Germany. It was named T-4 due to the location where they initially operated from, Number 4 Tiergarten Street, Berlin. Some 70,273 German citizens had already been murdered in this way, but due to courageous public opposition led by the Catholic Bishop of Munster, Clemens August Count von Galen, this euthanasia programme was significantly impeded in late August 1941.[17]

The virtual cessation of the programme now left a body of scientists who had gained considerable expertise in gassing large numbers of people without a task. Some of these scientists were then employed by the SS to develop gas vans in which large numbers of people could be killed by using carbon monoxide. Such gas vans could be taken to various locations in the East.

Other forms of gassing were also experimented with, primarily in order to be used at a stationary location, such as a concentration camp. These experiments included the use of Zyklon B, a cyanide-based insecticide which was used on Soviet POWs and some Jews at a former Polish army barracks in Ocwiecim (renamed Auschwitz) in the region of Silesia.

The result of these experimentations meant that by the end of 1941 three components were converging in the context of the Nazi solution to 'the Jewish problem' of Europe:

1. the use of the concentration camp system;
2. the application of these new more efficient and 'humane' killing mech-

---

[16] Browning, *Origins*, p. 283.

[17] USHMM, Euthanasia Programme, www.ushmm.org.

anisms;

3. and the combined experience of the various Nazi institutions and entities who had gained experience in moving large numbers of people.

Order for a death camp at Belzec to be established

That a line had been crossed by October 1941 is apparent when viewing certain events then occurring. The mass murder at Stanislawow on 12 October (and there were other smaller killings in the region of Galicia) was one such event. Then on 13 October Odilo Globocnik, SS commander and Police Chief based at Lublin, received orders to begin construction of a mass extermination camp near the small village of Belzec, west of Lwow. Construction began on 1 November 1941.[18]

During the same period preparations began on other specialised camps at Chelmno (named Kulmhof by the Germans), north-west of Lodz (named Litzmannstadt by the Germans); at Sobibor, east of Lublin; and at Treblinka, east of Warsaw. Additionally the Auschwitz Camp was to be enlarged, and a second camp was to be built nearby, known as Auschwitz II or Birkenau.

Bazyli and Anna survive

This oppressive chain of events meant there was now no chance at all for any Jew to survive – unless they were hidden by sympathetic Gentiles, or managed to find some other ingenious way of surviving. While Bazyli was being hidden by a member of the local Evangelical congregation, he was safe, and while Anna could maintain the ruse of being a Polish woman, she too was safe. However the daily tension they were under must have been extremely difficult to bear.

Jakob Jocz wrote later that after the German soldiers billeted in Anna and Bazyli's home had been sent to the front, one man with an administrative job stayed behind.[19] Anna told more of the story:

> Among other people, a postman named Mathes was designated to live at my house. He was an older man that I did not get along with very well. I had fur coats and other precious garments that I could not leave in the

---

[18] Browning, *Origins*, pp. 359-360.

[19] Memorandum regarding reparation from the German Government of Mrs. Anna Jocz, deceased. By Jacob Jocz. No date, German File, p. 1.

kitchen and so I hid them under his divan. Once, he drove to Germany for a vacation and someone developed suspicions concerning my situation. So they ordered a house search. In the room where Mathes stayed, they found my things. Thereupon someone screamed at me that I had hid Jewish property and slapped me so violently in the face that I fell. After that the state of my health significantly deteriorated but I was resilient, after all I still had to feed my husband.[20]

Anna hides a young Jewish girl named Roma Piotrowska

Yet despite these hardships Anna was still able to perform an act of great heroism. In an envelope belonging to Anna which is now part of the Jocz Private Collection are a set of photographs. On the envelope are written these words:

> Mother Jocz kept this girl hidden during the Nazi occupation of Lwow (Lemberg). She survived the persecution & is now happily married.

Inside are several photographs of the young girl in question, Roma Piotrowska. That she survived, in part due to Anna's care, is revealed by other photos in the envelope: Roma with her husband on her wedding day; one of her husband; one of her as a young lady with a group of young people, possibly her confirmation; and also one of her in an orchestra where she is obviously the lead singer. Roma married in 1960 in Wroclaw and became Roma Dominik.[21]

How, where and exactly when Anna hid Roma are not known, but this matter provides further evidence that Anna Jocz was one remarkable woman.

Life in the Warsaw Ghetto

Throughout this very same period life was becoming increasingly difficult for the 350,000 or so surviving Jewish people in the Warsaw Ghetto.[22] The five thousand or so Jewish Christians in the Ghetto were for the most part enduring the same conditions, except that for some time they received extra support from the Roman Catholic Church.[23] But their ultimate fate would be the same as all other Jews.

[20] Statutory Declaration of Anna Jocz, Toronto, 8 January 1959, German File, p. 55.

[21] Information from Jocz Private Collection.

[22] Some 100,000 Jewish people died while in the Ghetto.

[23] For some time the Roman Catholic charity, Caritis, operated in the ghetto.

A small number of these Jewish Christians, though, received better treatment especially if they were in the *Judenrat* and Jewish Order Service (Police). One who was despised was Jozef Szerynski, a self-hating Jew and one time commandant of the Jewish Police. Tragically the actions of some non-Aryan Christians such as Szerynski only strengthened the perception in the Warsaw Ghetto that converts were enemies of the Jewish people. There seems little evidence though of other instances where a noticeable number of non-Aryan Christians cooperated with the Germans.

One of the assimilated Jewish Christians who was quite well received was the medical scientist Ludwik Hirszfeld, who offered his services to assist the distressed of the Ghetto. Hirszfeld 'discovered' his faith while in the Ghetto. He wrote: 'Never had I such close contact with the church as when I lived in the Jewish district. For a year, every day, morning and evening, I soaked up the atmosphere of quiet in the church.... On Sunday all Christians – not only Catholics, went to Mass.'[24]

It seems too that there was some kind of a revival within the Ghetto. Hirszfeld also wrote: 'Many people were baptized in the district – both older and younger people, sometimes even entire families. Among them were some of my students, both men and women. Sometimes I was invited to be the godfather. What motives could they have had? No profit was to be had: the change of faith in no way changed their legal status. No – they were drawn by the charm of religion...'[25]

In 1943 Hirszfeld was offered the opportunity of escaping from the Ghetto, together with his wife and sick child. He accepted the offer. While in hiding he compiled his recollections of life in the Warsaw Ghetto, and it is partly due to his narrative that we have first-hand information relating to the Jewish Christian community in the Ghetto.

Ultimately though there were very few survivors from that community, they were almost completely wiped out in the unfolding events.

---

[24] Hirszfeld, p. 363 and n.22.
[25] Ibid, p. 365.

Chapter 18

The final solution to 'the Jewish Problem'

The Reich's Chancellory meeting and Wannsee Conference

The new, 'humane' approach to the solving of 'the Jewish problem' was close to being fully developed by the end of 1941. What the Nazi leadership now needed was to have this plan officially activated, in order to implement their final solution, not just in the Soviet Union and Poland, but in all of Europe.

Hitler provided the lead for this by summoning a meeting of the leading Nazis to his private office in the Chancellory on 12 December 1941. After alluding to his 'prophecy' of 1939, Hitler then stated, as Joseph Goebbels wrote in his diary: 'The world war is here, the destruction of the Jews must be the inevitable consequence.'[1]

Although Hitler never supposedly gave written orders concerning the murder of the Jewish people, his desires were being acted upon by the end of 1941 by his adjutants.

This comprehensive plan for the destruction of the Jewish people was then outlined at a high level meeting in a mansion in the outer Berlin suburb of Wannsee on 20 January 1942. The meeting was presided over by deputy-SS head Reinhard Heydrich, together with his assistant Adolf Eichmann, and included the heads of many of the German governmental departments.

The meeting concluded with a decisive endorsement of the plan to murder all eleven million Jews in Europe – and surrounding regions. All levels of German bureaucracy were now implicated in this plan. Thereafter not only were the Jewish people living under German occupation in the Soviet Union in danger – but all Jews everywhere. This included the Jocz family in Lwow.

Following the Wannsee Conference more precise planning occurred relating to how the Jews of Europe were to be murdered. There were four major

---

[1] Diary of Joseph Goebbels, cited in Browning, *Origins*, p. 407.

ways in which this plan was to be fulfilled:

- Despite the need for a more 'humane' and 'mechanised' form of murder, the murder squads would continue shooting Jewish people in the occupied regions of the Soviet Union. This method would also be employed in Poland as well from 1942 onwards as part of *Operation Reinhardt.*
- The majority of the Jewish people living in central, southern and western Europe would be sent to Auschwitz camp. Some also went to Sobibor and other locations.
- The 200,000-300,000 or so Jewish people in the annexed part of Poland, most of whom were now inside the Lodz Ghetto, were to be taken to a large mansion in the village of Kulmhof (Chelmno). They were then to be placed in gas wagons which would be driven to a nearby forest. By the time the vans arrived at the destination the occupants would be dead. The bodies would then be buried in mass graves in the forest. Chelmno had actually been operating since December 1941.
- The two million or so Jewish people in the General Government area, which included Lwow, were to be annihilated in an operation named *Operation Reinhardt.* They would either be shot by execution squads, or transported to and murdered at Treblinka, Sobibor and Belzec death camps. The first of these camps to be operational was Belzec.[2]

Hitler's 'prophecy' of 30 January 1939 was being fulfilled, not through relocation to Lublin, or Madagascar, or to any literal East, but to a metaphoric 'East', which was a SS euphemism meaning death.

Operation Reinhardt and deportation from the Lwow Ghetto

The administrative centre of *Operation Reinhardt* was based at Lublin, which became a large SS dominated city. It did not take long before Lwow felt the consequences of this final Phase in the Nazi solution to 'the Jewish problem.'

The round-up and deportation of Jews to a death camp was known as an *Aktion.* In what became known as the March *Aktion,* Jewish people in Lwow were assembled at the Sobieski school building and then taken to the city's

[2] The above information has been gleaned from numerous sources, including the Wannsee House Historic Display; Yad Vashem, Jerusalem; the Documentation Center Nazi Party Rally Grounds, Nuremberg; as well as historic displays at the Death Camps of Auschwitz, Treblinka, Belzec and Chelmno.

Kleparow train station. Kahane wrote: 'They were loaded onto cars and the train departed. To where? For the time being, no one knew its destination.'[3] This *Aktion* continued for two weeks and ended at Passover. Altogether some 15,000 people were 'relocated.'

Relocated to where? 'Slowly the bitter truth, the terrible secret', wrote Kahane, 'filtered back to us. Railroad workers who worked on that train revealed to us that the victims had been transported to Belzec, near Rawa Ruska.'[4] Belzec, Kahane explained, was a small station on the Lwow-Warsaw line. He continued:

> In the woods some distance from the township the Germans had erected many shacks and buildings, giving the impression of a camp. They surrounded the place with a high, impenetrable fence, reinforced with barbed wire. Off the main railroad they built a siding leading to the camp. Upon arrival at Belzec station, the train stopped and the engine driver and his assistants disembarked. A German driver climbed in and drove the train into the camp. On the same day he drove the empty train back to Belzec station. The Jews disappeared into the camp and were never seen again.[5]

Although at that time there were no survivors, no escapees, from this camp to tell others what was happening, it soon became clear that death awaited those who disembarked from those trains at Belzec. Kahane summarised the situation thereafter: 'After the March *Aktion* the Jews of Lvov never knew peace again. Disasters came in rapid succession, one following close on the heels of the preceding one. It could be said that until June 1943 when the ghetto was finally liquidated, we lived in the midst of one large continuous pogrom.'[6]

During the months after the March *Aktion* many thousands of Jews were taken away to slave labour camps, foremost being the Janowska Camp, where a very large number were treated mercilessly. Life in the Lwow Ghetto was no better. Kahane paints a picture of what ghetto life consisted of:

---

[3] Kahane, p. 44.
[4] Ibid., p. 47.
[5] Ibid.
[6] Ibid., p. 48.

> Early in the morning, between five and half past six, the whole Jewish district comes to life. All streets turn into rivers of people on their way to work. Haggard, emaciated by hunger, dressed in tatters, they move on. Everyone carries a knapsack or a pouch with bread. Ninety percent of this living matter streaming nervously through the ghetto streets and alleys have blue swollen faces and blue rings, swollen like pillows, around their eyes. Their bodies are simply bloated by hunger. Their daily diet consists of 70 grams of bread and a plate of thin, lukewarm, watery soup cooked by their wives at home… Between 7:00 A.M. and 5:00 P.M. no living soul can be seen on the streets…
>
> At five in the evening the ghetto comes back to life. Slowly the streets fill up with workers returning home. Oh, Lord, how terrible are their countenances! Worn out and tormented, their eyes are almost invisible in their swollen faces. They pass slowly, dragging their feet, stopping to rest against the wall. Most terrible of all is the appearance of young boys… skin and bones, skeletons wrapped up in bloated skins…[7]

This was the environment in which Bazyli, Anna, Pawel and Elzbieta Jocz were living, and having to somehow survive in. When one considers that Bazyli had been beset by poor health in the previous years it must have been an incredible ordeal for him to be living in a rodent infested wood shed during these months – and ultimately years.

For Anna it must have been a constant ordeal - somehow aiding Bazyli without drawing attention to his whereabouts, and at the same time maintaining her own guise as an ordinary Polish housekeeper. At this stage the whereabouts of Jan was unclear, but most likely he was in a labour camp, perhaps in Germany.

Concerning those trying to escape the encircling rope, Kahane states:

> Under Nazi rule … No apostasy could help. Every Jew, or apostate, or descendent of Jews down to the third generation was under the sentence of death, and all had to disappear from this world. A Jew seeking to save his life had to vanish and resurface as an Aryan or a "100% Aryan." This feat could be accomplished by means of forged documents called Aryan

[7] Ibid., p. 52.

> papers. Individuals lacking characteristically Jewish facial features and gesticulation and having a fluent command and unaccented pronunciation of Polish or Ukrainian arranged for themselves a set of forged documents: birth and marriage certificates, an old Polish passport, a special document testifying to the Aryan origins of its bearer, and a certificate of residence approved by the police....
>
> Those Jews who stood no chance of passing as Aryans due to their characteristically Jewish appearance or accent, or because they wouldn't dare to live as Aryans, endeavoured to hide in the houses of Aryan acquaintances for astronomical sums of money. They buried themselves behind walls to hide from German eyes.
>
> I doubt whether anyone is capable of understanding the feelings of these phony Aryans or of those hiding in mouse burrows, waiting for the defeat of Hitler. A passing car, a stir, a suspicious noise sent shivers down their spines, their hearts would start thumping, their imaginations would go wild, and their limbs go numb. And, in fact, only a handful of these phony Aryans survived to the end of the war. All powers joined against the Jew.[8]

A similar situation was now also confronting all the other non-Aryan Christians and Jewish people who were living in the Warsaw Ghetto, including Jerzy Jocz, if indeed he was incarcerated in the Ghetto which seems likely at this time.

Mass executions throughout the region

While tens of thousands of Polish Jews were being sent to Chelmno, Belzec, Sobibor and later Treblinka, many more were still being shot in the forests of Belarus, Ukraine and elsewhere. Jewish Christians were not exempt, as can be seen from the story of the Lubtshanski family, who were executed in the forest near Leida in Belarus on 8 May 1942.

A Polish Baptist minister named Rev. Niamolowski was then the minister in Leida (and later in 1946 was in Lodz), and told Fanny Rosenberg after the War:

> In the town of Leida, I had the privilege of fellowship with Brother and

[8] Ibid., pp. 54-55.

> Sister L. When the Germans occupied our town, the Jews there were used for all kinds of manual and hard labor. Brother and Sister L, too, worked hard. While working in the officer's canteen, the commandant, a Lt General, took a fancy to Br. L., who always did any job he was asked to do, without resentment, willingly and with a smile. The Gestapo, however, decided to destroy the Jews. The General tried to protect the Lubcianski family, but to no avail. This became known to the L's – but, praise God, they were prepared to meet the Lord. I shall never forget when shortly before they were assassinated, I was summoned to their home. Mr L. said, "Br. M., I have a great desire to partake of the Lord's Supper, which will be the last for us on earth." It was a most solemn event to commune with Hebrew Christians upon such an occasion.
>
> After our celebration at the Lord's table, dear Paul, embracing his only child, a girl of twelve years said, 'Darling Elizabeth, our hours or minutes are counted. When they shoot at us, do not cry. As soon as you hear the shooting, we will be with the Lord Jesus."
>
> Pastor M. could not continue further. Tears choked his voice and the last phrase was: 'Brother and Sister Lubcianski and child were killed shortly after that. They were shot.'[9]

On another occasion Rev Niamilowski again testified:

> I was eager to have the details of the execution. This is what I was told by a friendly policeman. Who was one of the guards at the place. He related the story about this Jewish couple with a little girl of about eight or nine years. The father of the child pleaded with the officer to permit him to die together with his wife and child. He said, "We are Hebrew Christians. We belong together." This tragic plea was granted. The father stood on one side, the mother on the other both holding the hands of their darling, Elizabeth. At the open grave, they bowed their heads in prayer. While still praying, they were machine-gunned, and the three fell into the grave.
>
> All the Jewish inhabitants of the ghetto, in Lida, numbering about six thousand men, women and children, were doomed to die. They were

---

[9] *The Bethel Witness,* European American Bethel Mission, Vol 10, No 1 & 2 1946, pp. 22-23.

> driven into the woods where graves had been prepared for them. These deep trenches were dug by Jews who were compelled to do it. When these masses arrived at the places, parents were ordered to undress their little children and to throw them into the grave. There the little bodies were torn by grenades. Fathers, mothers, brothers, sisters were obliged to undress and were driven to the edge of the trenches. Then machine-guns mowed them down.[10]

News of the murder of another prominent Hebrew Christian leader was broadcast by the IHCA in the July 1942 edition of *The Hebrew Christian* which stated: 'It was with deep sorrow that we received word from the Barbican Mission to the Jews that news had reached them via America of the death of Rev. Peter Gorodishz.'[11]

Mass murder of Jewish Christians in Chelmno

Apart from those associated with the Bethel Mission there were other Jewish Christians in the Lodz Ghetto. According to Andrzej Grzegorczyk, from the Radegast Ghetto Museum in Lodz, a group of some 260 German speaking Jewish Christians arrived in October-November 1941.[12] In this group there were some 150 Roman Catholics and 100 Lutherans who came from Berlin, Vienna and Prague. They had their own worship place, located on Jakuba 6 and their first service was held there on 24 December 1941.[13]

The *Bethel Witness* recorded about the Hebrew Christian community:

> Under God's Providence, the ghetto, Litzmanstadt, became a great center for Hebrew Christians, who were banished there with other Jews in 1940 and 1941 from countries occupied by the Nazis. Being treated as the other Jews, they were permitted to gather for their services. They, although belonging to different Protestant denominations, as well as a considerable number of Jewish Catholics, flocked about our missionaries with whom they had several services during the week. As the latter needed a different approach, and in order to talk to them freely of the one thing needful,

---

[10] *The Bethel Witness,* Vol 12, No 1 1947, pp. 18-19.

[11] *The Hebrew Christian,* Volume XV, April 1942-January 1943, p. 61.

[12] Conversation with Andrzej Grzegorczyk from the Radegast Ghetto Museum, Lodz, 27 July 2019.

[13] Obviously the remaining ten belonged to other denominations.

chiefly in the Polish tongue, our missionaries arranged special meetings for them. Many of the Catholic Jews were saved.[14]

In the following months a number of these people most likely died due to the privations of life in the Ghetto (over 40,000 people died of starvation and executions during the existence of the Ghetto). Grzegorczyk stated that between 4-15 May 1942 some 10,000 Jews were sent to Chelmno Death Camp. Within this number were the remnants of this group of 260 – who all went to their deaths together.[15] These Jewish Christians, together with those associated with the Bethel Mission were part of the 200,000 - 300,000 Jews who were murdered at Chelmno.

The deportations begin from the Warsaw Ghetto

On 22 July 1942 the Nazi high command sent the first of some 265,000 Jews from the *Umschlagplatz* railway station on the edge of the Warsaw Ghetto 'to the East.' This first transport, and subsequent transports until September 1942, did go East, but only as far as the specially build death camp near the village of Treblinka. There the occupants were unloaded and while a handful were selected to assist the Germans with some tasks, the vast majority were forced to undress and then were taken to the gas chambers. Afterwards their bodies were cremated.

Within that vast sea of humanity were the majority of the approximately 5,200 non-Aryan Christians who were in the Ghetto. These belonged to perhaps six of the seven categories mentioned in the Introduction. Victor Weisman and his family were among these, as well as the majority of the Hebrew Christian congregation from the Emmanuel Church. Additionally there were those associated with Roman Catholic parish churches in the Ghetto, especially All Saints, and other Jewish Christians including Nathan Sendyk, former head of the Mildmay Mission in Warsaw.

Roger Allison, who had remained in Romania until the German occupation in 1941 and then hurriedly left for Palestine, wrote concerning the Jewish Christians in Warsaw:

---

[14] *The Bethel Witness,* Vol 10, No 1 & 2 1946, p. 22. In this context 'saved' probably referred to these Jewish Catholics having been nominal and not having previously converted for reasons of conviction.

[15] Conversation with Andrzej Grzegorczyk.

> There never came further news from our fellow-workers in Warsaw. Most of them would have been shut up within the walls of the Ghetto, where without doubt they would have been 'faithful unto death' giving encouragement to their perhaps more fearful and suffering Jewish brethren. They left behind the tenderest, kindliest memories.[16]

News later reached Britain of Weisman's death and his obituary was published in the *Jewish Missionary Intelligence*, written by Martin Parsons:

> News has been received from Warsaw of the death of our senior worker there, Mr. Wiktor Weisman. No details are known. Mr. Weisman was a convert of the Mission and was baptized while on a visit to Palestine by the Rev. A. C. Martin. When he afterwards entered the service of the Mission he became one of its most devoted workers. Humble and retiring by nature, he could nevertheless become fired with holy zeal when preaching the Gospel or leading in prayer. As the administrator of the Mission House, the chauffeur on mission journeys, or the general helper of all in practical matters, he was highly efficient. But it is as a friend that many of us will always think of him. His was a lovable nature, and he responded to friendship. He was loyal to the core to his colleagues, his Church and his God. The writer and many others are the richer for having known him. If his wife and little boy are still living, theirs will be a lonely path, and we remember them in prayer. M.P.[17]

Weisman's wife and little boy also perished. Presumably all three were sent to Treblinka. Like the other death camps, estimates vary as to how many Jewish people were murdered at Treblinka. Numbers range from 700,000 to 925,000, which is the number given by the United States Holocaust Memorial Museum (USHMM).

The August *Aktion* in Lwow

In the weeks leading up to the middle of August a number of signs indicated that another *Aktion* was about to take place in Lwow. One of the signs was the visit of Governor Hans Frank, and another was the nullification of the coveted *Melde-karte* - work permit.

---

[16] Allison, *Journey*, p. 15.

[17] *JMI*, November 1943, p. 14.

Many understood the signs and made haste to either escape or hide. One of those was Rabbi Kahane, who approached Archbishop Sheptytsky. The aging Archbishop agreed to hide him, as well as to harbouring children. Concerning the children, Kahane recorded of the Archbishop's comment: 'As for saving our children, he stated his willingness to accept little boys and girls immediately, although it would be difficult to shelter circumcised boys.'[18] One of those little girls would be Kahane's three year old daughter who would be cared for at a convent. She would need to become what Kahane called 'a phony Gentile.'

Before Kahane himself could get to the Archbishop's palace he was rounded up in the *Aktion* which began on 10 August. Thousands of people were rounded up and taken to the Janowska Camp. There they were separated, with the able-bodied being kept for labour and the remainder being taken to the Kleparow railway station – and from thence to Belzec. This *Aktion* continued for some twenty-one days, during which time some 50,000 people were sent to Belzec.[19] None survived.

At one point, the SS Police chief, General Katzmann, 'warned the Aryan residents of Lvov against sheltering Jews and threatened such persons with severe punishment,' Kahane wrote. But, 'It turned out that many Aryans displayed compassion and sympathy for the tormented Jews.'[20] One of those brave people was the man who sheltered Bazyli Jocz in his wood shed – under the threat of severe punishment.

Kahane provided evidence of what would happen to those caught hiding: 'Night came and the streets were a little safer. People started leaving their burrows. We learned of terrible things. There were many victims. All those discovered in hiding were shot on the spot.'[21]

Pawel Jocz becomes a cook in a German camp

It is not clear what happened to Pawel Jocz after he recommended Roman Frister's mother to Kurt Brinker and the Jewishness of the Fristers was exposed. Was he able to continue working for a while as a Protestant pastor?

---

[18] Kahane, p. 59.
[19] Ibid., p. 72. Kahane says it was 60,000.
[20] Ibid., p. 71
[21] Ibid., p. 63.

Or did Brinker hold him in some way responsible for concealing the Fristers' Jewishness? Roger Allison perhaps provides a clue:

> For it was then that Paul … wheedled his way as cook into the mess of a Nazi military unit in the town. He looked Polish and spoke the language perfectly. In that employment, listening to the conversation of the soldiers, he received 'intelligence' information about forth-coming operations to round up Jews in specific areas which he was able to pass on and thus, at least temporarily, save the lives of many of his Jewish compatriots.[22]

One such *Aktion* which Paul may have informed the residents of the Lwow Ghetto about was in November 1942. Some 15,000 Jewish people were taken away during that *Aktion*, the majority to Belzec. Once again there were no survivors, and once again Bazyli, Anna, Pawel and Elzbieta were spared. Interestingly at this very time another Jocz was entering into the world when Joan gave birth to young Mary.

It was also in November that Rabbi Kahane, (with his wife and child already being cared for as 'phony Gentiles', by the nuns of the Greek Catholic Church), was sent to the notorious Janowska Camp. This vast complex on Janowska Street was nothing short of hell on earth.

Two types of Christians

One day while in the Janowska Camp, Kahane and his work crew walked past the Roman Catholic Church of Saint Anna just as the worshippers were exiting. It was 24 December 1942. Kahane recalls that upon seeing the Jewish slaves, the exiting congregants quickly sang a chorus to the tune of 'Glory on high and peace reigns on earth', but inserted these words: 'Glory on high, they broke the Jews' bones, and peace reigns on earth.'[23]

Rabbi Kahane was witnessing before his very eyes what most Jewish people perceived to be the true face of Christianity. Yet his wife and daughter were also being hidden by Christians, as he too would soon be. One could well imagine that this would be both a mental torment and a challenge for him. Similarly, one could well imagine the mental torment the Jewish Christians experienced, such as the Jocz family, when they also witnessed such events

---

[22] Allison, *Journey*, pp. 14-15.
[23] Kahane, p. 103.

and attitudes.

Several months previously the Nazis had begun deporting Jewish people from the Netherlands 'to the East.' The Roman Catholic Archbishop of the Netherlands Johannes de Jong and other Protestant Church leaders took a strong stand against this Nazi order.

The Nazi authorities then put tremendous pressure upon these leaders to back-off from their stance. Some Protestant leaders remained firm in their opposition. Archbishop de Jong took the strongest stance. In response, and in order to reveal to all who was really in charge, the Nazis ordered the immediate round up of dozens of Jewish Catholics, including nuns and monks. Within a matter of days over one hundred Jewish Catholics had been murdered at Auschwitz, including Edith Stein, and five members of the Lob family.

At about this time another profound article by Jakob was printed by *The Hebrew Christian,* entitled 'The Christian Church and the Jewish People in Nazi-occupied Europe.' Few people could grasp the dynamics of what was happening in Europe between the Nazis on one hand and the Church on the other, as well as Jakob could.

In reference to the Nazi attitude in Germany, Jakob stated: 'A recent document which is connected with the name of Alfred Rosenberg puts the aim of the Nazi Party "to extirpate by all possible methods the Christian faith introduced in the year of disgrace 800."'[24]

Jakob was highlighting how the Nazis aimed at completely neutralising the Church in Germany, and throughout Europe. For Christians, he stated, there were but two possibilities - apostasy or persecution. Nazism, he wrote 'cannot tolerate ... the spiritual independence of the Church', which is, Jakob said 'a constant challenge to its own existence. To it the Church can only be a servant to the State. We stand before the clash of two totalitarian claims diametrically opposed to each other: the claim of Christ and the claim of Hitler.'[25]

---

[24] *The Hebrew Christian,* Volume XV, April 1942-January 1943, p. 75. The year 800 AD being when Charlemagne was crowned emperor and Roman Catholicism officially received into Germany.
[25] Ibid., p. 76.

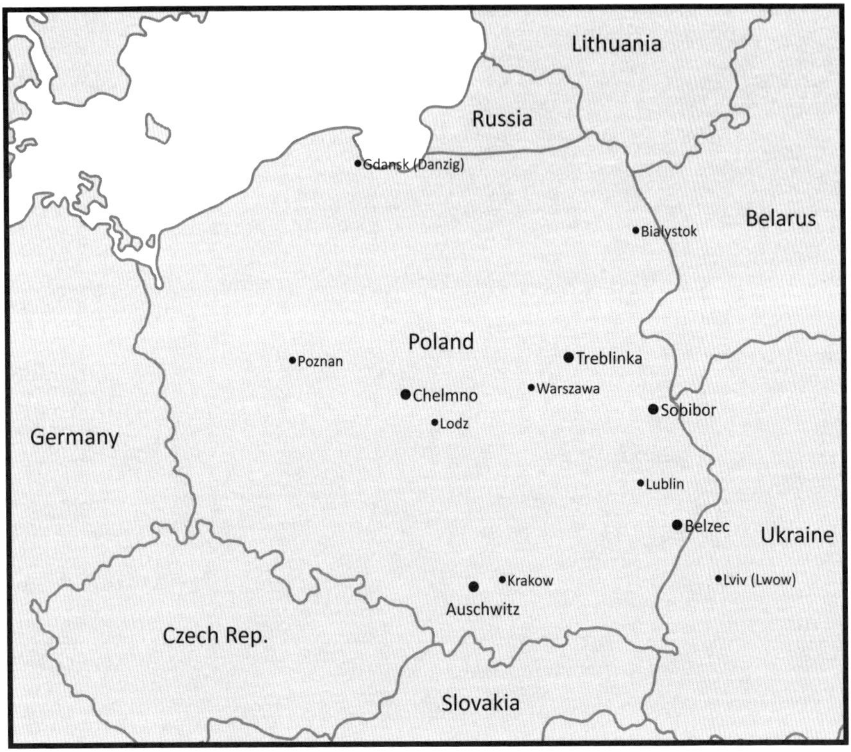

Locations of death camps
(Map of contemporary Poland)

Chapter 19

The death of Bazyli

Surviving through 1943

The final major round-up or *Aktion* at the Lwow Ghetto occurred between 5-7 January 1943, when a further 15,000 or more Jewish people were sent to their deaths at Belzec.[1] By this time the vast majority of the Jewish people in greater Poland had been murdered by the Nazis. Village after village, city after city, region after region was being decreed *Judenrein* – Jew-free. *Operation Reinhardt* was slowly coming to an end.

For those still alive, either in hiding or in the few ghettos and labour camps still existing, the next danger to survive was the winter of 1942-43. It was this winter that the German Army also had to survive in the far eastern region of the front line. Then came news of the surrender of the huge German Army at Stalingrad on 2 February 1943. It was now just a matter of time before deliverance would come.

The Warsaw Ghetto Uprising

Those in Warsaw, however, decided it was time to bring about their own deliverance. After witnessing the thousands of deportees being taken to their deaths at Treblinka many of the remaining 55-60,000 Jews decided to stage an uprising.

As the German troops entered the Ghetto to carry out a deportation on April 19, which happened to be during the time of Passover, they were fired upon. The Warsaw Ghetto uprising had begun. It continued until 13 May. There were a number of Hebrew Christians still in the Ghetto during the uprising. Stasiek Eisenberg and Mr and Mrs Wolfin were among them. Wolfin had been part of that 'happy time together' with Jakob, Viktor Weisman and Pawel back in July 1939.

---

[1] This information is sourced from the United States Holocaust Memorial Museum (USHMM), Washington.

Rachmiel Frydland, who had managed to get into the Ghetto, recorded Stasiek's final days:

> But now as he waited in the small Ghetto, death seemed near. He was in touch with the Jewish underground and had reliable information that within a few days the police would kill the rest of the Jews. The young people prepared to resist in desperation, knowing full well that they could do little against a power that had conquered almost all of Europe. Many of the older people were carrying cyanide to poison themselves instead of being killed in cruel manners by the S.S. Stasiek wanted to know whether he as [a] Christian could join the underground or carry the cyanide poison in his pocket. He wanted to know what was happening outside. Were Christians really singing and rejoicing as though nothing had happened, while cruel Nazis committed atrocities- such as dashing children and babies against the walls, or throwing babies from an upper room for another soldier to catch on their bayonets—just for fun. To these and other questions he put to me I had no answer. I, too, was a new believer and was not able to decide for him;. so I just listened. Then I told him of the decision I had made to stay with him and with the Jewish people in the Ghetto. He did not even want to listen but adjured me not to stay any longer. "Our days are numbered," he said "There is no escape from here."
>
> He felt that since God had kept me safe for such a long time outside the Ghetto that He wanted me to live. Perhaps I was the one destined to tell the story of the Jewish Christians who perished at the hands of people who considered themselves a Christian nation!
>
> I asked if he would join me in living outside the Ghetto, but he felt that his features were too Jewish. He could not exist as I had, by day in cemeteries, churches, or travelling aimlessly, and by night without a sure shelter. He would soon be recognized and made to give an account of how he escaped. If a Christian family would be found to hide him, he would be grateful; - otherwise he preferred to die with the Jewish people…
>
> Stasiek knew only too well what was to happen. The next week-end the Ghetto was aflame. The three or five thousand Jews that remained decided to resist the Nazi armies who came to exterminate them with tanks and airplanes. Though the outcome was certain, they were able to inflict heavy casualties on their exterminators. Stasiek and Mr. and Mrs. Wolfin were

killed as Hebrew Christians had been previously.[2]

When the uprising was finally suppressed the Germans destroyed the Ghetto, symbolically completely destroying the Warsaw Synagogue as the final act. Some 7,000 Jewish people had died in the uprising, and the remaining 50,000 or so were then led away to various camps. Few ultimately survived the War.[3]

The liquidation of the Lwow Ghetto – June 1943

On 23 May David Kahane was informed that the inmates of the Janowska Camp were being liquidated in order to replenish the camp with healthier workers from elsewhere. This was his cue to escape. That night he managed to enter the palace of Archbishop Sheptytsky (known as Jura Mountain and associated with the Church of Saint George) in the centre of Lwow. There he was welcomed and given refuge.[4]

A week later Kahane was moved to a nearby monastery. It was there that one evening two monks came to his room and told him: "There is great tension in the city. Rumours abound about a terrible and dreadful *Aktion*. People talk about the total liquidation of the camp and the ghetto. The Aryan residents are warned not to shelter Jews under pain of death. The Germans are conducting searches in private houses, public buildings, and monasteries. We cannot be certain that they will not search our monastery too." Kahane was led to a secret hiding place in the attic.[5]

Among the hundreds of Jews in hiding at this time were David Kahane (a rabbi) and Bazyli Jocz (a Jewish Christian evangelist). One was secreted away by Greek Catholic monks in a monastery and the other was hidden in a wood shed by a sympathetic Polish Christian. If either were found, they would be shot, as, most likely, would those who harboured them.

The Lwow Ghetto was finally liquidated in June 1943.[6] The Jocz and Kahane

---

[2] Frydland, R. *Joy Cometh in the Morning*, pp. 41-42. It is difficult to reconcile Frydland's figures with the official numbers of those in the Ghetto at that time.

[3] encyclopedia.ushmm.org/content/en/article/warsaw-ghetto-uprising

[4] Kahane, p. 118.

[5] Ibid., p. 129. During this time in hiding Kahane wrote: 'My only reading material consisted of the … Ukrainian newspaper, the Bible, and the New Testament in Delizsch's translation.' Kahane, p. 132.

[6] This information is from the United States Holocaust Memorial Museum (USHMM), Washington.

families were now perhaps even more vulnerable. Their situation, and of those who sheltered them is explained by Rabbi Kahane:

> … The Aryan city residents lived in constant fear, particularly those who sheltered Jews in their homes. Upon discovery of such a hideout the Germans executed both the hiding Jew and their protectors.[7]

The *Judenjagd* – 'Jew Hunt'

Throughout 1943 there were continuing attempts to locate and execute those still in hiding. This was known as the *Judenjagd*, or 'Jew Hunt.' Thousands of Jewish people were hiding in the forests, or like Bazyli, in a wood shed.

Polish historian Jan Grabowski, in his book *Hunt for the Jews,* stated that there were several phases of this operation. Although he was specifically dealing with matters in the region of Dabrowa Tarnowska, the principles were applicable elsewhere. The first phase was in the period immediately after the closing of the ghettos and involved locating bunkers used for hiding within the various ghettos and other hiding places in nearby forests. Concerning those found, he wrote: 'Some Jews were executed on the spot, immediately. Others were taken to the local execution site— usually the nearest Jewish cemetery.'[8]

Grabowski added: 'Jewish and Polish descriptions of this initial phase of the *Judenjagd* testify to the incredible level of violence, which evolved into an orgy of murder. For the local population it was also a lesson of obedience: the Germans were the masters of life and death, and Jewish life had no value at all.'[9]

During this period each day would have been one of constant trepidation for both the Jocz and Kahane families – and those hiding them. Quite unbelievably though, the situation actually got worse. Grabowski continued:

> The first phase of the Jew hunt came to an end as soon as the Jews hidden in bunkers in the ghetto, or those wandering in the nearby woods, had

---

[7] Kahane, p. 132.

[8] Grabowski, Jan. *Hunt for the Jews: Betrayal and Murder in German-Occupied Poland,* (Indiana University Press. Kindle Edition), Kindle Location 1155-1156.

[9] Ibid., Kindle Location 1183-1185.

been discovered and killed. In order to find the rest, the Germans needed new methods and a new strategy. From the German standpoint, this phase (which was to last until the end of the war) required significant involvement of the local Polish population. To achieve their goal, the Germans developed a system of prizes and penalties, and combined it with a constant barrage of propaganda, making the Poles even more sensitive to the "Jewish threat." The system of penalties for hiding Jews has been discussed at length in the historical literature.[10]

The foremost threat was the penalty of death, and although material incentives were also offered to Poles for delivering Jewish hideaways, now more so than ever the death threat hung over any Pole harbouring a Jewish person. This greatly reduced the chance of survival for those Jews who had made it thus far in hiding.

Operation Harvest Festival (Aktion Erntefest)

By the end of 1943 two matters were becoming clear. Firstly, the Germans were being defeated on the battlefield and were being driven back by the Soviets on the Eastern front. Secondly, the Nazis were even more determined to complete Phase Seven of their final solution for 'the Jewish problem.'

By now the vast majority of the Jewish people in Poland and the regions under German control in the East had been murdered. There still remained, though, many thousands in various labour camps. On 3-4 November 1943 the Germans instituted *Operation Harvest Festival* and murdered those still in these labour camps. Some 43,000 Jewish people located in such camps at Majdanek, Poniatowa and Trawniki alone were shot in this operation.[11]

The Soviet Red Army drawing near

It was by now all too evident that the Soviets were soon to cross into Poland. All three of the death camps at Treblinka, Sobibor and Belzec were dismantled and great efforts were made to destroy all evidence of the atrocities the Nazis had perpetrated there. This was part of Himmler's 'Operation 1005', which was directed by the assassin of Babi Yar, SS commander Paul Blobel.

---

[10] Ibid., Kindle Locations 1213-1221.

[11] One can see today the execution site and where the bodies were buried at Majdanek.

News of the Soviet advance brought hope that the surviving Jews had not felt in a long time - for Bazyli as he was facing the harsh winter of 1943-44 in the wood shed, as well as for Anna in her guise as a Polish Gentile, while Pawel and Elzbieta remained safe in whatever disguise they had chosen. Yet despite this change of fortunes for the Germans, they became even more determined to rid the region of all Jewish people. In the monastery where Kahane was hiding, Brother Teodosy informed him that, 'A bunker with hiding Jews was discovered and its occupants shot. In several places Christian families were shot together with the Jews they had been sheltering.'[12] Could the Jocz and Kahane families hold on a little longer?

Bazyli is betrayed

Alas it was not to be. On 28 February 1944 Bazyli was discovered – only a few months away from deliverance. Jakob Jocz wrote later that at some point 'my father quietly rejoined mother, keeping indoors and out of sight.'[13] This visit was obviously of only a very short duration.

Anna Jocz recalled the tragic chain of events at this time:

> In February 1944 we already felt that the Germans would evacuate the city. Many soldiers and civilians left the city and it had gotten around that even the Gestapo prepared to leave. My husband's state had gotten much worse. When I went to visit him he said that he could not bear staying in the room any longer. There were mice and rats that jumped into his hair. Having assumed the worst was already over, I told him to come to the apartment in a few days, since everything would be over soon. He left his room and came home for only one or two days until he said that he had recovered and could return to his hiding place. I told him that I would make him coffee and then he could go. At that moment men in uniform stormed into the house, asked my husband if he was Jocz and he admitted that he was. They searched his body. When they saw that he was a Jew, they arrested him immediately.[14]

---

[12] Kahane, p. 147.

[13] Memorandum regarding reparation from the German Government of Mrs. Anna Jocz, deceased. By Jacob Jocz. No date, p. 1. Jocz Private Collection, File - 'Cries for Help- Hebrew Christians in Poland.'

[14] Statutory Declaration of Anna Jocz, Toronto, 8 January 1959, German File, p. 55.

Like the young boys whom Archbishop Sheptytsky knew would be so difficult to shelter, the mark of circumcision was undeniable evidence of Bazyli's Jewishness. For Bazyli Jocz it mattered not that he had been baptised in a Lutheran Church in Vilna, nor that he had worked for the German Lutheran Church. His faith mattered nothing at all. What mattered was that he was circumcised, and therefore he was Jewish.

Anna continued:

> When my husband was taken away, I fainted. I was unconscious for the whole day. Late at night the men came again and also wanted to arrest me. I could neither move nor speak, but heard one man say they should leave me and they all left. For about three months my whole body was paralyzed. Afterwards, I was able to move my torso, but until this day both of my legs are paralyzed. I suffer from heart disease and acute digestion problems. I am 100% an invalid.[15]

Jakob's account of this event, obviously conveyed to him by Anna, added other details, although some details, especially the date, are not correct:

> I think it was early 1945, a prostitute who regularly visited the German soldier, discovered my father's presence and denounced him to the Gestapo. She did it for gain. The Germans burst into the house, found father's hide-out and began to drag him away. Mother, who was an unusually courageous woman, began to shout: "I am also Jewish, take me with him." She was hit in the face, knocked to the ground and left unconscious. When she came to everyone had left. My father was never seen again.[16]

Bazyli's execution

Following his arrest Bazyli was taken to the local prison. Anna recalled: 'On our street lived a woman, whose brother worked in the prison. He delivered

---

[15] Statutory Declaration of Anna Jocz, Toronto, 8 January 1959, German File, p. 55.

[16] Memorandum regarding reparation from the German Government of Mrs. Anna Jocz, deceased. By Jacob Jocz. No date, p. 1. Jocz Private Collection, File - 'Cries for Help - Hebrew Christians in Poland.' The soldier referred to was most likely the German administrator or postman.

the news that my husband was shot there the following day.'[17]

Several other sources validate that Bazyli Jocz was arrested by the Gestapo on 28 February 1944,[18] and that he was executed by shooting the following day, 29 February 1944, in Lwow.[19] There were also two actual witnesses to these events, namely Janina Derdacka and Ing. Zadislaw, who 'confirmed the killing in Lemberg [Lwow] on the 28th of February as well.'[20]

In their sworn (solemn) declaration they also testified: 'We have always lived in Lemberg, also during the years of the German occupation in 1941-1944. We knew that the claimant and her husband Basilius Jocz were baptized Jews. Mrs. Jocz disguised herself to be an aryan while her husband Mr. Jocz hid himself. However, in 1944 he was found, taken to the prison and shot. We also remember that after these events the claimant was paralyzed.'[21]

Anna's severe injuries

Anna may have had some health problems resulting from her fall in the village when she was young – the fall associated with her father encountering the Hebrew New Testament in Dr Frohwein's surgery. However, the physical violence she was subjected to by the Gestapo agents resulted in her receiving very severe injuries. Jakob later recorded concerning his mother's injuries: 'As a result of shock and injury mother remained paralysed from the hip down for the rest of her life. She was confined to a wheelchair and required constant medical attention.'[22]

Some years later when Jakob was attempting to receive compensation from the German Government, a doctor by the name of Dr Irene Moore testified: 'Basilius Jocz was arrested and shot by the Germans because he was of Jew-

---

17 Solemn declaration from Anna Jocz, German File, p. 55.

18 Rocholl to Pozel, 20 January 1959, German File, p. 47.

19 Physical Damage (Paragraph 28-43 BFG), probably attached to letter, Rocholl to Ministry of Financial Compensation (Germany), 3 June 1958, German File, p. 20.

20 Letter of the Attorney Rocholl to the Ministry of Financial Compensation, 17 November 1960, German File, p. 109.

21 Solemn declaration by Janina Derdacka and Ing. Zadislaw, 20 February 1959, German File, p. 60.

22 Memorandum regarding reparation from the German Government of Mrs. Anna Jocz, deceased. By Jacob Jocz. No date, p. 1. Jocz Private Collection, File - 'Cries for Help-Hebrew Christians in Poland.'

ish descent. His wife Anna Jocz did not have a Jewish name and did not look Jewish, so she pretended not to be Jewish. She had to serve German soldiers without getting recompensed. Because she was still a suspect, the Gestapo abused her several times… Her legs are paralysed.'[23]

Another who was a witness to these events was the 'postman named Mathes.' His full name was Alexander Matthes, and the German authorities tracked him down after the War in order to obtain his sworn testimony in the case of Anna seeking compensation for injuries sustained by the Gestapo agents.[24]

It was somewhat of a miracle that Anna was not shot at the time when Bazyli was arrested, but that could have been little comfort. After the long battle to survive, which involved the daily risk of the Germans in her home discovering she was Jewish and providing for Bazyli while he was in hiding, and now realising that Bazyli was dead and that she was partly paralysed, Anna had a long road to recovery ahead of her.

Outside of the available information, it is somewhat difficult to put all the pieces together. What became of the young Jewish girl Roma during this time? Was Anna then cared for by Pawel and Elzbieta after the death of Bazyli?

The Polish Home Army and Soviets re-take Lwow

At the time when Bazyli was executed 'for the crime of being Jewish' as Martin Parsons stated, the Soviet Red Army was marching westwards and the German resistance was beginning to collapse. Rabbi Kahane described this period: 'Lvov suffered heavy bombardment nearly every day. Everyone including the Germans saw the approaching end. Hitler's defeat was inevitable. But Jew-hatred did not abate even for a moment.'[25] In early May a bunker containing twenty-eight Jewish people was discovered in the cemetery. All were shot.

Once again one could well imagine the daily anxiety which Anna, Pawel and Elzbieta were experiencing, as well as the Kahane family, when they heard of

[23] Letter from Dr Irene Moore, German File, p. 21. Dr. Moore worked at a private practice owned by Dr. Sopel and Dr. Robinson.

[24] Letter to J. Jocz by the attorney. 15 December 1958, German File, p. 35.

[25] Kahane, p. 150.

such events. No doubt they were all praying for a speedy deliverance by the Soviet forces.
Then on 21 July 1944 the leadership of the Polish Home Army ordered an uprising to begin in Lwow and the city fell to a combined Home Army and Soviet force on 25 July 1944. Kahane savoured the moment: 'Lvov was liberated. The Red Army took over the city. At long last I am free again like any other man.'[26] No doubt the Jocz family were experiencing similar feelings, albeit still grieving the death of Bazyli.

The end result

It is estimated that of a Jewish population in Lwow of over 150,000 in June 1941 only 200-300 had survived.[27] This included Anna, Pawel and Elzbieta, as well as Rabbi Kahane and his wife and daughter. Many of the survivors were children hidden on order of Archbishop Sheptytsky.[28]

Alongside Bazyli most of the other Hebrew Christians of Lwow seemingly perished in the Holocaust, either in the ghetto, in the Janowska Camp, shot in the nearby forests, or gassed in the Belzec death camp.

Unfortunately life would still present many challenges for the Jewish survivors. For the remaining Jocz family members one major challenge was how to survive under the returning Soviet regime.

---

26 Kahane, p. 151.

27 Holocaust Education & Archive Research Team, Lvov, www. holocaustresearchproject.org/ghettos/lvov.html

28 Archbishop Sheptytsky died of natural causes in November 1944 aged 79. In his book *Why?*, Peter Hayes (Apple Books), describes how as many as two-thirds of the convents in Poland offered sanctuary to Jewish people, especially children. Another Jewish child who survived the War was Hava Nistel, who was cared for by partisans in the region of Turka. Her mother died at Belzec and her father died of sickness while in hiding. After the War Hava lived first in Israel and after marrying Jim Salter, lived in Britain. Their son, Ben, served as Chairman of the CMJ Board in England for many years.

Chapter 20

Anna, Pawel and Elzbieta escape from Poland

The Soviets return – 1944

Some years later Pawel wrote of the period following the Russian return:

> After the second entry of the Soviet Russian army in 1944 into Lwow (Lemberg) the old investigations and retributions as to the whereabouts of her (Mrs Anna Jocz') husband and children as well as her religious and democratic views were concerned, were resumed by the communist authorities with great vehemence.[1]

Clearly the patriotically Polish Jocz family was still very much under scrutiny by the atheistic Soviet authorities. In such circumstances, what would the future hold for them? Any thoughts they entertained of leaving Soviet-controlled territory, though, would have to wait until the Germans were defeated.

Although the Germans had been ousted from Lwow in July 1944, the War was still far from over. Despite suffering severe losses - of territory, manpower and prestige - Nazi Germany not only kept fighting but also continued to murder Jews in great numbers.

Murder of Jewish people continues

By 1944 almost all of the Jewish people of Poland had been murdered, but there still remained many more elsewhere in Europe, including some 825,000 in Hungary. The *Yad Vashem* Holocaust Museum states that within this number there were some 100,000 Jewish people who were registered as Christians,

---

1 Attestation by Rev Paul Yates (Pawel's Anglicised name), 3 March 1960, Jocz Private Collection. There is an interesting piece of information relating to this period of time. It is a letter dated 10 October 1944 and written in Russian and Ukrainian and translated into German, testifying that Anna was baptised in the Lutheran Church, and that she was of Aryan descent. This second point, as Jakob stated, was written in Russian in order to hide her Jewish descent. Cf. 'Translated letter from Russian and Ukrainian to German'. Original Russian letter dated 10 October 1944, German File, p. 13. See Jakob Jocz to Attorney Rocholl, 20 December 1958, German File, p. 39.

but who were 'racially' Jewish.[2] The Nazis now turned their attention upon this large Jewish population. Ultimately some 568,000 or so were murdered. While most of these were sent to Auschwitz, around 80,000 were shot in Budapest, while thousands more died on the infamous Death Marches.[3]

On 27 January 1945 the vast death camp at Auschwitz was captured and liberated by the Soviet troops. By this time the Nazis had deserted the camp, forcing thousands of prisoners on further excruciating Death Marches. Although the Nazis made attempts to cover up their crimes at Auschwitz as they had done elsewhere in Poland, they did not succeed, and much evidence remained of their heinous crimes against humanity.

It is estimated that more than 1,100,000 Jewish people were gassed and cremated at Auschwitz. Within that huge number were many Jewish Christians.[4]

Yalta Conference, end of the War, and Potsdam Conference

As the War was nearing its inevitable conclusion three of the Allied leaders, Joseph Stalin, Winston Churchill and President F. D. Roosevelt of the United States, convened at Yalta in the Crimea between 4-11 February 1945 to discuss their plans for post-War Europe. Several decisions made, which were strongly insisted upon by Stalin, could potentially affect the Jocz family:

- that citizens of the various Allied nations were required to return to their home countries at the conclusion of the War. The Soviets insisted that all Soviet refugees in zones to be administered by the British, French and Americans who at one point had been Soviet citizens, had to return to the Soviet Union.
- Stalin clearly stated that the Soviet Union intended retaining control over that part of Poland which they had gained following the Molotov-Ribbentrop Agreement – which included Lwow.

Three months later the Germans were ultimately defeated and the last of several surrenders took place in Berlin on 8 May 1945. By that time soldiers of

---

[2] www.yadvashem.org, 'Historical Background: The Jews of Hungary During the Holocaust.'

[3] www.yadvashem.org/articles/general/jews-of-hungary-during-the-holocaust.html.

[4] One Gentile Christian who died at Auschwitz was Jane Haining, a Scottish lady who worked among Jewish girls at the Church of Scotland Mission in Budapest.

the Western Allies were occupying much of the western region of Germany, while Soviet soldiers were occupying all of Poland and the eastern region of Germany. With these factors in consideration, the Allied leaders met at Potsdam, not far from the Wannsee House from 17 July to 2 August, to discuss exactly how Germany would now be occupied and administered. Roosevelt had died and the United States was now represented by President Harry Truman, while Churchill was replaced half-way through the Conference by Clement Attlee, who had just won the British election. The Soviet Union was still represented by Joseph Stalin.

One of the main points to be determined was that of future boundaries – where the demarcation lines would be drawn in Germany between the Soviet occupation region, or zone, and the Western Allies (United States, Britain and France) occupation regions, or zones. It was also agreed that some regions of eastern Germany would be transferred to Poland, while the Soviets retained areas of eastern Poland, including Lwow. Concerning this time Jakob Jocz wrote in the article 'Hebrew Christians in Poland':

> After the Russians had occupied part of Poland the population was given the chance to stay or leave. Many left for the territory of reconstituted Poland. They were taken to the Western frontier and settled in what was once part of the German Reich. As the new settlers moved in, the German inhabitants were evicted.[5]

Pawel, Elzbieta and Anna make their escape from Lwow

At that very time the Jocz family decided they would need to make their escape from Soviet-occupied Poland. If they didn't make their move then, they might not be able to once clear boundary lines had been firmly established. Pawel later described their attempt to escape:

> Seeing no other way out, we decided to flee this part of the country. By bribing some Soviet army men who hid us (Mrs. Anna Jocz included) in their covered military truck, we were deposited in Bytom (Beuten), in the western part of the annexed territory of Poland.[6]

---

[5] *The Hebrew Christian*, Volume XIV, 1946-1947, p. 71.

[6] Attestation by Rev Paul Yates, 3 March 1960, Jocz Private Collection.

The Jocz Family History states that an 'evacuation certificate dated July 17 1945 issued by the government representative for Ukraine SSR confirmed their arrival in Bytom.'[7] Bytom had until just recently been the German town of Beuten and was in the southern part of Poland in the region of Silesia, about half way between Lwow and the present German border. This move, and the date (on the first day of the Potsdam Conference) indicates that they sensed that because of their democratic and religious views the Soviet authorities might be considering actions against them.

Writing some years later, Pawel (then known as Paul Yates) stated that they lived initially with a Mrs Grzeska but were then 'found by the Polish government.'[8] After the conclusion of the War the Soviets installed a puppet Communist government in Poland known as the People's Republic of Poland.

Pawel on another occasion wrote: 'However, the Communist secret police soon discovered us again and subjected us to even severer discrimination and harassments... For fear of further retributions and possible deportation to Syberia [sic] we all had to flee from the country.'[9]

Although at this point there was no physical barrier separating the Soviet-controlled region from the Western-controlled region, the crossing into Germany nevertheless must have been a complicated and even dangerous ordeal. Their movements would have been all the more difficult considering that Anna was paralysed from the waist down.

After entering Germany they were sent to Meppen in north-western Germany where they were placed into a Polish Displaced Persons camp (DP camp). The reason for the Polish DP camp being located at Meppen was because it was in this region that the 1st Polish Armoured Division was based, following their victories over German forces in the north-west of Germany in April 1945.

Bitter and sweet for Jakob

With the cessation of hostilities the full extent of the atrocities committed by the Nazis became apparent to all. Families began hearing about what had

---

7 *A Brief History*, p. 10.

8 *Ubersetzung*, Rev. Paul Yates, 30 March 1960, German File, p. 87. 9 Attestation by Rev. Paul Yates, 3 March 1960, Jocz Private Collection.

happened to their loved ones. In most instances, however, entire families had in fact been murdered. Jakob was deeply concerned as to the whereabouts of his father and mother, as well as Pawel, Elzbieta, Jerzy and Jan as well as his extended family in Lithuania. Sadly Jakob was to discover that Bazyli's brother Moishe and sister Janina had 'both perished in the concentration camp.'[10]

More bitter news was to follow when word was received in Britain of Bazyli's death. The CMJ General Committee recorded on 16 November 1945:

> Having reported murder by the Gestapo of Mr B. Jocz, missionary at Lwow,
>
> Resolved, that the Committee record the tragic death of their missionary with great sorrow, and offer their truest sympathy to the widow and to her son the Rev. Dr. Jacob Jocz, and the other members of the family.[11]

Such news would have been extremely difficult and bitter for Jakob, coming the same year as the birth of his third daughter, Chris. Joan recorded of this time period, and, although there are several inaccuracies in her description, she somehow encapsulates the bitterness and sweetness of their lives then. Joan wrote:

> J [Jakob] became the head of the London Mission & a chief speaker for the Society [CMJ] & began to write and study for his doctorate at Edinburgh University. It was at this time we learned that his father who was also a missionary for the CMJ, & a dear & gentle man, was denounced as a Jew by the door-keeper (a Pole) at Sewerynow & taken away & shot by the Germans a month before the War ended. His mother survived …A lady of great courage & humour…[12]

Jakob received his doctorate from Edinburgh University in 1945. The title of his thesis was: *A Study in the Relationship Between the Jewish People and Jesus Christ.* This was the sweet. The Polish Jewish Christian who happened to be in London and not Warsaw in 1939 and who had weathered the storms of

---

[10] Myers, p. 12.

[11] CMJ General Committee, 16 November 1945, Minute 2089, Bodleian Library, Dept CMJ, c. 186.

[12] *Memoirs of Joan Jocz*, p. 8. Jakob received his PhD in 1945 and became head of the London Mission of CMJ in 1946.

mental anguish during the following years concerning the plight of his family, friends and congregants – had attained this high academic honour despite these circumstances. It was an exceptional achievement.

On one hand a Jocz family member, and part of the CMJ staff, had just attained this high academic honour, while on the other hand another Jocz family member and CMJ staffer was being mourned after being tragically murdered at the hands of the Nazi Gestapo.

No doubt Jakob was now determined to do his utmost to locate and extricate his mother from this large Jewish cemetery, known as Continental Europe.

Attempts to leave Meppen

While located at Meppen DP Camp the Jocz family sought to enter into Britain. This would be very difficult, especially for Elzbieta who was German by birth, although she had worked in Poland for a British-based missionary society. It could have been easier for Pawel as he had studied in Britain prior to the War. Anna was very much dependent upon the movements of Pawel and Elzbieta.

On 4 March 1946 CMJ sent a letter to the Aliens Department of the British Home Office seeking permission for Elzbieta to enter Britain. On 14 March an official from the Home Office wrote on behalf of the Secretary of State stating that 'he regrets that this is not a case in which he is able to make any exception from his general policy regarding the admission of foreigners by authorising the grant of a visa to Mrs JOCZ.'[13]

With this door now closed the Jocz family had to re-adapt their plans. Pawel (and later Elzbieta) managed to become attached to the 1st Polish Armoured Division which was part of the British Army of the Rhine (B.A.O.R.). Pawel's identity card, dated 16 May 1946, reveals that he was identified as 'Protestant Chaplain, rank 2nd Lieutenant.' Elzbieta's identity card states that she 'began employment on 2 November 1946 at the DP/PWX Branch, 1 Pol. Armd. Div, as a private.'[14]

---

13 Home Office to the Secretary Church Missions to Jews, 14 March 1946, J. 14639/2, located in Bodleian Library, dept CMJ, 91/1-16, Staff Files 1935-37.

14 *A Brief History*, p. 10. See also Jocz Private Collection, Photos of Pawel and Elzbieta. Elzbieta, interestingly, was issued her ID card on 30 April 1947.

To their surprise help then arrived from another quarter. Pawel received three letters dated 12 September 1946 and addressed to him at B.A.O.R (Camp Meppen Rose). These letters were from Victor Buksbazen, who was then the Director of the Friends of Israel Missionary and Relief Society based in Philadelphia. Buksbazen was writing to ask Pawel 'to become our missionary and representative in Belgium.' One of those letters was directed towards officialdom, stating that The Friends of Israel was offering employment in Belgium to Pawel.[15]

Pawel must have immediately set matters in motion as the family history states that the Joczs had been issued four separate passes dating between 16 September to 27 November 1946, which were 'issued by the 1st Polish Armoured Division authorizing travel between Meppen (Germany) and Frankfurt, Dusseldorf and Brussels to consult with Belgian Liaison Officers.'[16]

The Belgian Ministry of Justice provided a certificate dated 11 October 1946 which permitted them to enter and reside in Belgium.[17] Once they were in Belgium they began efforts to get Anna into Britain to be with Jakob. The Jocz family history states: 'It was there with help from the British Embassy that Paul was able to make contact with Jakob and in 1947 they completed arrangements for Anna to travel to England.'[18]

Pawel later testified of this period:

> Through a miracle which we until this day cannot understand, Mrs. Anna Jocz, who at that time was 66 years old and broken in body, was able to secure a passport, and join her son, Dr. Jacob Jocz, then residing in London, England.[19]

In view of all that Anna had to endure during the previous years it was a great relief to all that she was now able to leave Europe and go to live in Britain,

[15] Jocz Private Collection, Photos from Pawel and Elzbieta.
[16] *A Brief History*, p.10.
[17] *A Brief History*, p.10. As Elzbieta's Polish Army ID card is dated 2 November 1946, it might be that she remained for the time being in Germany, or worked for the Polish Army in Belgium.
[18] *A Brief History*, p. 10.
[19] Attestation by Rev Paul Yates (Pawel Jocz), 3 March 1960, Jocz Private Collection.

and to once again be with her oldest son Jakob.

Anna moves to London

Although Britain hadn't suffered the full-scale murder and killing that had taken place across the Continent, she had lost many thousands in the fighting and aerial bombings and was now struggling to recover economically. Against this background Anna now moved into the small home of Jakob and Joan. Jakob later wrote to the attorney Mr Rocholl that at this time Anna was treated at the Mandmay Hospital and the German Hospital in London and received a small pension of $28 a month from CMJ, and that his mother had no papers, had problems with her heart, digestion and nerves.[20]

Anna's reunion with Gottfried Frohwein

Several years after arriving in London Anna had a very special visitor – Gottfried Frohwein, the son of Dr Paul Frohwein. Gottfried and his mother and sister had also somehow survived Hitler's onslaught. Gottfried later was able to provide testimony to the German authorities that both of Anna's legs were paralysed. His statement read:

> I, Gottfried Emil Hermann Frohwein born in Wilno, 7th of November 1902…
>
> I lived in Wilno from 1902 until 1918 and knew the claimant Mrs. Anna Jocz as well as her husband Basilius Jocz, which came often to my father's office, who was a doctor in Wilno. I knew that both had Jewish parents and that they converted to Christianity.
>
> … I am a doctor and studied in Berlin. I met the claimant in 1948 in London and can confirm that she lost the ability to walk, needs a wheelchair to move about and suffers from other serious illnesses. She is completely unable to work.[21]

It was almost as if the wheel had turned full circle. The Frohweins and the Joczs together again. Gottfried and Anna, both Jewish Christians, both under the threat of death for their Jewish identity, yet both managed to survive

---

[20] Letter Jacob Jocz to the attorney Rocholl, 9 May 1958, German File, p. 17.
[21] Solemn declaration by Gottfried Emil Hermann Frohwein, German File, p. 59.

the Nazi onslaught. Most other non-Aryan Jewish Christians in Europe, and especially in Poland, however, did not survive.

Pawel and Elzbieta in Belgium and then the US

Pawel and Elzbieta, now better known as Paul and Elizabeth, remained in Belgium from 1946 to the end of 1949 where Paul was associated with the Reformed Free Churches of Holland and Belgium. He continued his work on behalf of The Friends of Israel ministering to the Jewish people but in June 1949 he received another letter from Victor Buksbazen, which stated:

> . . . yesterday our board of directors met in session and upon my recommendation, decided to invite you to the United States as our missionary and representative. The city in which you will work will be decided upon later. I am so happy for your sake, and for Elizabeth's and especially for her mother. Last night I called up Mrs. Singer to tell her the good news. She was so excited and thrilled she could hardly talk.[22]

En-route to the United States they stopped in Britain where they were re-united with Jakob, Joan and Anna. While there Paul was also ordained (or re-ordained) by the Polish Reformed Church on 8 January 1950. They then departed Britain shortly afterwards and arrived in New York on 18 January. From there they made their way to Oakland in California where Paul began his work for the Friends of Israel.

Several years later when Paul applied for naturalisation he changed his surname to Yates, as the Americans were finding it too difficult to pronounce Jocz. Pawel Jocz now became Paul Yates. Then in 1956 Paul became the minister at the United Presbyterian Church in Oakland, and served there while also working with The Friends of Israel and endeavouring to introduce Jesus to his kinsmen according to the flesh.[23]

Jerzy survives the War, but dies shortly after

In 1947 CMJ requested the Anglican Chaplain in Warsaw, Rev Adolph Sergeant, to seek information about any survivors from the Hebrew Christian community previously associated with the Emmanuel Church. On 11 February 1948 Sergeant wrote to Rev. Gill of CMJ: 'George Jocz, the younger son

---

[22] *A Brief History*, p. 11.
[23] Ibid., p. 12.

of your former missionary is married, works in a government printing shop and earns a small salary.'[24]

Although little is known of Jerzy's movements during the War, there is a 'Holocaust Survivor Card' in the Jocz Family Collection, testifying that he had endured the horrors of the Nazi occupation of Poland.

More than likely Jerzy had suffered from the effects of the War as he prematurely. The Jocz family history states that he 'wrote a letter to his mother dated Oct. 11 1949 telling her not to worry about his illness but he died on Oct. 31 1949 at the age of 40.'[25] His wife Lucia died shortly afterwards, in January 1950.[26]

Jan arrives in Britain

Little is known of Jan's life during and after the War. His nephew Philip Jocz, wrote that Jan (John) had left the family in Lwow at some point in time and had survived the War somewhere in Europe. 'I remember a story', Phil wrote, 'that suggested he spent some time in a German munitions factory where he sabotaged bombs intended for England.'[27]

The Jocz family history states: 'As for John, who was only 16 when war broke out, there is no record of how he survived. He never spoke about his experiences which must have been traumatic in the extreme and affected him for the rest of his life.'[28] Jakob's daughter Anne recalled that about the year 1950, when she was about eleven years old, her uncle John visited their home in England.[29]

John remained in England and initially stayed with Jakob and his family. It must have been quite a houseful, with Anna as well as the growing number of children, with the arrival of Philip in 1948. John pursued 'a course of study leading to a pharmacy degree.'[30] He then met Doris Hawkins 'a former

---

[24] Rev. A. L. Sergeant to Rev. Gill CMJ, 11 February 1948 No. 183, Bodleian Library, Dept CMJ c. 233 Correspondence Si-Z.

[25] *A Brief History*, pp. 10-11.

[26] Ibid.

[27] Email from Philip Jocz to the author, 11 June 2020.

[28] *A Brief History*, p. 11.

[29] Email from Phil Jocz to author, 11 June 2020.

[30] *A Brief History*, p. 13.

teacher who was completing her medical degree' and they married in 1958. Following this he then established his own chemist shop in Worthing.[31]

Jakob meanwhile continued to work with CMJ in London, as well as being a parish priest at St. John's, Downshire Hill. In 1949 his doctoral thesis was printed as a book under the title *The Jewish People and Jesus Christ.* It was an immediate success. He would later begin working on a sequel, entitled *The Jewish People and Jesus After Auschwitz.*

No doubt the presence of Anna was a daily reminder of this dynamic of the Jewish people, Jesus, and the Holocaust. Throughout this same period Anna, while enjoying the benefits of a peaceful existence, was also attempting to come to grips with the traumatic events of the last few years. In this she was not alone.

---

[31] Ibid.

Chapter 21

The Hebrew Christian community is decimated

The CMJ–related Hebrew Christian communities are no more

Like the Jocz family, every Jewish family in Europe had been affected by the Nazi onslaught. Often there were only one, perhaps two survivors from entire families, and only one, perhaps two surviving families from entire communities. The same was true with the various Hebrew Christian communities, especially in Poland.

The CMJ-related Hebrew Christian communities in Warsaw and Lwow were decimated. At the time when Jakob departed from Poland in August 1939 it was recorded there were some one hundred and twenty congregants in the Hebrew Christian congregation at the Emmanuel Church in Warsaw. This number is most probably just the adults, so by any standards this was a sizeable Evangelical congregation. Joan Jocz wrote in her memoirs that only a few from those present at the Christmas function in 1936 survived the Holocaust.[1]

The leadership of CMJ did their best to locate survivors in Warsaw.[2] Although Rev. Sergeant did locate some survivors from the Hebrew Christian congregation, it is clear that the vast majority of the former members of that once vibrant community in Warsaw had perished. There did not appear to be any remnant of the small Hebrew Christian community in Lwow.

It seems that only one former CMJ staff member from Warsaw, apart from Jakob, survived. This was John Enis. After the War Enis had managed to get into the American zone in Germany and was being sheltered at the DP Centre at Lampertneim-Hessen. From there he wrote to CMJ on 26 February 1946, stating: 'Thanks God I saved from this terrible war and especially per-

---

1 *Joan Jocz Memoirs*, p. 5.

2 It seems that Herman Carpenter (alongside H. L. Ellison, vice-President of the IHCA), visited Warsaw some time in 1947. *The Hebrew Christian*, Volume XX, 1947-1948, p. 54.

secution of Jewish race. Alas, very few of the Mission workers saved. From our Mission I know nobody who saved.'[3]

From what Enis stated and from the available materials it would seem that all of the CMJ staff at the Emmanuel Centre died, including Mr and Mrs Weisman and their child, Mr and Mrs Wolfin, and Nathan Szuman and his family.

Letters from two survivors from Warsaw

In his capacity as the former pastor of the Hebrew Christian congregation in Warsaw, Jakob still had concern for the Jewish survivors from the congregation. He received a letter from one such survivor, which reveals the deep anguish, agony and confusion she felt, which was similar to so many of the survivors. This lady wrote to him in March 1946:

> I do not know what impression my letter will make upon you but I can assure you that it is not a ghost who is writing but a living person who regards Dante's hell as nothing compared with what has been taking place in our midst during the reign of the "ingenious" madman.
>
> But I am still the same person … who used to attend your Services at Sewerynow on Sundays. The Mission House is nothing but a shell – nearly nothing is left of it, as is the case with the rest of my beloved Warsaw…
>
> Pastor … I am so discouraged, as nothing will convey in human language my experiences, and yet there were others who suffered more. I [can] therefore modestly hold my peace. One thing, however, I know with certainty, the Great Spirit of Love accompanied me everywhere & kept me; in order to manifest His Power to those who put their whole trust in Him. I have learned to be happy in suffering, to give thanks for it, & even ask for more if so be His Will…
>
> I am glad you were not in Poland; the Jewish ghetto makes a terrible impression – I am not able to find the place of my mother's house. As I stood where once was our street, I tried to strain the air through my fingers in an effort to fondle it, seeing that my mother and my sisters breathed the same air in their last moments. But I could not even cry; the

---

[3] John Enis to CMJ, 26 February 1946, Bodleian Library, Dept CMJ, c. 226, Correspondence C-F, No. 121.

rain, however cried for me, weeping on the walls erected by the hands of the crazy Hitlerites…

As I write this letter, my little boy asks me: "Mummy, have you still somebody to write to?"[4]

Another letter from a Hebrew Christian survivor was written in July 1948 and addressed to the CMJ Secretary Rev. Gill, and is representative of the struggles faced by the Jewish Christian survivors:

My name is Regina Ruth Kucinska. My parents were Paul and Mary Wajs. I was born in Warsaw, Poland. I was baptised in the Church of the Anglican Mission at Warsaw by Rev. H.C. Carpenter. I spent all of my young years within the Mission. My parents also belonged to the Anglican Church and in that Church they were baptised. Till his premature death in 1926 my father worked for the Mission preaching among the Jews. After my father's death my mother, in appreciation of his work, was granted life rente [sic] amounting to one hundred pounds sterling a year. She was receiving money till the outbreak of the war. The influence of my parents accounts for my early devotion to the missionary work. I was very young when I started working among the Jewish women and children. First I was married to Joseph Zomer, the Mission's missioner, who turned Christian being 16 years old after the advanced studies in the Jewish rabbinstic school.

When the war of 1939 broke out I was in Lodz, Poland. Early in 1940 we were displaced from the city and sent to a detention camp. We left behind us all we had. After a month we were released and after another month we reached Warsaw, where my mother was living.

Here in Warsaw my husband got seriously ill. After months of hardship and starvation he developed pulmonary tuberculosis which ended his days in 1941. I had to overcome many difficulties from the part of the Jews to arrange his interment at the Christian cemetery.

This same year, 1941, I succeeded to escape from the ghetto with my

---

4 Letter to Jakob Jocz, no date, which he then translated into English. Bodleian Library, Dept CMJ c. 230 Corres L-N. Letters from Warsaw.

son George. He was 7 years old. Words cannot express difficulties and miseries which I met with on the other side of the walls. Among the unfriendly people, without documents, money, work, roof under which I could shelter my head I had to depend only upon God on whom I put all my hope. The reasons of safety forced me to place my son at an protestant orphanage. Unfortunately, after 3 months of stay there he was discovered by the Gestapo and taken away for ever.

At the same time in 1943 the Warsaw ghetto was liquidated and my mother found her death at the hands of the German Hitlerites.[5]

Despite these struggles Regina Ruth managed to survive the ordeal and was now writing to seek assistance, especially payment from CMJ for the rent owed to her mother from the period 1 September 1939 until her death in 1943. CMJ did assist Regina Ruth and the few other survivors as best they could.

When survivors did return to their home locations they were often very disorientated, and with Poland being under either Soviet or Polish Communist control, communication with the outside world was not easy. As the months and years passed, however, it became progressively clear that the CMJ-related Hebrew Christian communities at Warsaw and Lwow would never rise again.

All Hebrew Christian communities are decimated

The losses sustained by the two CMJ-related Hebrew Christian communities were replicated elsewhere. All of the Evangelical missionary societies which had been operating in Poland pre-September 1939 were decimated, while the Jewish Roman Catholics fared similarly. Although a larger number of non-Aryan Christians in countries such as the Netherlands and Germany either managed to escape before the War began, or somehow managed to survive the War, such was not the case in Poland. Once the War began on 1 September 1939 the Jewish people in Poland were trapped – including the Jewish Christians.

The work of the Bethel Mission in Lodz suffered terribly. Although Leon and Fanny Rosenberg survived, most of their close family who worked with

---

[5] Ruth Kucinska to Rev. Gill, 23 July 1948. Bodleian Library, Dept CMJ, c.230, Correspondence L-N, Number 193-194.

them in Lodz were murdered. Fanny wrote to her husband Leon while he was still in the United States on 10 August 1945:

> The tragedy which has befallen our BETHEL family cannot be described. Most of our missionaries in Lodz and Litzmanstadt, as well as most of those who belong to the BETHEL family, together with the children, were assassinated by the Nazis. Of our workers, only Br. Choinacski, Brother and Sister Bakalarz and Esther Narve are alive.[6]

Shortly later Fanny wrote to her sister, Helena Weinmann (who herself had left Yugoslavia before the onslaught of the Holocaust there). The *Immanuel's Witness* journal stated:

> Mrs Rosenberg, writing to her sister Miss H. Weinmann, relates of three hundred Hebrew Christians in Lodz who were murdered. She herself survived, but members of her family and many relatives were all murdered.[7]

Samuel Wilkinson, the General Director of the Mildmay Mission to the Jews, wrote:

> First and foremost there is the naked fact that six out of seven of our workers in Poland and the Baltic countries have perished. We have had definite information about four of them and the deaths of the other two must be assumed. The only survivor, Mr. R. Friedland, of Warsaw, lost his young wife at the hands of guards when, after a three-foot fall of snow, they were forced to leave the woods where they had been existing – not living – and try to find food in a neighbouring village. When they came to the road they were met by a hail of bullets ; he escaped, but she was shot![8]

Frydland not only survived but also wrote an invaluable record of what befell the Hebrew Christian community in Poland in his booklet *Joy Cometh in The Morning.*[9] After the fighting ended in Poland he was invited by the Polish Evangelical Baptist Church to work for them as an itinerant preacher. Of

[6] *The Bethel Witness*, Vol 9, Number 4, 1945, p. 6.
[7] *Immanuel's Witness,* Barbican Mission to the Jews, April 1945 – March 1946, p. 109.
[8] *Trusting and Toiling on Israel's Behalf*, 1946, p. 171.
[9] This booklet is now available as *When Being Jewish Was A Crime* (Thomas Nelson, 1978).

this time, he stated:

> It brought me in contact with many pastors and from them I heard the stories of other Hebrew Christians who had died and remained faithful to the very end… There they rest even now in the unknown graves of Poland and Western Russia with no one molesting them any more. No more are they with us, Mr. Mandelbaum, Mr. and Mrs. Leibovich, with their little children, Mr. and Mrs. Sofer with their five little children, Mr. Mehlsack and many others …[10]

Frydland offered this sobering assessment:

> The Hebrew Christians to survive were those that escaped to foreign countries and a few who married non-Jewish women were somehow preserved by them. All of the leading Hebrew Christians, missionaries, pastors, teachers, scholars, who remained in Poland, perished.[11]

The Barbican Mission to the Jews (BMJ) suffered a similar experience. They reported that their leader Rev. Peter Gorodishz 'and his son died in a concentration camp.'[12] The fate of the other staff from their centres was unknown, although the wife of J. Klajn who was in charge of their work in Lublin informed the BMJ that her husband had been murdered. The BMJ stated: 'We have not received any details, but we can imagine the circumstances. The largest concentration camp was at Lublin, and one of the earliest to be established by the Germans in Poland. Our deepest sympathy is with Mrs. Klajn and her children.'[13]

They also reported: 'As far as we know, Mrs. Fajans, the widow of the Rev. J Fajans, is the only survivor of all the workers in Bialystok, and is still on the spot. She lost her husband, a very valuable missionary and her son and daughter. Both promising young people.'[14]

The fate of the many thousands of Jewish Catholics no doubt was the same as the Jewish Protestants, and of all Jewish people in Poland. As previously

[10] Frydland, p. 44.
[11] Frydland, p. 48.
[12] *Immanuel's Witness,* April 1945 – March 1946, p. 42.
[13] *Immanuel's Witness,* ibid, p. 82.
[14] *Immanuel's Witness,* ibid, p. 117.

stated there were about 5,200 Jewish Christians in the Warsaw Ghetto, most of whom were Jewish Catholics and the vast majority of whom perished either in the Ghetto or in Treblinka.[15] Such a fate would also have befallen Jewish Catholics elsewhere in Poland, including Lwow as attested to by Rabbi Kahane.[16]

Representative tributes

A statement perhaps representative of all of the murdered Jewish Christians, and the pain of those left behind, was published in the Editorial from the Barbican Mission magazine *Immanuel's Witness*:

> We in the Barbican Mission too, know the bitter pain of loss, and mingle our tears with those who have survived. Our Hebrew Christian brothers and sisters, our children in the Lord, were as cruelly tortured and put to death as the rest of the Jews. What toil and sweat, what pain and anguish, before these were begotten in the Lord! What emotion and affection deposited. Cruelly they were wrenched from us, and we were left in a helpless state. We were not there to comfort them in their sorrow and cheer them to the gates where enemy can no longer reach or touch. At least they rest, but we are left to contemplate.[17]

In its own tribute, the Mildmay Mission to the Jews detailed its losses, which were similar in ration to the fate of the Jewish population generally:

> The foregoing brief survey is tragic enough in itself, but it is only this Mission's own cross section of the tragedy of European Jewry: six workers out of seven gone, and the seventh bereft of his wife, hunted and driven to the extreme limits of human endurance. This tallies almost exactly with the fate of the Jews of Eastern Europe as a whole, where some six million out of seven have perished at the hands of the Nazis, and the survivors have experienced what is little better than a living death.[18]

That the majority of the Hebrew Christians and Jewish non-Aryan Christians died in Poland there is little doubt. In his article on 'Hebrew Christians in

---

15 Dembowski, p. 66.
16 Kahane, p. 9.
17 *Immanuel's Witness,* ibid, p. 109.
18 *Trusting and Toiling on Israel's Behalf,* 1946, p. 171.

Nazi-occupied Poland' Jakob wrote of one murderous episode which also presented a glimmer of light and hope to those Hebrew Christians who survived, or who were outside of Europe and were despondent when hearing of the tragedy. He wrote:

> How do Hebrew Christians die? What follows is an authentic story.
>
> It happened in a township on the Polish side of Volhynia during the Nazi occupation. The Germans had already shot father and mother, a devoted Hebrew Christian couple. Now they drove up in a lorry packed with terrified Jews to take their children. They were thrown into the quivering and screaming human mass on their fatal journey. Suddenly, above the heart-rendering cries of frightened humanity there arose a joyous song of hope and faith and triumph – the children of our Hebrew Christian brother broke out in hymns of praise to God![19]

Is there life after death?

In the period from 1945-48 the survivors had to pick up the pieces, but in Poland especially, life for these Holocaust survivors was not easy. On numerous occasions there were outbreaks of anti-Jewish sentiment, the worst of which was a pogrom at Kielce on 4 July 1946, when forty-two Jews were murdered.

These events seemed to confirm that Europe was still not a healthy place for Jewish people to live. Jewish life had virtually ceased there - Jewish life which included the Hebrew Christian movement.

In view then of all that had just taken place in Europe, could anything rise from these ashes? Could the Jewish people ever overcome this physical tragedy of all tragedies, and could the Hebrew Christian movement ever rise again?

---

[19] *The Hebrew Christian*, Volume XIX, 1946-1947, p. 71.

Chapter 22

The Nazis did not succeed

The remnant arises

Although the Nazis succeeded in murdering Bazyli and other members of the Jocz family, as well as another six million Jews including most of the Jewish Christians, they did not succeed in their overall objective.

There was indeed a resurrection of Jewish life from the ashes of Europe.

The survivors from Europe, the remnant, for the most part managed to ultimately leave and establish new lives, in North America, Australia, South Africa, Britain and elsewhere.

In those mostly free and democratic countries these survivors joined the existing Jewish communities and grew and prospered.

Many found a safe haven in the land of Israel, where the Jewish state of Israel was officially founded on 14 May 1948. As the Jewish people say, *Am Yisrael Hai* – 'The people of Israel live.' The dream of countless Jewish people, both before Theodor Herzl and after him, had now been accomplished.

Although none of the four Jocz sons moved to live in Israel, one other survivor from Lwow did. After the War David Kahane and his family managed to migrate to Israel where he later became the Chief Rabbi of the esteemed Israeli Air Force.

Nazism also did not succeed in destroying the Hebrew Christian movement. Although much of the movement had been snuffed out in Europe, the remnant for the most part also moved to other parts of the world and joined with Jewish followers of Jesus in those lands.

From the ashes of the European Holocaust a new type of Hebrew Christian movement began to emerge. Much of this new beginning was in North America, a new beginning which Paul and Elizabeth, Victor Buksbazen and

Rachmiel Frydland were part of. They were soon to be joined by Jakob.

Jakob seeks new beginnings in Canada

By the mid-1950s Jakob, although he was enjoying his work with CMJ, was nevertheless experiencing some challenges in his parish from some 'who could just not accept the exotic "foreigner" as their spiritual leader.'[1] He was seeking new horizons.

Then came an offer to work for the Nathanael Institute, an Anglican-based work in Toronto Canada endeavouring to introduce Jewish people to Jesus.[2] The offer was accepted and Jakob and Joan, together with the four children, left Britain for Canada in October 1956. Anna joined them there in December 1956.

Jakob becomes President of the IHCA

Interestingly at this time Jakob was also elected to the position of world-wide leader of the Hebrew Christian movement. In 1957 he became President of the International Hebrew Christian Alliance. This appointment was a clear testimony to Jakob's character and intellect, following in the footsteps of such illustrious men as Sir Leon Levison and Arnold Frank.

Few Jewish followers of Jesus were as equipped as Jakob for this position. Under his leadership the Hebrew Christian movement, in North America and world-wide, began to break out into a new form, a form which Hebrew Christians of previous generations had often sought for but not been able to find and which gave space for distinctly Jewish expressions of faith.[3] This modern-day movement became known as the Messianic Jewish movement.

Appeals to the Germans and Anna's last journey

In 1957 Jakob appealed for financial compensation from the German Government for the injuries sustained by his mother Anna at the hands of the

---

[1] *A Brief History,* p. 12.

[2] Theresa Newell states in her booklet *The Rev. Dr Jakob Jocz* that the Nathanael Institute was initially formed in 1882 as part of the work of CMJ in Canada. Theresa Newell, *The Rev. Dr Jakob Jocz,* An Olive Press Research Paper, Issue # 36, 2018, p. 2.

[3] An exception to this was the late nineteenth century movement in Kishinev in today's Moldova initiated by Joseph Rabinowitz, whose adherents were known as 'the Israelites of the New Covenant.'

German Gestapo agents. This would prove to be a protracted and frustrating affair. Throughout all the years that Anna had been with Jakob and the family they had received little, if any, government assistance.

It was in the midst of this legal challenge that Jakob was invited in 1959 to become a part-time lecturer at Wycliffe College, also in Toronto. It wasn't long before this College recognised Jakob's giftedness, broad experience and knowledge and in 1961 he was offered a full-time position there.

With the new position also came a new, more spacious house to which Anna moved together with Jakob and Joan and the children. The Jocz Family website states that: 'Anna occupied a large room on the second floor with a balcony overlooking the back yard. It had everything she needed but sadly she lived there only a few months. In early November 1961 she had to move to a nursing home.'[4]

That same month, on 24 November 1961, there was finally a breakthrough with the application for compensation, and the German Reparations Commissions at last approved the application for Anna.[5]

Sadly, Anna though would never benefit from these reparations. She died in the nursing home on 11 December 1961, three weeks after her eighty-first birthday.

This bold, humble and unassuming woman who had endured endless challenges - especially in Vilna, in Warsaw and in Lwow - and who had been about to enjoy some financial comfort and the pleasant surroundings of the new family home, died without being able to enjoy either.

But this outcome perhaps reflects Anna's very life and character, a life of constantly living on the edge. In their brief history, the Jocz family summed up Anna's remarkable life which had spanned such tumultuous decades:

> What a journey brought her to this place. She grew up in horse and buggy

[4] *A Brief History*, p. 15.

[5] Ibid., p. 17. Unfortunately there is a very sad and unjust ending to this episode. Not only did Anna fail to receive any compensation, but the German Government afterwards charged Jakob with legal expenses involved in several court cases associated with the affair.

> days and she lived to travel on jet aircraft. She survived two world wars, pogroms, physical infirmity and many other deprivations. Seeing her in later life one would never have guessed that she faced down the Nazis and risked her own life to shelter others. A woman of indomitable courage and unwavering faith.[6]

Anna Jocz was indeed a testimony and a proof that the Nazis did not succeed. Not only did she survive the Holocaust but she witnessed the survival and flourishing of her own people and lived to see the founding and early days of the State of Israel. She also witnessed two of her sons continuing the legacy of her murdered husband as they presented Jesus as the Messiah to the Jewish people, as well as witnessing a fourth generation of Jewish followers of Jesus within her own family.

Life had indeed sprung forth from the ashes of the Holocaust.

---

[6] Ibid., p. 15.

Epilogue

By the time Jakob died in 1983 he had become one of the intellectual giants of the Hebrew Christian movement, which in time has become synonymous with the Messianic Jewish movement. Today the International Hebrew Christian Alliance is known as the International Messianic Jewish Alliance.

This movement of Jewish followers of Jesus, already very strong in North America and Britain, is also increasing in size and vitality in Israel – and, has seen a resurrection in some regions of Europe itself.

CMJ, the organisation in which Bazyli, Anna, Jakob, Joan, Paul and Elizabeth were involved, is still in existence. Today though it operates in a more limited capacity compared to the pre-1939 period.

It is the desire of CMJ to honour those who were associated with them and who lost their lives during the Holocaust, even as it is the desire of Jewish followers of Jesus to honour their brethren who perished in that tragedy of all tragedies.

This publication, therefore, is dedicated to Bazyli Jocz, Victor Weisman and family, M. Wolfin and family, Nathan Szuman and family, Peter Gorodishz, the many members of the Rosenberg family, Nathan Sendyk and the thousands of other Polish Jewish Christians and the thousands of Jewish Christians from elsewhere in Europe, such as Isaiah Feinstein, John Rottenberg, Edith Stein, the Lob family and many many more.

May their lives and testimonies never be forgotten.

Selected Bibliography

Books

Adeney, J. H. *Digest of the Annual Reports from 1908 till 1952,* (No publication details, original copy in Conrad Schick Library).

Allen, R. *Arnold Frank of Hamburg,* (James Clarke & Co Ltd, London, no date).

Allison, R. *Journey to Jerusalem,* (Fastprint & Design: St Leonards-on-Sea, 1988).

Browning, C (and Jurgen Matthaus), *The Origins of the Final Solution*, (Arrow Books: London, 2005).

Browning, *Police Battalion 101,* (Harper Collins, New York, 1992).

Churchill, W. *The Grand Alliance*, (Houghton Mifflin; Boston, 1950).

Ciano, Galeazzo, *The Ciano Diaries 1939-43,* (Simon Publications, Florida: 2001).

Czerniakow, A. *The Warsaw Diary of Adam Czerniakow*, (Elephant Paperbacks, Chicago: 1999).

Dembowski, P. *Christians in the Warsaw Ghetto*, (University of Notre Dame: Indiana, 2005).

Desbois, F. *The Holocaust by Bullets*, (St. Martin's Griffin, New York: 2008).

Documents on German Foreign Policy, Series D, Vol. V, VI, XI.

Dylewwski, A. *Where the Tailor was a Poet – Polish Jews and their Culture,* (Krakow, 2003).

Encyclopaedia Britannica, (Chicago, 1975).

Frey, J. *Narrative of the Reverend Joseph C.F. Frey*, (London, 1809).

Frister, R. *The Cap*, (New York: Grove Press, 1993).

Frydland, R. *Joy Cometh in the Morning*, (Rachmiel Frydland, no date).

Gidney, W. T. *The History of the London Society for Promoting Christianity amongst the Jews,* (London, 1908).

Goldhagen, D. *Hitler's Willing Executioners*, (Abacus, London: 1997).

Grabowski, Jan. *Hunt for the Jews: Betrayal and Murder in German-Occupied Poland,* (Indiana University Press. Kindle Edition).

Hertz, D. *How Jews Became Germans*, (Yale University Press, 2011).

Hirszfeld, L. *The Story of One Life,* (Kindle, University of Rochester).

Hitler, A. *Mein Kampf,* (English translation, Pimlico, London, 1969).

Jagodzinska, A. *Duszozbawcy*, (Wydawnictwo Austeria: Krakow, 2017).

Jocz, J. *The Jewish People and Jesus Christ*, (Baker Book House: Grand Rapids, 1979).

Kahane, D. *Lvov Ghetto Diary,* (University of Massachusetts Press, 1990).

Kuschnir, V. *Only One Life*, (American European Bethel Mission: Santa Barbara, 2000).
Levison, F. *Christian and Jew – Leon Levison*, (Edinburgh: The Pentland Press, 1989).
Newell, T. *The Rev. Dr Jakob Jocz*, (An Olive Press Research Paper, Issue # 36, 2018).
Pileggi, D. A *Narrow Bridge,* (Jerusalem 2018).
Ringelblum, E. *Notes from the Warsaw Ghetto,* (ibooks, New York: 2006).
Sacher, H. *A History of Israel,* (Alfred A. Knoft, Inc: New York, 1996).
Sacher, H. *The Course of Modern Jewish History*, (Delta Publishing: New York, 1977).
Sevener, H. *A Rabbi's Vision,* (Chosen People Ministries, 1994).
Shirer, W. *The Rise and Fall of the Third Reich,* (Simon & Schuster, New York, 1960).
Snyder, T. *Bloodlands,* (Vintage, 2011).
Wilson, M. *Our Father Abraham*, (Dayton, 1989).
Wurmbrandt, R. *Christ on the Jewish Road,* (Hodder and Stoughton, London, 1970).

Articles

Arthur F. Glasser, 'The Legacy of Jakob Jocz', *International Bulletin of Missionary Research,*April 1993.
Havi Ben-Sasson, 'Christians in the Ghetto: All Saints' Church, Birth of the Holy Virgin Mary Church, and the Jews of the Warsaw Ghetto', in *Yad Vash-em Studies XXXI,* edited by David Silberland, (Yad Vashem Jerusalem, 2003).
Joan Jocz Memoir, www.jocz.ca
Patrick Cockburn, 'To look at Ukraine's future might be, just look at its shameful past.' *Independent,* 9 March 2014.
Russian troops seize Lwow from Nazis, find the Jews gone, *Haaretz*, 5 May 2020, www.haaretz.com.

Journals

Annual Review of the British Jews Society (BJS)
CMJ Annual Reports
The Jewish Missionary Herald, British Jews Society.
Jewish Missionary Intelligence (JMI), CMJ.
The Chosen People, ABMJ.
The Bethel Witness, European American Bethel Mission.
Immanuel's Witness, Barbican Mission to the Jews,
The Hebrew Christian, Hebrew Christian Testimony to Israel (HCTI).

The Hebrew Christian, IHCA.
Trusting and Toiling, Mildmay Mission to the Jews.

Dissertations and unpublished works

Martin Parsons, *Autobiography,* Chapter 7, unpublished work, www.parsons-family.co.uk.

Mitch Glaser, *A Survey of Missions to the Jews in Continental Europe 1900-1950,* (Fuller Theological Seminary, 1998).

Elizabeth Myers, *The Literary Legacy of Jacob Jocz,* (Fuller Theological Seminary, 1989).

Websites

Yivo Encyclopaedia, www.yivoencyclopedia.org
Yad Vashem, www.yadvashem.org
A Brief History of the Jocz Family, www.jocz.ca
USHMM, (United States Holocaust Museum Memorial), www.usshmm.org.
Wikipedia, www.wikipedia.com

Archives, Museums, Memorials and Libraries

ABMJ – American Board of Missions to the Jews (Chosen People Ministry, New York).
Auschwitz-Birkenau Death Camp, Poland.
Barbican Mission to the Jews, CWI, Eynsham, Oxfordshire.
Belzec Death Camp, Poland.
Bethel Mission, Santa Barbara, USA.
Bodleian Library, Oxford, Department CMJ.
Chelmno Death Camp, Poland.
Conrad Schick Library, Christ Church, Jerusalem.
Documentation Center Nazi Party Rally Grounds, Nuremberg.
Drancy Internment Camp, France.
Gurs Concentration Camp, France.
Hebrew Christian Testimony to Israel (HCTI), Reading.
International Missionary Council Archives, Yale University.
Jocz Private Collection, Toronto Canada.
Madjanek Concentration Camp, Lublin region, Poland.
Mildmay Mission to the Jews, Reading.
Polen Museum, Warsaw.
Topography of Terror Exhibition, Berlin.
Treblinka Death Camp, Poland.

USHMM – United States Holocaust Memorial Museum, Washington.
Wannsee House Museum.
Wycliffe College, Toronto.
Yad Vashem, Jerusalem.

Interviews
Andrzei Grzegorczyk, Radegast Ghetto Museum, Lodz, Poland
Philip Jocz, Toronto

Other resources connected to the overall research study have been accessed, but the above stated are those from which material has been accessed for this particular publication.[1]

The life and work of Rev. Dr Jakob Jocz

The life and work of Jakob Jocz is worthy of a fuller explanation, but it is not within the remit of this publication. For those interested in knowing more about Jakob's academic life I would refer you to:

- Glasser, A. 'The Legacy of Jakob Jocz', *International Bulletin of Missionary Research,* April 1993, pp. 66-71.
- Jocz family website, www.jocz.ca
- Myers, E. *The Literary Legacy of Jacob Jocz*, (Fuller Theological Seminary, 1989).
- Nessim, D. *Jewish Believers in Jesus in the Canadian Protestant Church from 1759 to 1996*, MA Thesis, 1996.
- Newell, T. *The Rev. Dr Jakob Jocz*, An Olive Press Research Paper, Issue 36, 2018.
- David Barron of Jews for Jesus Canada is also working on the literary life of Jocz.

[1] For further information on the work and publications of Rev. Dr Jakob Jocz please see the Jocz family website, www.jocz.ca